T0340345

Improving Business Process Performance

Gain Agility, Create Value,
and Achieve Success

Improving Business Process Performance

Gain Agility, Create Value, and Achieve Success

JOSEPH RAYNUS

CRC Press
Taylor & Francis Group
Boca Raton London New York

CRC Press is an imprint of the
Taylor & Francis Group, an **informa** business
AN AUERBACH BOOK

CRC Press
Taylor & Francis Group
6000 Broken Sound Parkway NW, Suite 300
Boca Raton, FL 33487-2742

First issued in paperback 2019

© 2011 by Taylor & Francis Group, LLC
CRC Press is an imprint of Taylor & Francis Group, an Informa business

No claim to original U.S. Government works

ISBN-13: 978-1-4200-7249-5 (hbk)
ISBN-13: 978-0-367-38262-9 (pbk)

Visit the Taylor & Francis Web site at
http://www.taylorandfrancis.com

and the CRC Press Web site at
http://www.crcpress.com

Contents

Foreword

It's always a challenge to balance the strategic and tactical views of the work your organization is doing. Too often the strategic view becomes academic and encumbered by the assumptions required to make some chosen methodology workable on your specifics. Similarly, the no-nonsense tactical work involved in solving day-to-day problems and executing projects sometimes loses sight of what's important in the big picture, strategic perspective.

This book presents an approach to a workable process to help an organization maintain clarity of purpose, bridge the gap between the strategic and tactical views, and apply structure to how it monitors its progress. The eight-step process brings discipline to the organization's planning, establishes links between activity and effect, and allows the organization to develop a framework that is useful at various levels of investment. You can make it more or less detailed as you see fit for your organization's requirements; you can mature it over time.

Joe Raynus speaks directly to issues of goal setting, performance measurement, and responsive action. In doing this, he examines the concepts of management scorecards, innovation curves, and measurement frameworks. His purpose is to provide a strategic framework that maintains flexibility, balance, and alignment. This is a solid approach to organizational management.

Terry Balven
Director, Acquisition Business Systems
Headquarters US Air Force

Introduction

Since I wrote my first book ten years ago, not much has changed in the field and concepts of continuous process improvement, quantification, and metrics.

What we need is a new paradigm—a new vision of business reality, a fundamental change in our approach in value delivery and management. At the beginnings of this change is the shift from the static to the holistic understanding of the dynamic business processes. The approach that could lead to this paradigm shift is the subject of this book.

I do not like the word *reengineering*. For me it sounds like this: we already screwed up once, so let's try something else and hope this time a miracle will happen.

The traditional business process reengineering cycle starts with process identification. The process as-is analysis follows, and the next step is to design the to-be process and go back to the process identification. Sounds good, but without considering the value delivered to the customer, it is just an endless exercise delivering just a minimum effect.

Why Value?

- The creation of value is the primary goal of managers in leading companies
- Organizations exist to create value for all constituencies/stakeholders
- Stakeholders include customers, owners, managers, employees, suppliers and society in general
- Organizations determine the degree to which they will prioritize the interests of each stakeholder group and will therefore balance performance goals accordingly

—Sumantra Ghoshal, Christopher A. Bartlett, and Peter Moran
"A New Manifesto for Management," Sloan Management Review, 40(3), 1999

The creation of value is the primary goal of an organization. Unfortunately, we are mixing value creation with solution implementation and product development. This is not a simple issue: just go to the root cause of the problem to solve it. The real issue is different: What do we expect after the problem is solved? Is it going to contribute to the value of the company?

Organizations have to change constantly to meet different expectations from many stakeholders. The executive's performance is judged now by the delivered value internal and external to the enterprise. The growth in market value is directly connected to the development of new skills, swift reaction to the changes in value definition and value delivery, and effective decision making.

Arnold J. Toynbee (1889–1975), in his *A Study of History*, put forward a philosophy of history based on an analysis of the cyclical development and decline of civilizations. Toynbee examined the rise and fall of twenty-six civilizations in the course of human history, and concluded that civilizations rose when the leaders, in his own words, "creative minorities," "responded" successfully to "challenges," and declined when the leaders stopped responding creatively. He saw the rise or fall of civilizations as depending on the success or failure of the leaders' response to the challenges. In other words, a civilization can last as long as the leaders continue to succeed in responding to successive challenges.

With the civilizations as units identified, he presented the history of each in terms of challenge and response. Civilizations arose in response to some set of challenges of extreme difficulty, when creative minorities devised solutions that reoriented their entire society.

He wrote that as humans we have the distinct ability to anticipate the consequences of our individual actions for our collective future and to change our behavior accordingly. He also wrote that we have the capacity to discern repeating patterns in evolutionary processes and to distill from those patterns insights into how to maximize our own evolutionary potentials.

According to Toynbee, the genesis of a civilization consists of a transition from a static condition to dynamic activity.

Toynbee defined a pattern of interaction, which he calls "challenge and response." A challenge from the natural or social environment provokes a creative response in a society, or a social group, which induces that society to enter the process of civilization. It involves what is now often called a paradigm shift (from the Greek *paradeigma*, meaning "pattern")—a profound change in the thoughts, perceptions, and values that form a particular vision of reality.

The Chinese philosophers saw reality, which they called Tao, as a process of continual flow and change. Delivering value to a customer is a process of continual flow and change as well.

Value focus and delivery is a key. Without that, it does not matter how well we plan and design our processes, align to the organizational strategy, goals, etc. We will endlessly talk about process improvement and performance management. Have we ever asked: Can we quantify the required effectiveness and efficiency of the organization? What are the expected benefits from our performance and process improvement effort? To keep value delivery and profitability under control, but ...

One of the main reasons that we, as humans, can be easily fooled is that we like to promote and follow the illusion of control every day of our lives. So, what is the illusion of control? We believe that we control, or at least influence, the outcomes that we have no influence over. Some people say that this has a positive effect on people and increases motivation and persistence. Others argue that those people learn significantly less and become a barrier for applying common sense, risk management, and control and performance analysis. It becomes a big source of frustration and does not motivate the rest of the organization, which looks at this exercise with mistrust, feeling that management is gambling with the future again and again.

There is always a distinction between ends and means. The performance measures and metrics are about the ends. The means are the strategies to achieve your goals and objectives. The performance indicators show whether your individual strategies work in real time, and how you progress toward the intended outcomes.

All of us who, at least once in our career, have been involved in strategy development, mission and vision definition, and organizational planning have become increasingly frustrated, recognizing that these have nothing to do with reality, but are just case studies from MBA textbooks. The main purpose of this exercise is to increase the profitability of the organization. In most cases, the imagined linkage between strategy and operations, strategy and profitability, and strategy and continuous process improvement is broken as soon as strategy is approved and is in the process to be implemented. Very soon the strategy becomes inefficient and obsolete, showing a large disconnect with the dynamic, highly volatile and highly competitive outside environment.

The value created and delivered to the customer not by the organizational performance but by the process, which focuses on evolution and supports customer needs.

And guess what? At this point, we feel like we are losing control over the situation and something should be done as soon as possible to restore our faith in humanity. This is when organizations start to turn to the methodologies that, from their point of view, will be able to give them all the right answers, but the questions they ask are wrong. We are getting the right answers on wrong questions because we do not know the right questions to ask. And by the way, the questions should be answerable. The environment is very volatile. The situation changes all the time, and what is right today may be wrong tomorrow.

Change demands a response. Response means decision making to react on change. Decision making requires information, facts, and data. Even if we have these, we do not know what to do with them, how to correlate them, and how to cross-reference them. We want ready-made decisions, prescriptions, because we got used to survival in a one-dimensional problem space, which reduces organizational agility, and not in a value space, where the show stoppers can be avoided, allowing the organization to constantly and continuously increase value.

There is a critical question to ask: What information/data do we need for the critical decision making? And another question: Will an aggressive attitude help in making a decision? We cannot afford anymore the trial-and-error approach to decision making. The published results are not really convincing.

So, what do we want and what are we dealing with? Do we want to be agile or do we want to be resilient? According to Jim Highsmith, "Agility is the ability to both create and respond to change in order to profit in a turbulent business environment." What is resiliency? "Dealing effectively with pressure (real or perceived) and capably perform and meet requirements while managing in stressful situation."

Are we agile or are we resilient? Can we answer the question? Can we really identify and structure priorities for strategy development and problem resolution? Do we describe *how* a project is delivered, not *why* it will work or what *effects* it will have? Do we evaluate produced value, which includes product and service by outputs, not by outcomes/effects? Output evaluation is necessary, but not sufficient, to show delivered value to the marketplace.

We have to connect value creation with strategy development and continuous process improvement and management. Where is the connection between action and the outcome?

- Which processes that I work in are key to the success of the organization, the customer, or are in need of improvement?
- What specific problem can I solve to improve the performance of this process or my company?
- What is the current baseline level of performance that quantifies this problem or process performance?
- By how much and by when do I want to improve the performance? What is my objective?
- How much money would I save if I improved the process performance to the level stated in the objective statement?
- If I make an improvement, which of the company's goals and objectives does it support?

There are three domains described in this book. They all unite in one holistic framework that I call IMPACT (interactive measurable pervasive aligned collaborative traceable), to keep the process of value delivery stable in an unstable environment. The purpose of the framework is very simple: respond to the challenge with skill, strategy, and capability. The purpose of this model is to help management to apply the holistic approach to solve management issues and to provide the ability to operate and execute on all three levels: strategic, tactical, and operational.

The new approach should be dynamic and requires flexibility in response to the challenges. It should be structured around the process value delivery rather than functions.

The eight-step framework approach focuses on up-front planning using already developed and mature methodologies for the purpose of translating dynamic strategy into action. The eight-step approach is a logical sequence of steps that can be grouped into three domains:

- Value creation
- Value management
- Value sustainment

It applies equally well to the management corporation or the running of a small business, to the process execution or to the project development activities.

Problem is bad.
Opportunity is good.
What is in the middle? Probletunity.

> No one knows where the borderline between non-intelligent behavior and intelligent behavior lies; in fact, to suggest that a sharp borderline exists is probably silly. But essential abilities for intelligence are certainly:
>
> - To respond to situations very flexibly;[*]
> - To make advantage of fortuitous circumstances;
> - To make sense out of ambiguous or contradictory messages;
> - To recognize the relative importance of different elements of a situation;
> - To find similarities between situations despite differences which may separate them;
> - To draw distinctions between situations despite similarities which may link them;
> - To synthesize new concepts by taking old concepts and putting them together in new ways;
> - To come up with ideas which are novel.
>
> **—Douglas R. Hofstadter,** *Godel, Escher, Bach: An Internal Golden Braid*[†]

---

[*] Stephen R. Covey. 1989. *The seven habits of highly effective people*. New York: Free Press.
[†] Stuart A. Vise. 1997. *Believing in magic: The psychology of superstition*. New York: Oxford University Press.

Businesses spent a huge amount of resources for massive change management programs with the objective to prevent potential problems of the transformation process. In a lot of situations, they have no idea how a transformed organization is supposed look. Even if they have a (blurry) vision of their future, they have no concept how to approach change management.

In reality, change management and transformation management should be represented by the same concept, be symbiotic, and have the ability to answer one question: Are we creating an organization with the capability to renew itself (to have some kind of self-healing and sustainable capabilities) when the next crisis presents itself.

Transformation has become a very popular word. We like this word and have adapted it. We have to transform this, we would like to transform that, and we have to do it now! Nobody has time to think. Transformation now! It sounds even better if it has a label of Lean. Lean sounds more meaningful and important, and proves that management is up to date on everything, particularly on the subject of processes and process improvement. Lean brings importance to the cause.

Whatever we do, it is all about achieving the outcomes, not doing the activities. In many projects, there is a tendency to measure the value of the solution being delivered, rather than the business results.

The law of unintended consequences states: "Any intervention in a complex system may or may not have the intended result, but will inevitably create unanticipated and often undesirable outcomes." *Unintended consequences* are outcomes that are not (limited to) the results originally intended by a particular action. The unintended results may be positive or negative, but they should be unforeseen by the actor. The concept has long existed but was popularized in the twentieth century by Robert K. Merton.

Unintended consequences can be grouped into roughly three types:

■ A positive unexpected benefit
■ A negative unexpected drawback
■ A perverse effect (which may be contrary to what was originally intended, i.e., when an intended solution to a problem only makes the problem worse)

The law of unintended consequences has a much broader focus than just judging by results; it directly relates to the decision-making process or the ability of management to make decisions focused on how they will impact the realization of desired outcomes (results). The expected outcomes are at the end of the process of capabilities delivered, where the capabilities mean product and services delivered to a marketplace.

The broad umbrella of these techniques and methods to ensure that outcomes are planned and realized is referred to as value management. Value in this context means the set of outcomes desired by the organization that can be a combination of qualitative or quantitative. Management refers to proactive planning, organizing of activities, tracking of information, and reporting on desired outcomes.

This expanded focus requires the incorporation of two key principles into an organization's mindset:

1. Organizations are not transforming in a vacuum. There are myriad connections to the outside environment.
2. We want to stay pragmatic. We can reference but cannot literally apply a natural systems approach to organizations. It is very difficult to accept the concept that an organization is a living system. It is difficult because we have immediately rejected the management concept of command and control. The rejection of command and control immediately puts us in a position of uncertainty—what's next? The application of ancient wisdom to management science is not exactly supported by leading MBA programs.

So, where do we start? Where is the root of the new approach, such as business ecology? Probably, at the beginning; we have to reconsider our view of what constitutes success and failure. Can failure be a sign of health? Does "equilibrium is death" apply to organizations as well as the living organisms with which they are compared? Begin at the end: focus on outcomes.

References

Stephen R. Covey. 1990. *The 7 habits of highly effective people. New York: Fireside.*
Jim Highsmith. 2002. *Agile software development ecosystems*, Addison-Wesley Professional.
Douglas R. Hofstadter. 1979. *Gödel, Escher, Bach: An eternal golden braid.* New York: Basic Books.
Arnold J. Toynbee. 1987. *A study of history.* Oxford University Press.

Acknowledgments

There were multiple discussions, conversations, arguments, presentations, frustration and inspiration. There were good and exciting months and disappointing stretches of time. It was a long journey which would be impossible to complete without help and support of my wife, Gail.

I wish to thank all those who helped through this journey and inspired me on the way.

I especially want to thank Terry Balven (USAF), Randy Nunley (Odyssey Consulting Group), Steve Dempsey and Jim Doody (IPT Associates), Joe Defee (CACI), Dr. Richard Soley (OMG), David Russo, Natasha Volf, John Wyzalek (Taylor & Francis), and Dr. Kal Bugrara (Northeastern University).

Special thanks to my students from Northeastern University Graduate School College of Engineering for the diligent research and hard work: Kun Xiao, Rui Xue, and Anukriti Lal.

I would also like to thank my daughter, Natasha, for catching me off guard and taking my picture in Paris.

To all of them my deepest thanks.

Joe Raynus

The Author

Joseph Raynus is a founder and principal consultant at ShareDynamics. ShareDynamics is an information technology process performance management consulting company that helps organizations achieve their strategic goals by translating them into realistic indicators to monitor, balance, and adjust process performance. ShareDynamics has partnered with the Software Engineering Institute at Carnegie Mellon University to deliver training and consulting services in the area of measurement and analysis.

Joseph is certified by the Software Engineering Institute at Carnegie Mellon University and has conducted many assessments, training, and implementations of processes across all phases of a project life cycle.

As a principal consultant, Mr. Raynus provides industry consulting, mentoring, and training for quality and process improvement initiatives, management of conflicting business objectives and strategy goals, development of measurement frameworks, and balanced scorecard and Lean Six Sigma methodologies. He has developed an eight-step strategic alignment and governance framework methodology that supports capabilities-based planning, resource allocation, and monitoring and control by use of strategically aligned performance metrics and key process indicators. He also runs seminars and hands-on workshops to introduce participants to the eight-step framework components and teach them how to develop measures and metrics that are tightly aligned with organizational goals and objectives and provide a reliable mechanism for monitoring and controlling business vitality. Mr. Raynus's consulting clients include Sun Microsystems, Oracle, the U.S. Air Force, the U.S. Marine Corps, and the U.S. Coast Guard R&D Center.

Mr. Raynus is a pioneer in the computer industry and an early champion of software metrics, measurements, software quality, and reliability. Mr. Raynus was a founding member of the National Software Council, supporting the recognition of software as a critical resource and economic force (1995), and a member of its advisory board. In the early 1990s, Mr. Raynus founded and was CEO of SBM (Software Business Management). Their revolutionary product, DecisionVision, was a project management, systems, and automated software metrics tool, which was used by both industry and the U.S. Department of Defense.

Mr. Raynus is a frequent speaker at industry events and the author of several books, including *Software Process Improvement with CMM* (Boston: Artech House, 1999), which is also available in Japanese and Chinese, and his latest, *Improving Business Process Performance: Gain Agility, Create Value, and Achieve Success* (New York: Taylor & Francis, 2010), which is dedicated to the issues of quantitative performance management, strategy definition, and organizational alignment.

In addition to his work as principal consultant at ShareDynamics, Mr. Raynus is an adjunct professor of information systems at Northeastern University College of Engineering, where he teaches courses in information systems planning and management and business process engineering.

Mr. Raynus was awarded a master of science in systems engineering from the State Marine Technical University of St. Petersburg (SMTU), St. Petersburg, Russia.

Chapter 1

The Paradigm

> The future ain't what it used to be.
>
> **—Yogi Berra**[*]

The Paradigm

The dictionary definition of *paradigm* is a key model, pattern, or method used to achieve certain goals or objectives. Historian of science Thomas Kuhn, in his influential book *The Structure of Scientific Revolutions*, gave "paradigm" its contemporary meaning: the set of practices that define a scientific discipline during a particular period of time—in other words, a habit of reasoning at a given moment in history, the standard model for how people are expected to conceive and solve problems.

However, in his book, Kuhn defines a scientific paradigm as:

- *What* is to be observed and scrutinized
- The kind of *questions* that are supposed to be asked and probed for answers in relation to this subject
- *How* these questions are to be structured
- *How* the results of scientific investigations should be interpreted

The usage of paradigm goes beyond that. A paradigm is a set of assumptions. It is how we view the world. The paradigm explains the world and helps us to predict

---

[*] Allen Barra. 2009. *Yogi Berra: Eternal Yankee.* W.W. Norton & Co., xxxv.
Thomas S. Kuhn. 1996. *The structure of scientific revolution.* University of Chicago Press.

its behavior. When we are in a middle of the paradigm, it is hard to imagine any other paradigm.

In his book *Powers of Mind*, Adam Smith describes a Stanford experiment. A team of psychologists raised batches of kittens, some of whom were brought up seeing only vertical stripes and some of whom were brought up in a horizontally striped world. After they grew up and were allowed to move anywhere, the vertical stripers thought the world was vertical and the horizontal stripers thought the world was horizontal. The horizontal stripers could not see the vertical world, and vice versa. The psychologists wrote: "Functional neural connections can be selectively and predictably modified by environmental situation." In other words, our experience shapes our perception. We adapt to our environment without really understanding it.

Science progresses not gradually, but by paradigm shifts that are dramatically revolutionary—shifts that uproot the old habits of mind. And the biggest obstacle to a paradigm shift is paradigm paralysis, when people cannot or will not think outside the prevailing models of thinking

A paradigm—a prevailing set of assumptions—explains the world and helps us to predict its behavior. When we are in the midst of the paradigm, it's pretty hard to imagine any new paradigm.

In the history of science, the classic example is a change that, when it finally comes, literally alters the way we see the universe. For an amazing number of centuries, people believed that the sun and planets all moved around the earth, which was (obviously) the center of the universe. Not only that, but scientists could prove it. These were the limits of the knowledge at that time. Within those limits, scientists explained orbital revolutions somewhat geometrically, calculating cycles and epicycles.

As astronomical data became more accurate, the scholarly community resisted the new evidence. Instead, they calculated more and more complex cycles and epicycles. They were desperate to prop up the old worldview, to keep their calculations in sync with the observations, so that accurate predictions could still be made. The toolbox of cycles and epicycles was stretched beyond limits. To explain observable phenomena, astronomers resorted to a proliferation of increasingly useless calculations.

If you think you see a parallel with today's corporate cultures, that's all right with me. As a paradigm is stretched beyond limits, the holes in the Swiss cheese get bigger and bigger. All the rationales and "innovations" won't work any more. As people keep thinking inside the box, the corporation loses its ability to reach its goals, or even to measure its performance.

All right, so what happened in astronomy? Along came more modern scientists who were not afraid of risk: first Copernicus, then Galileo, then Kepler. Thinking outside the box for the first time in ages, these pioneers tossed out the entire toolbox and declared, "You guys, the earth moves around the sun." They started a revolution by proving their heretical theory, without using cycles, epicycles, and epi-epicycles.

The whole paradigm shifted, and a new one took its place. At last, counterforces had boldly restored the balance and made continued growth and success possible.

Just because the new paradigm is a lot better and makes more sense than the old one, it does not necessarily get adopted right away. Paradigms don't change easily. We always want to keep on investing in the old paradigm. We have lots of reasons for not moving to the new paradigm, even when its outlines become clear.

Practices that are repeatable—good or bad—become true. Even failures get explained away. What can be measured easily prevails over what cannot. What is measurable and repeatable becomes true; this "truth" is our paradigm. If something comes along that doesn't fit the prevailing paradigm, we get uncomfortable because it doesn't ring true. How many times do we assume a cause-and-effect sequence without any objective connection, just based on our perception?

We love to quantify everything. In business management, we have to. Yet at the same time, do we understand what the data are presenting? I say again: when we're in the midst of the prevailing paradigm, we cannot imagine any new paradigm. Our understanding of the situation is based mostly on unbalanced and uncorrelated information.

What makes the situation even worse is that we are afraid to ask questions. Questions put us out of balance because answers could put us out of the paradigm. The business environment furnishes a wide range of examples, from financial indicators to quality indicators. Paradigm influences our thinking very heavily.

There is an old story that makes the point well. At a gathering of rabbis, the wise men were debating a passage of holy law. One rabbi found that he was in disagreement with the rest of a group on a point of implementation. The others put great pressure on him to concede, but he knew that he was right and that God would be on his side. So he called upon the Almighty to help him to prove his case. "Please, God, if I am right, let the streams of Israel flow uphill," the rabbi begged. Immediately, the waters of the land changed direction. Unfortunately, his adversaries were unmoved.

"Please God," the rabbi asked again, "if I am right, may the trees bend to the ground." And they did. But his fellows were unmoved.

"Dear God," the rabbi called out in growing frustration, "may you speak aloud and support me in this painful dispute." The clouds parted and a great voice from heaven boomed: "Rabbis, hear my words—you others are wrong and this man is right. Such is my will and intention."

The lone sage smiled in triumph, but the group remained unimpressed. "Oh, we pay no attention to heavenly voices," they said. "After all, the correct determination on this point was written down long ago."

If you listen to the heavenly voices for a change, you will discern two criteria for conceiving the new paradigm: distinguishing between organization and structure, and the process focus.

Criterion 1: Organization versus Structure

With a classical paradigm, as with any complex system, there is a belief that the dynamics of the whole can be understood from the properties of the parts. Once you know the parts—their properties and the mechanisms through which they interact—you can derive the dynamics of the whole. Or so the thinking goes. Therefore, the rule is: in order to understand the complete system, we have to break it up into smaller pieces. The pieces themselves cannot be explained any other way, except by splitting them into smaller pieces.

As far as you go into this procedure, you always end up with fundamental building blocks, all the way to data elements whose origin and sources you can no longer explain. You get all the way to atomic particles, then subatomic particles, then chaos. From these small building blocks, you would then reconstruct the whole. You would try to explain its dynamics in terms of the properties of the data components.

But there's a disjunction here. There's an old saying in cybernetics and systems theory that for a system, the whole is more than the sum of its parts. Someone observing the set of constituent elements comprising a composite unity can see "the sum of the parts," while the "whole that is more" can only be seen if that observer shifts to addressing the system as a unified whole—a simple unity.

The organization-structure dichotomy is graphically illustrated in the work of the sixteenth-century Italian painter Giuseppe Arcimboldo (Figure 1.1), who devised remarkable portraits, known as composite heads, in which the faces may be composed of vegetables, fruit and tree roots, animals, flowers, etc.

Figure 1.1 Giuseppe Arcimboldo, Vertumnus (1591).

Figure 1.2 The complementary distinction between organization and structure is very useful in delineating and analyzing systems' form and function, for example, describing enterprises as having a generally invariant form in spite of specifically changing components.

How are we able to recognize this composite of fruits and vegetables as a face? Because it is organized to correspond to the conventional, symmetrical, recognizable model (or structure) that we have perceived as a human face since earliest infancy. Arcimboldo's fanciful art achieved a discernible facial organization by arranging novel components according to a conventional structure (Figure 1.2).

Speaking of changing components, Dr. Randall Whitaker writes: "In my long experience with team decision processes and other collaborative activities: I've found that the lack of consensus orientation tends to be the rule and not the exception. For example, meeting participants are often operating with very different views of topics, intentions, and outcomes. These in turn may be quite different from the views or orientations of an observer watching the interaction."*

In the new paradigm, the relationship between the part and the whole is more balanced. While the property of the part contributes to the understanding of the whole, at the same time the property of the part can only be fully understood through the dynamics of the whole. Once we understand the dynamics of the whole, we can derive the property and patterns of parts and data interactions.

Criterion 2: Process Focus

The second criterion for conceiving the new paradigm involves a shift from thinking in terms of structure to thinking in terms of process. Why do we have to focus on process instead of structure? Focusing on process, not structure, we should agree on what our processes are. We have to know how the processes interact and what each process delivers. It should be very clear to us how and what each process delivers,

---

* http://www.enolagaia.com/Tutorial1.html.

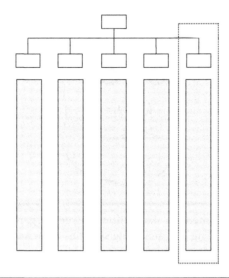

Figure 1.3 Traditional methods of performance management focus on department and functional unit performance.

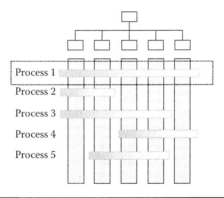

Figure 1.4 PM focuses on the management of cross-functional processes. This involves continuous monitoring, evaluation, measurement (e.g., cost, quality, cycle time), and process innovation.

what skills are required for each process, and how well each process performs. The most important point is that we should measure our processes effectively and manage by these facts (Figures 1.3 and 1.4).

In the old, traditional paradigm, there is a fundamental organizational structure, and then there is a way in which this monolithic structure interacts through organizational processes and procedures. In the new paradigm, the process is primary, and any organization is a display and a manifestation of the underlying process.

In his book *The Synergism Hypothesis*, Peter Corning gives two examples of process focus from Adam Smith's *Wealth of Nations*. In the first example, Smith (not the contemporary commentator, but the eighteenth-century father of modern economics) described a pin factory that he personally observed, in which ten workers together were able to produce forty-eight thousand pins per day. They did this by dividing the production process into component tasks, each of which lent itself to specialization. If each worker were to work alone, attempting to perform all of the tasks associated with making pins, Smith thought it unlikely that on any given day they would be able to produce even one pin per worker.

We can look at the pin factory in another way by considering how various specialized skill and production operations were combined in an organized, goal-oriented system. The system described included not only the roles played by the ten workers. Those roles had to be precisely articulated with respect to one another. The description also included the appropriate machinery, the energy to run the machinery, sources of raw materials, a supporting transportation system, and markets in which production costs are recovered through sales.

Finally, the pin factory operation was also dependent on an existing communication and control subsystem (on top of the technical advances) through which planning, the hiring and training of workers, production decisions, and coordination, marketing, and bookkeeping could be affected.

The success of the pin factory was the result of the total organization, the total configuration of functional relationships between worker and worker, worker and machine, worker and society, and worker and environment. Remove any one of these components and the system, as a system of cooperative interaction and interdependencies management, would not work.

In the second example, Smith compared the transport of goods overland from London to Edinburgh in "broad-wheeled" wagons and the transport of goods by sailing ships between London and Leith, the seaport that serves Edinburgh.

In six weeks, two men and eight horses could deliver about four tons of goods to Edinburgh and back. In the same amount of time, a ship with a crew of six or eight men could carry 200 tons to Leith—an amount of freight that would require 50 wagons, 100 men, and 400 horses for overland transport. What was the critical difference here?

It was not the division of labor alone, not the technical advances embodied in ships as opposed to horses and wagons, and not the capital needed to finance the building of a ship. It was, in part, all of these things: the total configuration of factors integrated in one system and one process associated with shipborne commerce. Working together, these components created a system that tied together a number of formerly independent operations. They created a system of people for allocating resources and regulating activities of the business.

Later that system came to be called business process management. Those involved in the process interdependence, each contributing different skills, understood that their synergy led to the achievement of a common goal.

More Process Focus: The Tale of Hora and Tempus

One final example, famously described by the late Herbert Simon, the Nobel Prize winner for pioneering research on organizational decision making, illustrates achievement of the main goal by setting incremental subgoals. (Setting subgoals enhances the adaptability of the process.)

There once were two watchmakers, named Hora and Tempus, who manufactured very fine watches. Both of them were highly regarded, and the phones in their workshops rang frequently. New customers were constantly calling them. However, Hora prospered while Tempus became poorer and poorer and finally lost his shop. What was the reason?

The watches the men made consisted of about one thousand parts each. Tempus had so constructed his that if he had one partially assembled and had to put it down—say to answer the phone—it immediately fell to pieces and had to be reassembled from the elements. The more customers liked his watches, the more they phoned him, and the more difficult it became for him to find enough uninterrupted time to finish a watch.

The watches Hora handled were no less complex than those of Tempus, but he had designed them so that he could put together subassemblies of about ten elements each. Ten of these subassemblies, again, could be put together into a larger subassembly and a system of ten of the latter constituted the whole watch. Hence, when Hora had to put down a partly assembled watch in order to answer the phone, he lost only a small part of his work, and he assembled his watches in only a fraction of the man-hours it took Tempus.

In this example, Hora organized the components into a stable subsystem and therefore created a process that was flexible enough to adapt to outside disturbances. What is most important to understand is that Hora set up systematic subgoals, which were then translated into the interdependent subassemblies. Setting subgoals led to achievement of the ultimate final goal, which was not attainable otherwise. Hora was able to achieve success in three very important steps of gaining knowledge:

- Obtain knowledge of how each individual part works.
- Obtain knowledge of how each part works with those to which it is connected.
- Obtain knowledge of how all of these interactions combine in the system to produce the desired effect.

Business Performance Engineering and Management

> It is not the strongest of the species that survives, nor the most intelligent that survives. It is the one that is the most adaptable to change.
>
> **—Darwin**

Let's go to the root: In 1905 and 1911, Frederic Winslow Taylor published the monographs *Shop Management* and The *Principles of Scientific Management*. Those two publications gave the beginning of so-called scientific management, which is also called Taylorism or the Taylor system. In a nutshell, this is a theory of management that analyzes and synthesizes, and optimizes workflow with the objective to increase productivity. He wrote in the introduction to one of his monographs:

> PRESIDENT ROOSEVELT, in his address to the Governors at the White House, prophetically remarked that "The conservation of our national resources is only preliminary to the larger question of national efficiency."
>
> The whole country at once recognized the importance of conserving our material resources and a large movement has been started which will be effective in accomplishing this object. As yet, however, we have but vaguely appreciated the importance of "the larger question of increasing our national efficiency."
>
> We can see and feel the waste of material things. Awkward, inefficient, or ill-directed movements of men, however, leave nothing visible or tangible behind them. Their appreciation calls for an act of memory, an effort of the imagination. And for this reason, even though our daily loss from this source is greater than from our waste of material things, the one has stirred us deeply, while the other has moved us but little.
>
> We can see our forests vanishing, our water-powers going to waste, our soil being carried by floods into the sea; and the end of our coal and our iron is in sight. But our larger wastes of human effort, which go on every day through such of our acts as are blundering, ill-directed; or inefficient, and which Mr. Roosevelt refers to as a lack of "national efficiency," are less visible, less tangible, and are but vaguely appreciated.*

Today, this has become synonymous with the improved and efficient way to do business. Many believe that in the same time it was a root of performance management and business process engineering. But what is performance management? Somebody called it management by 2 × 4—"variations of the age old practice of whacking people upside the head to get them to do what they are supposed to be doing." Performance management systems are used to track and evaluate everyone in the organization to make sure they are performing to the standards set for them.

But who sets performance goals in the first place? Usually they are designated at the top of the organization and cascade down through the ranks. Proponents of performance-based management assume that these objectives are derived from objective data and judgments. Cynics suspect they are based on the performance goals the CEO needs to make his or her bonus. But are performance management systems enough to ensure that there will be satisfactory performance? Perhaps, but

---

* Frederick Winslow Taylor. 1911. *Principles of Scientific Management.*

the fact that so many of these management approaches fail to produce the results expected suggests there may be other, more productive and less stressful ways to keep an organization on the right performance track.*

It goes without saying: To compete in the present environment of globalization, organizations must change. Those that fail to see the need for change will not survive. This change, in nearly every case, involves business performance engineering.

Back in the 1990s, business reengineering was a very popular subject. For example, *Reengineering the Corporation* by Michael Hammer and James Champy was published in 1993. This trend spawned two remedies:

■ Reengineer the business through IT
■ Align IS (information systems) and corporate goals

The assumption was that organizations would set their focus on business reengineering, and on development of information systems that directly support company strategy. Management would then be able to assume control and gain competitive advantage.

Organizations were rushing into business process reengineering (BPR) to improve effectiveness and efficiency in order to achieve competitive advantage. As Scott Adams memorably summarized it in *The Dilbert Principle*, "Businesses flocked to reengineering like frat boys to a drunken cheerleader."

What happened next? Downsizing. Big time. In a lot of companies, middle managers were "reengineered." The middle management had two main job responsibilities: to provide senior management with the information needed for decision support, and to implement internal policies and procedures that would reflect the directions and critical success factors set by senior management.

A big gap developed between the goals and objectives defined by senior management—and expressed in quantitative targets for achievement—and actual measurable information gathered from the operational level. Companies had changed strategies, but its business processes (if they even defined them) stayed the same.

BPM and the Hot Hand

Traditional performance management decision making was based on organizational hierarchies. But when the companies changed organizational structures, their performance management never changed. When this happens—and it often does—traditional key performance indicators are distorted. These measures do not have predictive capabilities and do not reflect changes until it is too late.

---

* Tony DiRomualdo, "The Myth of the Performance-Based Management," Wisconsin Technology Network, May 26, 2004, http://wistechnology.com/articles/858/.

The outside environment is always brimming with potential opportunities, problems, and threats that make any business forecasting and planning extremely difficult. Sometimes even gazing into a crystal ball would be more accurate.

One company—let's call it Atroxx Solutions—unexpectedly achieving a good fourth quarter in a short period of time, expanded their "human capital" by 40%. They didn't realize that this additional revenue was not a trend, but a spike caused by effective sales effort and ready-to-buy market conditions. Eight months later, Atroxx realized that its big expansion effort was a bad move. (The realization came from the balance sheet and a heated directors' meeting.) Guess what? The company decided to reduce its costly "human capital" by a big percentage.

What went wrong? Atroxx had all the needed state-of-the-art tools and applications to support intelligent decision making, and boasted trained MBAs from top business schools. Yet they didn't read their fourth quarter results properly. Senior management did not have in place a corporate-wide strategy that would prevent individual organizational growth at the expense of overall corporate performance. The company's business analysts and sophisticated business information applications couldn't prevent the fiasco, for the simple reason that top-level strategic objectives were not aligned with bottom-level initiatives and operational performance.

The moral of the story is that there's a human tendency to discover patterns in random data to support a self-fulfilling prophecy. In professional sports, this is called the "hot hand" phenomenon. This is the compelling, yet illusionary perception held by fans and players alike that some players have "hot streaks" such that one successful shot is likely to be followed by another successful shot, while a miss will be followed by another miss. In an experiment, university basketball players were asked to place bets predicting the results of their next shot. Their bets showed strong evidence of a belief in the hot hand, yet their actual performance offered no evidence for its validity.

Applying this example to corporate life, it is clear that a real-time system is needed that will alert management to problems and opportunities, and that will empower them to react through quantitative information and company-wide collaboration. That is exactly the purpose and function of business process engineering.

Strategy, Strategic Management, and BPE

Strategic thinking and strategic actions reflect a company's ability to construct the picture, recognize patterns and trends, establish priorities, anticipate issues and outcomes, and have alternatives to fall back upon. Strategy directs action.

Strategy planning and strategy readjustment that are based on a dynamic relationship to the outside environment are what enable a company to survive and thrive in any given situation. (Strategy is different from tactics. Think "head" and "hands." Tactical refers to hands-on monitoring—getting the job done and making sure those goals are met.)

In every enterprise, it is difficult to link strategy to execution—to align strategic and operational issues. There is a gap in between the day-to-day performance that seeks to achieve measurable goals and the guiding strategic vision. That gap, if it widens, can be fatal to the enterprise. The performance-strategy gap occurs whenever the present execution of organizational processes is driven by historical motivation instead of present realities.

Strategic management requires us to focus on achieving long-term objectives while performing operational activities. Managing the execution of operational strategy is a key component supporting the enterprise's overall vision and strategy.

Components of BPE include all the practices, technologies, methodologies, and metrics used to gather and apply relevant information, displayed as graphical scorecards and dashboards, to deliver corporate information. It usually displays figures for key performance indicators so that management can track organizational performance relative to corporate goals and strategies. Some companies use established management methodologies with their BPM systems, such as balanced scorecard or Six Sigma. The main objective of business process engineering is to have an ability to generate information for decision support.

This leads me to discuss today's surge of activities and tools around business intelligence (BI) and enterprise data integration projects. A lot of applications and tools on the market claim to help you turn information into higher business performance.

Competition at the Crossroads

In 2007, a landmark study by the BPM Forum and Deloitte Consulting, "Competition at the Crossroads: Strategic Planning and Action in Disruptive Markets," described a business crisis. The report found that most technology executives are constrained in their ability to identify and respond to major market change because of a focus on immediate, short-term business priorities, an institutional bias against taking risks, and a lack of resources.

The executives surveyed said that the biggest value-based impediments to course-correcting action are a focus on short-term profitability, a fixation on existing business, and a lack of a quantitative business case for major change, with clear short-term return on investment (ROI).

The report cited "insufficient investment in strategic planning, getting the right information, and having the required talent that can look beyond today's sales, profitability, current products, customers and technologies."

The same report quotes one executive in the B2B space who argued that, while staying close to the customer is critical to business competitiveness, it's imperative to identify and work most closely with customers on the leading edge of technology adoption and use: "It's about aligning yourself with innovative customers, so that you, yourself, can be on a leading edge of innovation."

In a survey conducted by BPM Partners, BPM initiatives are being driven by an internal demand for greater accuracy and accountability and transparency of financial reporting, including a focus on having "one version of the truth." Nearly 40% of respondents questioned the accuracy and integrity of the financial data available to them from their existing systems.

The business-critical importance of BPM was a key finding in a global survey of 450 CFOs from 35 countries that was undertaken by IBM Business Consulting Services. Sixty-five percent of the survey respondents rated BPM as a top objective, supporting the emerging role of CFOs toward more active participation in decision support and shareholder value creation, rather than the traditional focus on transactional activities (managing the balance sheet).

Today, Internet technology makes the diffusion of performance measurement across the business or across businesses much simpler than in the past. This has sparked interest in business information technologies at various levels of management.

Wayne Eckerson, director of education and research at the Data Warehouse Institute, summed it up in the BPM Standards Group report:[*]

> In order to drive a successful BPM initiative, companies should identify strategic business drivers up front, select metrics and measures derived from their drivers, and assess the ability of their current systems to support BPM. These are all important parts of the process companies should follow for BPM success.

BPM: A Brief History

What started as BPM systems has been transformed into business performance management processes.[†] The BPM Standards Group has developed a common definition of BPM that provides appropriate context for performance management, including the following principles:

> BPM is a set of integrated, closed-loop management and analytic processes, supported by technology, that address financial as well as operational activities.

---

[*] www.bpmpartners.com/documents/press032504.pdf.

[†] The definition of BPM was clarified in 2004 by the BPM Standards Group. John Van Decker of META summarized: "We've agreed upon the term 'BPM' for Business Performance Management. Others may use CPM and EPM as equivalents. The 'other' BPM (Business Process Management), BAM (Business Activity Monitoring), BI (Business Intelligence), EIS (Executive Information System) and analytic applications are not equivalent to this definition of BPM but may represent a portion of what BPM provides."

BPM is an enabler for businesses in defining strategic goals, and then measuring and managing performance against those goals.

Core BPM processes include financial and operational planning, consolidation and reporting, modeling, analysis, and monitoring of key performance indicators (KPIs) linked to organizational strategy.

In 2003, when the BPM Standards Group was being formed, business performance management had grown to a $1.1 billion industry and was expected to grow 15% to 20% in only one year. It grew to $1.6 billion in 2007, a compound annual growth rate of better than 10%. A META Group study also showed that 85% of enterprises surveyed planned to undertake a BPM project in the near future.

Today's major BPM applications include budgeting, planning, consolidation, activity-based management, and cross-functional scorecarding.

You get the message: business performance management became a very important component in a company's survival kit. Enterprises are getting more and more interested in BPM. They'd better—this is critical.

Not long ago, KPMG studied U.S. and European business and government executives. Vince Kellen, a BPM expert at DePaul University, tells what they found:

One of the most common disappointments reported was the lack of data integrity and the inability of their system to produce meaningful information to support decision-making. The study also discovered that BPM systems are not aligned with strategic business measures, dependent on lagging (not leading) indicators, are poorly integrated with internal and external information, and rely too heavily on financial measures.

Some factors for failed BPM systems included measuring things that are easily measured versus what should be measured, data inaccuracy, measures that were too complicated, and users not understanding the system and its measures.

Companies will switch and adopt the concept of BPE for various reasons. Mainly, they need to improve management's control over the formulation and execution of strategy—a process to which they are denied access by today's tool sets. The biggest issues these companies face are a poorly defined metrification process (including Key performance indicators) and a lack of people with sufficient analytical skill, judgment, and decision-making abilities. BPE would enable these companies to develop an enterprise-wide strategy that would alert them against optimizing individual business unit growth at the expense of overall corporate performance.

References

Scott Adams. 1996. *The Dilbert principle: A cubicle's-eye view of bosses, meetings, management fads & other workplace afflictions.* New York: HarperBusiness.

BPM Forum. 2007. www.bpfforum.org/csr

Peter Corning. 1983. *The synergism hypothesis.* New York: McGraw-Hill.

Michael Hammer, and James Champy. 1993. *Reengineering the corporation: A manifesto for business revolution.* New York: HarperBusiness.

Vince Kellen. 2003. *Business performance measurement: At the crossroads of strategy, decision-making, Learning and information visualization.* www.kellen.net/bpm.htm

Adam Smith. 1975. *Powers of mind.* New York: Random House, 24.

Chapter 2

The Change

More than any other time in history, mankind faces a crossroads. One path leads to despair and utter hopelessness. The other, to total extinction. Let us pray we have the wisdom to choose correctly.

—Woody Allen
Side Effects (1980)

The future is moving so quickly that you can't anticipate it ... We have to put tremendous emphasis on quick response instead of planning.

—Steve Kerr
Chief Learning Officer of General Electric
(Laufer, 2009)

Change

A theory of change is a description of how and why a set of activities—be they part of a highly focused program or a comprehensive initiative—are expected to lead to early, intermediate, and long-term outcomes over a specified period.

—Anderson, 2000
University of Wisconsin-Extension

Everything begins with change. In a lot of cases, we have little choice in influencing what, how, and when the change comes about. We always fight with the change even when the change is good.

Situations always change. One individual cannot predict everything in advance and decide everything in advance. There is a big gap called uncertainty in between information available, biases, decision-making ability, and decisions made. The decision-making process depends on business culture, leadership, processes, and strategic control. A decision-making executive must have a sort of control system, which will help him or her to detect compliance to the company strategic goals, as well as an ability to be proactive and quickly reposition the organization in case of unexpected changes. It could be called detect and control capability, similar to a closed-loop control system. When an organization stops to respond to outside changes, because of the inability to sense them at the right time, this organization will be dead soon. To react, you can afford to go "by the book." To prevent, you need something more than a book filled with policies and procedures. You have to define, improve, and develop business processes through a closed-loop measurement and analysis improvement process, but what is most important is a flexible framework that will support three main organizational components: people, process, and technology.

Why would organizations change? People are well paid, sometimes not held accountable, allowed to do their own stuff, and difficult to control. Is there any reason to change? Managers are hired, receive bonuses, and fired based on their short-term performance and their ability to deliver. It is probably very unreasonable to assume that the majority of management, with those ground rules, will choose to take a risk on long-term quality programs, where the potential result is very uncertain (unless it is pushed from above).

At the same time, the organization believes it needs change when it cannot deliver and sustain value delivery. The commonly used paradigm is to embark on change management activities and, in a lot of cases, not be able to understand the real situation and always confusing output and outcome. The gap between output and outcome creates a need of doing something. That something that will be able to fill the gap is often called change management. Is it again an illusion of control? Do we need change management, or do we have to consider a process of transformation?

We rarely *think* about process transformation. The thinking process starts with simple questions:

What is a process of transforming tangible outputs into expected outcomes?
What are the steps in between?
How is it going to impact us and our customers?

CATWOE

In 1990, Peter Checkland and his colleagues at the University of Lancaster developed soft system methodology (SSM), which could serve as a general problem-solving tool.*

---

* P. Checkland and J. Scholes, *System Methodology in Action*, Wiley, 1990.

Checkland related the word system to a way of doing things, and organization and resources and procedures and associated with it with properties typical for human activity systems and can be easy correlated with any organizational structure:

A system has a purpose(s). It exists for a reason and achieves some change, or transformation.

Its performance can be measured, and it can be shown to be more or less efficient.

There is a mechanism to control—a decision-making process.

It has components, which themselves can be taken to be a system.

Its components are related and interact.

It exists as part of a wider system(s)—its environment, with which it must interact.

It has a boundary that defines what is and what is not part of the system.

It has its own resources.

It has an expectation of continuity, and can be expected to adapt to or recover from disturbances.

Another governing principle is the principle of emergence—most often expressed as "a whole is greater than the sum of its parts." When the constituent parts of the system act together, they have properties that the individual parts do not have.*

In the core of each conceptual system lies a transformation process whose input is changed or transformed into a new form—the output. What follows transformation is a worldview—a powerful concept that defines the point of view that makes transformation reasonable and worth doing. Together they form the core for CATWOE. The components of CATWOE are as follows:

Customers (the beneficiaries of transformation)
Actors (those who do transformation)
Transformation process
Weltanschauung (the worldview that makes transformation meaningful)
Owners (those with the power to stop transformation)
Environmental constraints (components outside the system, which are taken as given but affect systems behavior)

This model specifies a way of regulating itself if desired performance is not achieved, and defines terms of efficacy, efficiency, and effectiveness:

E1—efficacy: Does the system work? Is the desired transformation achieved?
E2—efficiency: A comparison of the value of the output of the system and the resources needed to achieve that output.
E3—effectiveness: Does the system achieve its longer-term goals?

We will discuss how those three Es should be measured later in the book.

---

* Jeremy Rose, Soft Systems Methodology, Department of BIT, Manchester Metropolitan University.

Attempts to improve or change processes in large organizations usually are met with resistance. The "survival law" requires one to be a "team player" and not to make any waves. There is probably a very simple explanation to that. We always try to resolve a problem independent from the situation and how this situation affects the desired outcome.

Our shackle cloth: process, structure, and long-term policies are annoying and boring. We still prefer a creative art form. As it was said before, organizational structure should be built around the process, not function. Structure comes and goes and should support process. It should be created to fit the current situation and support the expected outcome, which is translated into the customer value and customer satisfaction. Structure should be flexible enough to support long-term organizational mission and vision.

Companies, like any living organism, must become learning organizations that change and adapt to suit their changing environment. "If you don't practice the change management that looks after the future, the future will not look after you," said Bill Gates. "The tendency for successful companies to fail to innovate is just that: a tendency. If you're too focused on your current business, it's hard to look ahead."

Change management talks became very popular in the corporate environment. The term *change management* spread so wildly that even when people came for an interview, they were always asked how they managed change. Change is expected, not stability.

Alan Weiss writes that people do not generally resist change per se. They resist venturing into unfamiliar and potentially harmful territory. Work with your client to establish not only the future state desired, but also the details of the journey.[*]

Change is a problem. When change is initiated, it means that an organization has to move from point A to point B—from "here" to "there," from the as-is to the to-be state.

If you do not have a vision of a bridge to build, you will stay here and will never be able to reach there. So forget the shining city on a hill.

Most of our here is a problem. There is something wrong with our here. Here is a graveyard of our good intentions, initiatives, projects, and management. It is dressed in shackle cloth and ashes and always asking for forgiveness.

So, why does the problem exist? One possible explanation was given by Richard Boland and Fred Collopy from Weatherhead School of Management (Case Western Reserve University and University of Cambridge). They write that managers are thrown into situations that are not of their own making, yet for which they are responsible to produce a desired outcome. They operate in a problem space that has no firm basis for judging one problem-solving move as superior to another, yet they must proceed. They also suggest that we are always trapped by our vocabulary, and we train our managers to work and make decisions in a problem space not in

---

[*] Alan Weiss, *Organizational Consulting*, Wiley & Sons, 2003.

the future. The problem space is dependent on the way the manager represents a situation that he or she faces. The first step in any problem solving is problem representation and, to a large extent, the solution hidden within it.

Successful change programs begin with targeted results, and your level of success is determined by your ability to deliberately respond to a challenge inside or outside the adapted business process and practices in a timely and cost-effective manner.

If we look at the two sayings above (Woody Allen and Steve Kerr), you can easily realize they contradict each other. The first saying is passive and receptive, while the second is active and creative. So, who is right? Both of them!

Lao Tzu writes that governing the large country is like cooking a small fish. A leader should not stir too often, or it will come apart. Can we apply the same statement to the corporations? How can we minimize the damage that unnecessary change might cause?

Lao Tzu suggests that the best way to govern a country is not to disturb people unnecessarily. A good government does not make many policies or issue many orders. It runs a country in such ways that when its work is done, people will say: "All this happened naturally."

If you wish to manage change effectively, you need to understand that the way people behave is a balancing act—they balance the forces that act upon them. Some of these forces are trying to get people to change their behavior, and others are trying to restrain or limit that change.

First, talk about adaptive changes: respond to external change, anticipate change, search for opportunities, and create an adaptive organization. Second, talk about change generation: create and lead change, create new business models, create new core of capabilities, etc. The real change management is achieving balance between adaptation to change and change creation.

Balance isn't an issue of time, but an issue of choice. It's about living your values by aligning your behavior with what you believe is really important. Let's look at what we are trying to balance. There are three main components in this balancing act: people, culture, and process. When all those components are integrated, they deliver value to a customer (Figure 2.1).

Leadership is imperative for molding a group of people into a team, and shaping them into a force that serves as a competitive business advantage. A leader knows how to make people function in a collaborative fashion, and how to motivate them to excel in their performance. Leaders also know how to balance the individual team member's quest with the goal of producing synergy—an outcome that exceeds the sum of individual inputs. Leaders require that their team members forego the quest for personal best in concert with the team effort (Figure 2.2).

Change constantly requires the balancing of effectiveness, efficiency, and improvement (Figure 2.3). We must survive and succeed in a constantly changing world. In order to do that, we have to treat change as a friend—a friend that presents as an opportunity for potential growth and improvement. If you wish your organization to be better able to survive and prosper in today's uncertain and

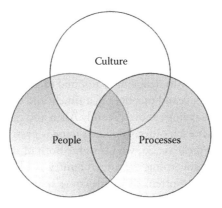

Figure 2.1   Object Management Group business architecture.

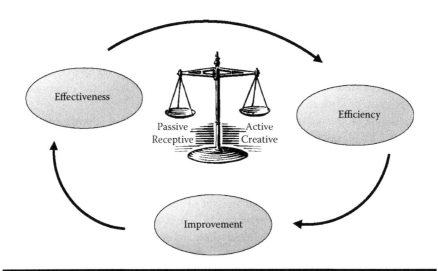

Figure 2.2   Balancing improvement.

turbulent times, you should raise a creative tension. To achieve this, you must move your organization to the point at which a natural balance is found between chaos and order.

It does not matter whom I'm visiting or talking to when people ask: "Mr. Raynus, how do you do change management?" I understand it's time to leave. They ask this question not because they really want to know, but because they want to blow you away. They know they do not have an answer, but they think they do. The reality is they really do not need an answer. The answer may not be what they expect, but the real question is still: "How would you define the change process?

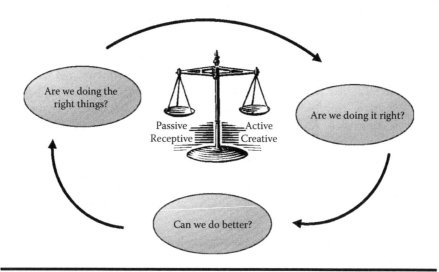

Figure 2.3 Connecting right and better.

Very often organizations view performance management as a linear environment. In the majority of cases, a significant percentage of performance goals and objectives impacting management do not fit the linear model. Approaching performance management in a linear fashion will not produce a success. The reality is not linear:

> What if being successful this year involves making sure you do not practice what you did last year?*
> What if the business environment is not stable, and therefore a sequence or known formula that worked yesterday is not a guarantee of success next month or next year?
> What if responding to a change is, with all of its unpredictability, more closely tied to success than dutifully working your plan toward the big objectives?
> What if you can't respond to the process and update information fast enough because of the challenges of information management?

There are few frameworks that try to answer this question. The first one is "unfreezing, changing, and refreezing." This framework for change management is based on Kurt Lewin's† adoption of the systems conception of dynamic stability. This framework could be useful if you plan the change and can afford it. Organizations cannot afford to stay lost over an extended period of time, i.e., "unfrozen."

The real change process is a process of problem finding prevention and solving. Managing change is a matter of moving from one state to another, specifically

---

* Fred Nickols, Change Management Primer 101, www.nickols.us.
† www.consultpivotal.com/lewin's.html

from the problem state to the solved state. And most important is a problem definition and a problem analysis. Goals are set and support defined organizational strategy. They are achieved at different levels and in various areas and functions. They are quantifiable and measurable—ends and means connected and related to each other. The net effect is transition from one state to another in a planned, orderly fashion. This leads us to the most important finding that the change has a process dimension. At the conceptual level, the change problem is a matter of moving from one state to another state. It is usually accomplished as the result of setting and achieving three types of goals: transform, reduce, and apply. Transform goals are concerned with defining differences between two states. Reduce goals are concerned with determining ways of eliminating these differences. Apply goals are concerned with putting into play operators that actually affect the elimination of these differences.*†

As the preceding goal types suggest, the analysis of a potential change problem will at various times focus on defining the outcomes of the change effort, identifying the changes necessary to produce these outcomes, and finding and implementing ways and means of making the required changes.

Fred Nickols writes that a change problem can be treated as smaller problems having to do with the how, what, and why of change. To frame the change effort in the form of *how* questions is to focus the effort on means. Diagnosis is assumed or not performed at all. Consequently, the ends sought are not discussed. To focus on ends requires the posing of *what* questions. What are we trying to accomplish? What changes are necessary? What indicators will show the success? What standards apply? What measures of performance are we trying to effect?

End and means are relative notions. They are not absolutes; that is, something is an end or a means only in relation to something else. Thus, chains and networks of ends-means relationships often have to be traced out before one finds the "true" ends of a change effort. In this regard, *why* questions prove to be extremely useful. To ask a *why* question is to get at the ultimate purpose of functions and to open a door to finding new and better ways of performing them. Why do we do what we do? Why do we do it the way we do it?

Strategy development and execution is a continuous process, the product of constant adjustment and readjustment. An operation is an established process driven by existing strategy. Operations generate today's value, while strategies create tomorrow's opportunities. The problem of successful strategy execution is misalignment between operations and strategy. It leads to miscommunications and uncertainty of strategy execution.

It includes planning, prediction, and containment. The change reaction and management are intertwined throughout the strategy definition process. Managing

---

* A.A. Newell and H. Simon, The Theory of Human Problem Solving. In *Readings in Cognitive Science*, A. Collins and E. Smith (eds.).
† www.nichols.us

change requires specific approaches. Managing change requires balancing between strategy and operations. The most effective way to deal with uncertainty contained in strategy development is to have a balancing process that constantly confronts the unknown and creates a new change.

Organizations should establish a connection between problem resolution and expected outcome!

What's changing or what needs to change in your organization?
What factors external to your organization are causing you to make these changes (e.g., lost market share, reduced product life, increased competition)?
What difficulties have you encountered in making changes?
What are your organization's strengths and weaknesses?

The Business Perspective

Belgian surrealist Rene Magritte painted a series of pipes entitled *Ceci n'est pas une pipe* ("This is not a pipe"). The picture of the thing is not the thing. In the same way, an organization chart is not a company, nor a new strategy an automatic answer to corporate grief. We all know this, but when trouble lurks, we call for a new strategy and probably reorganize. And when we reorganize, we usually stop at rearranging the boxes on the chart. The odds are high that nothing much will change. We will have chaos, even useful chaos for a while, but eventually the old culture will prevail. Old habit patterns persist. At a gut level, all of us know that much more goes into the process of keeping a large organization vital and responsive than the policy statements, new strategies, plans, budgets, and organization charts can possibly depict. But all too often we behave as though we don't know it. If we want change, we fiddle with the strategy. Or we change the structure. Perhaps the time has come to change our ways.

Peters and Waterman's *In Search of Excellence* set off a quarter century of management improvement initiatives. This admonition, found in the first paragraph of the first chapter of their book, is as valid today as it was in 1982:

> My previous book was published a few years ago pointing out the relationship between the process measurements and software capability maturity model (sw/CMM) and emphasized on the fact that measuring the process can enhance organizational behavior in a software development organization. A lot happened over the last few years. The economy was booming at an unbelievable speed. But only a few companies were successful in the improvement effort and unfortunately not too many changes have been noted.

Organizations are challenged to constantly reshape their operations and improve performance, and to adapt quickly to new markets and opportunities. With new methodologies and frameworks such as business activity monitoring (BAM), business process management (BPM), business process intelligence (BPI), Six Sigma, Lean, and executive dashboard, the real question becomes: How do I get started?

Alvin Toffler, in his book *Power Shift*, discusses the close relationship of knowledge, power, wealth, and the transformation in society. According to Mr. Toffler,

> a revolution is sweeping today's … world. No genius in the past … could have imagined today's deepest power shift; the astounding degree to which both force and wealth themselves have come to depend on knowledge.

Toffler defines a power shift as a transfer of power, as a deep-level change in the very nature of power. He further states, "Knowledge itself, therefore, turns out to be not only the source of the highest-quality power, but also the most important ingredient of force and wealth."

Before we can really understand the concepts behind Quantitative Business Performance Management (QBPM), we need to take a look at the conditions that spawned the need for this framework. The recognition of the importance of information as a major factor in changing organizations has grown considerably in recent years. Information is no longer viewed as a convenient way of getting work done; it is quickly being recognized as a critical resource essential for today's organizations to maintain their competitive edge.

In a 1958 article in the *Harvard Business Review* entitled "Management in the 1980s," Harold J. Leavitt and Thomas L. Wistler made predictions about management in the future. By the late 1980s, they predicted the combination of management science and information technology would cause middle management to shrink, top management to take on more of the creative functions of management, and large organizations to shrink again.

Peter Drucker, in a 1988 *Harvard Business Review* article titled "The Coming of the New Organization," suggests we look at a symphony orchestra. In an orchestra, several hundred musicians play for one director. There is no chain of command and no middle management. The director interacts directly with individual players. What enables a symphony orchestra to work effectively? What provides the glue to keep all of the players from going their own independent direction? What keeps them working to effectively and efficiently produce a common product? There are at least three factors that both of these horizontal organizations share that are critical to their success.

By the mid-1980s, businesses began to realize that automation alone was not the answer to increased productivity. Businesses realized that information is a resource that needs to be managed for increased productivity, and that automation is only a tool, although a very necessary tool, to provide managers access to the information that they need to make decisions. Furthermore, businesses realized that from an information point of view, the solution to productive organizations is not how much information can be automated. The solution is what information is necessary to support the functional processes that make up the business, thus allowing for efficient operations. While organizations were drowning in automated information, they were starving for the appropriate information, which was needed to perform essential business operations. Automation of unnecessary information inhibits productivity. However, automation of the appropriate information, which supports business processes, can be a productivity multiplier.

Twenty years ago it seemed to be a good idea to manage overall organizational and individual project performance by goals. The thought was if you track your goals with enough specificity and are able to quantify them, there is a good chance you will be able to achieve them. At the same time, the importance of the environment or the context in which the goals are set should not underemphasized.

In a 1991 comprehensive review of thirty years of research on the impact of management by objectives, Robert Rodgers and John Hunter concluded that companies whose CEOs demonstrated high commitment to MBO showed, on average, a 56% gain in productivity. Companies with CEOs who showed low commitment only saw a 6% gain in productivity. They defined high commitment as "enthusiastic support for" and "participation in" the MBO program. This is hardly a new observation, but it does provide compelling hard data for encouraging the CEO's full involvement in the MBO process. The key factors are goal setting, participation in decision making, and objective feedback to managers. Goal setting is critical since it makes clear to the manager what the organizational objectives are and what the role of the manager is in achieving those objectives. Feedback provides information regarding whether goals are still important and current and what should be done to improve effectiveness of the organization or individual process.

Do You Still Remember the Late 1990s?

This was the time of the dot com's gold rush, when people were making fortunes on technology, mergers and acquisitions, and any association with the Web business was a way (or seemed like) to make a fortune. Nobody really thought about improving management techniques.

Peter Drucker—who?

Deming's quality circles—what for? It's not more than an expensive thing of the past.

"We do not really have time for management education—we need managers."

There was no reason to change. People were well paid, not held accountable, allowed to do their own staff, and difficult to control. Any product development, and software in particular, is very labor intensive, which takes even more managers (they are also well paid). Is there any reason to change? Managers are hired, receive bonuses, and fired based on their short-term performance and their ability to deliver. It is probably very unreasonable to assume that the majority of management with those ground rules will choose to take a risk on long-term quality programs, where the potential result is very uncertain (unless it is pushed from above).

> Although we hear about many successful attempts to transform organizations, the overall track record is very poor. In recent surveys, CEOs reported again and again that their organizational change efforts did not yield the promised results. Instead of managing new organizations, they ended up managing the unwanted side effects of their efforts. At first glance, this situation seems paradoxical. When we observe our natural environment, we see continuous change, adaptation, and creativity; yet our business organizations seem to be incapable of dealing with change. (Fritjof Capra)

Inefficiencies in process management produce product quality issues and cause more testers to be hired. In a vast majority of the situations when requirements are not clearly defined, the customer is willing to accept mediocre quality product. Attempts to improve or change processes in large organizations are met with resistance. The survival law requires one to be a team player and not to make any waves. But in order to be a team player, you have to have an environment that supports the team.

Process, structure, and long-term policies are annoying and boring. We still prefer a creative art form.

In this environment, the process data are not managed or understood, and therefore are not used as the basis for management reviews. The problem is that the overall environment is viewed as a set of individual tasks as well as specific product and process knowledge, resulting in many unresolved issues. Practices and tasks are not well defined and measured in terms of effectiveness and efficiency.

The situation we have just described is not a system of managed processes based on a common goal. It is a clear way to failure, particularly if the organization is facing the situation of reduced cycle time to bring a quality product to market with limited resources.

Can we eliminate all problems and optimize the life cycle? Probably not; problems are normal for any given stage of the life cycle. Nevertheless, they are predictable and can be controlled by management. Management can deal with them and control the flow of the software development process. What kills the process is a different set of problems.

These problems are created when management does not face a problem to begin with and later is not capable of dealing with the ripple effect of failing quality, cost, and schedule performance. Management has to find a way to continuously prevent, understand, and solve the problems before they have a devastating effect. Analyzing the problems will help us to understand that problems are not caused by individuals but by the situation.

It is not the fault of an individual if the required software requirements are not identified, or if applicable standards are not applied or effectively tailored. It is not the fault of an individual if the quality of the product falls behind. These types of problems are the result of the poor-quality process. Why improve and manage processes? For these reasons:

Processes produce organizational products.
Processes are critical to maintaining a competitive edge.
Processes are the vehicles for meeting customer needs.
Processes are critical in achieving organizational goals.
The performance of individuals is only as good as the processes allow it to be.

Over the past few years it became obvious that organizational processes can, and should, be related in quantitative fashion in a dynamic model. It is possible not only to approximate the effect of processes' interaction inside the company, but also to define the effect of internal processes on the organization's interaction with the complex outside environments.

The managerial practices that drove industry for decades have become increasingly insufficient to support the increasing rate of change without adequate quantitative understanding of the progress made to achieve organizational goals. Somebody said: "If you can change a change, you can control the outcome."

Managers who can quantify their business goals and strategies, and integrate them with continuous process improvement, will be ahead of the game. Most organizations end up in an intensely competitive environment. This environment is subject to rapid changes, shifts, failures, and successes. Time and resources are limited. There is an increasing need for collaboration, information exchange, and in-time adjustment alignment of strategic and operational goals. It goes far beyond project scheduling and due dates. It should be a much broader and comprehensive approach.

Information from the outside environment should be used, but never is, to improve the decision-making process and serve as a foundation for process modeling and improvement activities. The nature of the decision to be made is influenced by many of the input parameters of the process. The incoming information should be used to set quantitative improvement goals in order to compare them with the actual result and derive strategy for the process improvement. Much of the performance management is a process of decision making. Most business managers would agree that if right decisions are made the first time, the outcome is almost virtually guaranteed. Those who manage their processes effectively and efficiently are in a much better position than those who do not.

In the summer of 1996, Peter Drucker gave an interview to *Leader to Leader* magazine. He was asked:

How does one learn to manage partnerships, joint ventures, and outside contributors? These things aren't taught in business school, are they?

PFD: Far from it. The present people in organizations are still stuck in the 19th-century model of the organization. When big business first emerged throughout the industrial world around 1870, it did not emerge out of the small businesses of 1850—it emerged independently. The only model available, the most successful organization of the 19th century, was the Prussian Army, which had just been reorganized and had learned from the inability of the Americans in the Civil War to organize, transport, and communicate with masses of people. It was the first modern organization. It defeated the Austrians in 1866, who had a much larger and better-armed army, and then, four years later, defeated the French, who were even better armed. The Prussians succeeded because they had created an organization. They were the first ones to use modern technology effectively, which in those days meant railroad and telegraph. Business copied the command and control structure of the Prussian army, in which rank equaled authority. We are now evolving toward structures in which rank means responsibility but not authority. And in which your job is not to command but to persuade.*

What Peter Drucker was referring to, the power of persuasion, is very true in modern organizations.

There is an additional reason why the systemic understanding of life is of paramount importance in the management of today's business organizations. Over the last few decades we have seen the emergence of a new economy that is shaped decisively by information and communication technologies. In this new economy, the processing of information and creation of knowledge are the main sources of productivity. Thus, knowledge management, intellectual capital, and organizational learning have become important new concepts in management theory. Applying the systems view of life to organizational learning enables us to clarify the conditions under which learning and knowledge creation take place and to derive important guidelines for the management of today's knowledge-oriented organizations. Organizational structure changes from a vertical hierarchy to a flat organization.

When you hear the terms *downsizing* or *restructuring* on the evening news, or read about them in the morning paper, you are learning about companies that are moving toward process management and away from hierarchical management. Process management includes a lot of concepts you are becoming familiar with: continuous process improvement (CPI), self-managed teams, business intelligence,

---

* "The Shape of Things to Come: An Interview with Peter F. Drucker," *Leader to Leader*, 1996.

and high-performance companies. Every one of these aspects of organizational enhancement starts with the concept of the business process.

In the traditional vertically structured organization, groups are arranged by function. In the horizontal organization, teams are arranged by process. How can horizontal organizations utilizing teams be managed? Since traditional business organizations are vertical, there are few examples in business to look at as a guide in managing horizontal organizations.

Second, in both organizations, all individuals have clearly defined roles. The players and actors know when to come in, how to do their part, and when to exit. They not only know what part they play, but also how their part interacts with other players and actors. The director also has a clearly defined role that is critical to the success of the enterprise. In fact, this role may be perhaps more critical than those of director positions in a hierarchical structure. The individual players are directly dependent on how the director interprets the strategic business goals.

The first factor is that each of the individual players/actors must have a common sheet of music by which to play or a common script from which to act. Put simply, they all must share a common vision, and each individual must know what needs to be done to accomplish the common purpose. Put into business terms, these organizations must have a detailed business plan of where the organization is going and a specific guide on how they are going to get there. This plan must be understandable, and each individual must know precisely how he or she fits into it.

Finally, the performance management must support strategic goals, which lay foundation for the processes that must be performed in order to accomplish the mission, and the individual roles. The performance management, be it automated or manual, must provide the common sheet of music so that each individual clearly knows how he or she fits into the organization and how he or she relates to others in the organization. In addition, the information system must provide each player, actor, and director the critical information needed to perform his or her individual roles. Each team member needs sufficient information on what is expected of him or her. If the system does not provide the essential information, confusion will result, and the mission of the entire organization will suffer.

The problem that still causes sleepless nights in the business community is undecidability.

A manager needs information about projects to be able to make decisions, plan and schedule, and allocate resources for the different activities. Sources of information are documents produced during the development and direct contact with the developers. However, these sources are not sufficient, and the manager must rely on experience and estimations. It would be better to know instead of estimating, but when this is not possible, the approach has to be to make as good estimations as possible. To be able to make good estimations, the manager needs to have in-depth information about the organization and the staff. Also, there is a need for validation of the estimations. The underlying problem for a manager is that it is very difficult to control something that one has little knowledge about.

Inability to make a decision or discriminate between different states of events affects the company bottom line and, as a result, drives the cost of doing business high and profitability low. This leads to the problem of the decision-making process and makes the questions below difficult to answer.

From the customer prospective: "How do our customers see us?"
From the financial prospective: "How do we get the best results for the funds?"
From the internal processes prospective: "What must we excel at?"
From the innovation and improvement perspective: "How do we continue to improve and create value?"

Therefore, if the management of the organization wants to minimize the number of problems it is constantly facing, it has to change its focus and learn how to "manage for results and by the process." The effect of change will give the organization a sense of control. If the process manages the organization, the organization can achieve continuous improvement, which, in addition, will be measurable.

The process-focused approach means that attention is concentrated on the process, rather than the product. For example, you would be able to identify (using planned schedule metrics vs. actual schedule) that your project is behind schedule and that the number of defects discovered is not acceptable. You then adjust the process, making sure that the design specifications contain enough detail, which helps developers translate designs into accurate code more easily. If instead you decide to increase the test cycle to improve the quality after the fact, you are using a product-focused approach.

What represents advancement in a process-focused approach?

- Progressive increases in data collection
- Development of measurement capabilities
- Analysis of informational content
- Subprocess interdependency management

If a project has a defined and quantified goal, you can tell exactly when you are off the track and when planned efforts have been diverted. A goal can also provide criteria by which to evaluate the organizational process and the adequacy of each step along the way. What is equally important is the setting of goals that can help us to improve our understanding by calling our attention to different possibilities or potential problems that might otherwise be overlooked.

It is difficult to learn from past experience and use the past to predict the future without a structure detailing how to interrelate data and events. The IMPACT framework captures the dynamic process of information and resource flow for a company within the context of its surrounding environment. This allows management not to operate on a crystal ball but on hard, verifiable information represented by key performance indicators.

The main purpose of IMPACT is to identify problems of not responding to challenges. Much time can elapse before the presence of a problem is detected. Even then, what the manager observes may be just a symptom of the basic problem rather than the problem itself.

The quantification concept of IMPACT integrates in a holistic manner people, process, technology, and organizational environment by providing quantifiable information for communication, collaboration, and decision making by translating business goals into measurement goals and refining them into the operational statement with a measurement focus.

The QBPM approach is to provide a knowledge worker with needed quantitative information for solution creation and knowledge management. Maintaining alignment between the measurement activities and the information needs of the organization helps the organization leverage information, which may otherwise not be captured, to enhance its performance. QBPM is not just process quantification or data management. QBPM also involves the management of information. When the way we manage information is the focus, the decision processes, management structure, and even the way work gets done begin to be transformed. When an organization focuses the management of information, whole layers of management can be reduced.

Although we hear about many successful attempts to transform organizations, the overall track record is very poor. In recent surveys, CEOs reported again and again that their organizational change efforts did not yield the promised results. Instead of managing new organizations, they ended up managing the unwanted side effects of their efforts. At first glance, this situation seems paradoxical. When observing our natural environment, we see continuous change, adaptation, and creativity, yet our business organizations seem to be incapable of dealing with change.

We can only expect an approximate representation of reality from such a procedure, and all rational knowledge is therefore necessarily limited. The realm of rational knowledge is, of course, the realm of science that measures and quantifies, classifies, and analyzes. The limitations of any knowledge obtained by these methods have become increasingly apparent in modern science, and in particular in modern physics, which has taught us, in the words of Werner Heisenberg, a German theoretical physicist, "that every word or concept, clear as it may seem to be, has only a limited range of applicability." For most of us, it is very difficult to be constantly aware of the limitations and the relativity of conceptual knowledge. Because our representation of reality is so much easier to grasp than reality itself, we tend to confuse the two and take our concepts and symbols for reality. It is one of the main aims of Eastern mysticism to rid us of this confusion. Zen Buddhists say that a finger is needed to point at the moon, but that we should not trouble ourselves with the finger once the moon is recognized. The Taoist sage Chuang Tzu wrote: "Fishing baskets are employed to catch fish; but when the fish are got, the men forget the baskets; snares are employed to catch hares; but when the hares are got, men forget the snares. Words are employed to convey ideas; but when the ideas are grasped, men forget the words."

In summary, four questions need to be asked:

What's changing or what needs to change in your organization?

What factors external to your organization are causing you to make these changes (e.g., lost market share, reduced product life, increased competition)?

What difficulties have you encountered in making changes?

What are your organization's strengths and weaknesses (highly flexible, dedicated employees/legacy accounting system)?

References

Woody Allen. 1980. *Side effects*. New York: Random House.

Al Anderson. 2000. Using theory of change in program planning and evaluation. Aspen Institute. PowerPoint presentation at the annual meeting of the American Evaluation Association, Honolulu, HI.

Richard Boland and Fred Collopy. 2004. *Managing as designing*. Palo Alto, CA: Stanford Business Books.

Rodney Brim. 2004. *The goal of management; from MBO to Deming to project management and beyond*. White paper. www.ManagePro.com

Fritjof Capra. *Life and leadership: A systems approach management seminar*. www.fritjofcapra.net/seminars.html

Timothy Conway. 2006. *Teachings from Lao Tzu and Chuang Tzu*. www.Enlighted-Spirituality.org

Peter Drucker. 1988. The coming of the new organization, *Harvard Business Review*, January-February.

Peter Drucker. 1996. The shape of things to come: An interview with Peter F. Drucker. *Leader To Leader Journal*, Summer.

Alexander Laufer. 2009. *Breaking the code of project management*. New York: Palgrave Macmillan.

Harold J. Leavitt and Thomas L. Whistler. 1958. Management in the 1980s. *Harvard Business Review*. November-December.

Thomas Peters and Robert Waterman. 1982. *In search of excellence*. New York: Grand Central Publishing.

Robert Rodgers and John Hunter. 1991. Impact of management by objectives on organizational productivity. *Journal of Applied Psychology* 76(2), April, 322–336.

Alvin Toffler. 1991. *Power shift: Knowledge, wealth, and violence at the edge of the 21st century*. New York: Bantam Books.

Chapter 3

Dynamic Balance of Strategy and Performance

> The situation gives rise to measurements. Measurements give rise to estimates. Estimates give rise to analysis. Analysis gives rise to balancing. Balancing gives rise to triumph.
>
> **—Lao Tzu (1973)**

For many years I have worked with many clients helping them to define and quantify performance parameters and relate them to the organizational strategy. We played a catch-up game: as soon as we define a way to measure performance, the strategy changes again. Always challenged, always changed, always in a hurry, and always late. But the high-level question always stays the same: "How do you stay profitable and competitive in business if everything changes around you so rapidly without any advanced warnings?" Strategies become obsolete as soon they are approved.

Dynamic Balance: The Way of Business Agility

Today, both the environment and the *business* environment face a critical challenge. The time between what is and what will be is getting shorter and shorter. The past, present, and future are getting closer.

The world is moving fast. The speed of decision making becomes critical to survive. Sometimes one feels like Alice from *Through the Looking Glass*. No matter how fast you run, you are not moving forward. In a fast-moving world you have to run for your corporate life. Do you remember what Red Queen said? "Now, here,

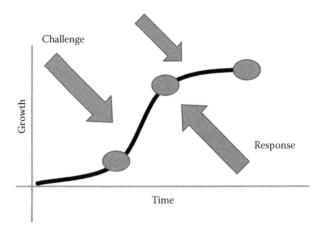

Figure 3.1 Challenge and response.

you see, it takes all the running you can do, to keep in the same place. If you want to get somewhere else, you must run at least twice as fast as that!"

But is speed the only condition and critical success factor to survive? The speed of the decision making is critical. Another critical condition is to know where you going and to know your directions well. The ability to move fast and knowing your direction are critical to the definition and execution of any strategy and goal achievement. It requires a lot of balancing between financial stability and organizational flexibility. It requires balance between change and challenge as well. If you can change the change, you can control the outcome. Well, easier said than done. But strategy and strategy change should constantly be revolved around the challenge presented to you by the outside environment. You respond to a challenge with the change, which in turn represents a challenge to your competitor.

In 1998 Michael Hitt and colleagues wrote that managers face the task of creating a balance between the stability necessary to allow development of strategic planning and decision processes and the instability that allows continuous change and adaptation to a dynamic environment. They also noted that managers must recognize and cope with multiple states of coexisting stability and instability, and the fact that most of these states are only temporary.[*] The authors argue that managers must break out of the traditional mold, and that the challenges and opportunities with which they must deal in a new competitive landscape are largely complex and nonlinear. They said that imputing linear and rational attributes to nonlinear problems will only lead to erroneous strategic actions (Figure 3.1).[†]

---

[*] Michael Hitt, et al., "Navigating in the New Competitive Landscape: Building Strategic Flexibility and Competitive Advantage in the 21st Century," *Academy of Management Executive*, 12(4), 1998.
[†] Ibid.

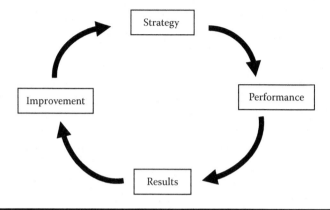

Figure 3.2 Strategy and results.

In order to withstand the pressure of the challenge, the organization should have the ability to provide the strategic response. Robert Lamb wrote that strategic management is an ongoing process that evaluates and controls the business and the industry in which the company is involved; assesses its competitors and sets goals and strategies to meet all existing and potential competitors; and then reassesses each strategy annually or quarterly (i.e., regularly) to determine how it has been implemented and whether it succeeded or needs replacement by a new strategy to meet changed circumstances, new technology, new competitors, a new economic environment, or a new social, financial, or political environment.[*]

There are number of good papers written on the subject of strategic flexibility and strategic responsiveness. In 1995 Richard Bettis and Michael Hitt published a paper describing the concept of "strategic response capability."[†] They wrote that strategic response capability can be related to the biological stimulus-response paradigm. The stimulus-response paradigm is a key for the survival of the organism. In this paradigm, the main component of survivability is development of better positions in the environment and to be in search of new opportunities. When faced with a crisis, our response should be to search for new opportunities (Figure 3.2).

Danger and Opportunity

The earliest citations I have found so far appear in the *Chinese Recorder*, a long-standing English language journal for missionaries in China. In the January 1938 issue,

---

[*] Robert Lamb, *Boyden Competitive Strategic Management* (Englewood Cliffs, NJ: Prentice Hall, 1984).
[†] Richard Bettis and Michael Hitt, "The New Competitive Landscape," *Strategic Management Journal*, 16, 7–16, 1995.

an unsigned editorial appeared under the title "The Challenge of Unusual Times." The person wrote: "The Chinese term for crisis is 'danger and opportunity' there should go forth a call to a Forward Movement in the Christian Church in China."[*]

Capra writes that the current crises of business we have recently encountered have driven our thinking processes into the quest for mere survival. Our community of business reverts to familiar patterns of slash and burn in an effort to support slim or nonexistent profit margins. Firing staff, cutting back on future development, selling off components, and reducing inventories are the typical reactions to difficult times. Most recently, financial manipulation has been exposed for the world to see, and react to with dismay and loss of trust.

These behaviors are not unique to the business community. Business activities of the early twentieth century were adopted as the "model" that works, and have permeated the very fiber of our being. Response patterns in politics and education echo this retreat into survival thinking. And so we blindly follow the mental lead of command and control that served so well in past times of unbounded chaotic growth and social extremes.

The Rules of Engagement Have Changed

But today's stakes are much higher than we perceive. The rules of engagement have changed and they are now changing continuously. The goal is to "see," for the first time, that it is our automatic behaviors and responses that push us into the command and control mode. The tough part for management is that self-awareness must come before changes in awareness of the enterprise and its purpose. Lacking this self-knowledge (how I act, respond, work with others), our efforts to lead an organization, from any level, will retreat to the safety of the comfort zone—the same place that has led us to our current crisis.

The Tao of Physics has profoundly influenced the ideas I have been developing and teaching to business leaders for years. We need this living systems vision to help us build and nurture sustainable *business* communities.

Tao in Chinese philosophy means "the way, the way of effortless action." It is the way of maintaining balance between opposing forces from without, and within Tao represents *balance during change*. Balance is the basis of stability. It is the basis of your survival and your ability to continue to grow, to prolong your level of stability—to balance the forces that are in opposition.

The Tao—the way the universe functions, the path taken by natural events—is sometimes called the way of *effortless action*. For instance, a characteristic of nature's path is the regular alternation *without effort* of phenomena, such as day and night. The classic example of effortless action is water, which unresistingly accepts the lowest level. From that position, water will nevertheless erode the hardest substance (Figure 3.3).

---

[*] "The Challenge of Unusual Times," *Chinese Recorder*, LXIX(1), 1938.

Figure 3.3   Image of yin-yang.

Balanced Growth

Yin: Looking at your business from the outside in, knowing your customer, understanding customer perceptions as well as the needs of all stakeholders, and working toward satisfying them.

Yang: Creating new market niches and customers by inventing "new to the world" products, mastering radical innovation, venture, competition, and differentiation strategies.

Balanced Change Management

Yin: Anticipating change, creating an adaptive organization, and adapting to change.

Yang: Being different, creating change and changing the name of the game.

Yin Yang, Big Bang

In 2005, Rich Karlgaard wrote:

> Google and Wal-Mart are the business world's version of yin and yang. Google is a hypergrowth, high-revenue, wildly high-margin company. Three thousand employees produce annual sales of $5 billion (at the current run rate), or $1.67 million per worker. Cash flow is north of $500,000 per worker per year. The typical Google worker possesses an IQ high enough to boil water. Half hold advanced degrees in science or engineering, most from elite universities. Google leaves no stone unturned in its pursuit of brainiacs, even asking to see prospects' SAT scores.
>
> Wal-Mart is the opposite of Google. It is the world's largest company by sales—$285 billion—but its profit of $10 billion is in line with low-margin retail. Wal-Mart sends the world's largest workforce into battle, 1.5 million (few of them SAT superstars) who generate $190,000 in sales apiece. Cash flow and profits per Wal-Mart worker are puny— only $16,000 and $6,700, respectively, or about 3% of those of Google.

Google and Wal-Mart have become huge successes in vastly different ways. But the yin and yang have this in common:

- Each company has a simple mission. Wal-Mart's is "always low prices." Google's is "to organize the world's information and make it universally accessible and useful." These companies know who they are.
- The brand and the mission statement of each are aligned. Picture Google and Wal-Mart in your head. There's no confusion about what these companies do.
- Each company's offerings are dirt simple to use. Shopping at Wal-Mart does not take a heroic intellectual effort. But neither does using Google, even though the search engine behind the curtain is the product of a prodigious intellectual feat.
- Both companies are technology leaders. The previous editor of *FORBES*, Jim Michaels, likes to call Wal-Mart the world's preeminent tech company. It pioneered the use of barcode scanners, slick supply chains, and inventory management tweaked to local purchasing preferences. The Bentonville, Arkansas, giant never sleeps. Now Wal-Mart is pushing into RFID chips. Wal-Mart's aggressive use of technology shows the lie of a recent *Harvard Business Review* article, "IT Doesn't Matter," that says it's okay to sit back and let others lead. Google, meanwhile, continues to attract the best tech brains in Silicon Valley.
- Both companies exploit the cheap revolution. Google's search engine runs on 100,000 cheap servers and a form of free Linux software. Wal-Mart searches the planet for low-cost production. It buys 10% of the goods China exports to the United States.

There are two concepts that I've mentioned earlier in the book: business resilience and business agility. Business resilience is the organizational ability to constantly manage critical success factors associated with flexible strategies as a response to the varying circumstances. Business agility requires unceasing effort, vigilant coordination, and prompt response. Nevertheless, a healthy living system, whether it's a body of water or a corporate culture, *naturally* marshals its inner resources to *match exactly* the force required to counteract any forces of destabilization. It is a strategic responsiveness that was defined by Bettis and Hitt as the ability to sense change in the environment, conceptualize the response to that change, and reconfigure resources to execute the response. The challenge to the businesses is to balance between agility and resilience.

Will Philips gives a good example. Business grows to multiple locations, and these multiple locations become a change that now impacts the organization with communication delays and coordination problems. Even if the business and markets are stable, success is likely to attract competitors. The business that learned to set prices based on cost plus or what the market would bear now finds itself competing with businesses that are satisfying the market at a lower price. This change demands a response. Yet, the most likely response is to complain about the competitor, believe the competitor's low prices will put it out of business shortly, and do nothing else. This failure to detect, then respect, then respond to the change adds viscosity of hysteresis to the change process. It shows up in declining performance, market share, growth, and profits. This delaying of detection, respect, and response is the underlying force that creates the S-curve.[*]

Balancing the S-Curve

The S-curve is a well-known management tool and depicts a paradox of growth (Figure 3.4). It consists in a display of cumulative costs, labor hours, or other quantities plotted against time. The name derives from the S-like shape of the curve, flatter at the beginning and end and steeper in the middle, because this is the way most of the projects look. The S-curve has been used to describe anything from demand for new toys to allocation of resources in a project. It is very useful to map a strategy of the organization.

Some time ago, Ichak Adizes drew the famous S-curve in his book *Corporate Lifecycles*. As a corporation matures, it grows along the S-curve and reaches the peak point of stability: maturity, best functioning, dynamic and responsive, and at the same time balanced (Figure 3.5).

The S-curve represents a trajectory of the execution of the planned strategy and the efficacy or ability to achieve the planned strategy. The measure of the efficacy is the volatility of the execution process.

What gives the trajectory its S shape? The two points of inflexion—the first point is when corporate growth really takes off, and the second when growth levels off to enter that state of balanced dynamism. At the first of these points, the corporation has successfully responded to greater and greater challenge, continuously and exactly matching force with force. This balance makes the upward trajectory possible, giving it the momentum it needs. At the second point, the balance of

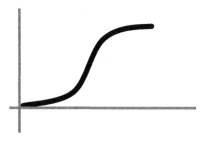

Figure 3.4   The S-curve.

[*] Will Philips, *The S-Curve.* qm2.org/scurve.html

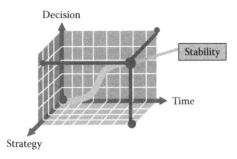

Figure 3.5   3-dimensional S-curve.

forces continues—growth is succeeded by a leveling off into stability. The corporation is maturing.

The S-curve can be considered an indicator, and it's used for many applications related to project management, such as target, baseline, cost, time, etc. That's why there is a variety of S-curves, such as:

Cost versus time s-curve.

Target S-curve. This S-curve reflects the ideal progress of the project if all tasks are completed as currently scheduled.

Value and percentage S-curves. Percentage S-curves are useful for calculating the project's actual percentage complete.

Actual S-curve. This S-curve reflects the actual progress of the project to date.

After that-all-too brief plateau of stability, in practically every business case, the triumphant S-curve is now followed by a downward, reverse S-curve as the corporation slides into an inevitable decline, responding more and more clumsily to challenges from the business environment (outside) and to forces in its own corporate environment (inside).

Inevitable decline? I don't think so! The critical issue is how to reach stability (maturity) *and stay there.* For as long as possible. The key is to identify and make use of certain other conditions that will allow you to manage this curve and leveling off. As you can imagine, it's a complex challenge.

What can be said about response to challenge in determining the corporate life cycle can also be observed in the evolution of civilizations on a global scale. Universal historian Arnold J. Toynbee did not believe that civilizations rise and fall according to an inevitable cycle. In *Change and Habit,* Toynbee observed that when a civilization responds creatively to challenges, it grows. When the counterpressure from within no longer matches the challenges from outside—when leaders lose the skill of creative response—civilizations go into decline. Toynbee saw entire civilizations as living systems—an organic network of internal social relationships. For

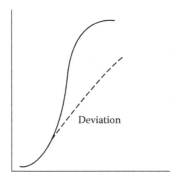

Figure 3.6 Deviation from the S-curve.

our own success and survival, we must look at our business environments in the same way.

So, how can we meet the complex challenge of reaching stability and prolonging that state of balance indefinitely? Let's take another look at the upward S-curve. This trajectory involves all your components as a corporation. It expresses your performance—how well you are achieving your goals.

As you know, key performance indicators (KPIs) are the tools by which management evaluates performance. If that is the case, then the overall synergy of your corporation, your living system, is the mother of all KPIs! It is the sum of all particular KPIs used in performance evaluation.

Whenever your living system deviates from the trajectory (Figure 3.6), you use your KPIs to let you know at what point you have to react, to correct that deviation. If your system's synergies are reacting with prompt agility, the corporation is back on track. The greater the agility, the sooner the alert will sound—and the more exactly the corporation will deploy the right forces to balance the challenge and restore the trajectory to its optimum upward path.

The Need for the Framework

"Strategy is a framework within which you make the decisions that determine the nature and direction of your business."[*]

Peter Drucker commented in one of his interviews, "The task of organizational leadership is to create an alignment of strength in ways that make a system weakness irrelevant." Does this mean that Drucker suggests that leading change is all about strengths? Does this mean that we have to create a change framework entirely based on any condition of change management by maintaining the strength of the

---

[*] Benjamin Tregoe and John Zimmerman, *Top Management Strategy: What It Is and How It Works* (Simon and Schuster, 1980).

organization? This framework should be able to maintain the level of organizational strength by adapting, learning, and engineering its performance.

This framework offers opportunity to management to better understand an organizational strategy by providing insight into how an organization interacts with its internal and external environments. The real issue is not that companies are having problems identifying where and how the operational efficiency can be improved. The real issue is how to better manage the efficiency of the process or subprocess delivering value to a customer. This is why the issue of constantly analyzing organizational performance is getting more and more critical for survival in a global economy.

In 2008, Ventana Research published a paper called "The Time for Performance Management Is Now, Not Later." In this paper, it said that two tenets of performance management are to respond quickly and decisively to changes in the business environment and to know you are working in a right set of activities. Immediate responsiveness is essential; the organization should be able to reprioritize and shift goals and targets as needed, not when some schedule says it should. Static reviews, whether annual, quarterly, or even monthly, do not reflect the real pace of business and will not enable you to act quickly. If you cannot respond with both agility and the certainty that your actions and decisions are the right ones, you likely will underperform or be outdone by the competition. Ventana says that its research shows that performance management processes are deployed tentatively or inadequately. Those sporadic efforts reflect the failure to realize the strategic importance of performance management and likely also lack of consensus on priorities among members of the executive team. One-third of the organizations react to change in an uncoordinated fashion. Ventana believes that organizations must act to deploy performance management in order to avoid failure and to deliver expected results. The need to manage performance is a reality when companies fail to hit their financial and operational targets.

There is no split between process and organization. Process and organization are one entity. Organization is a structure where the process resides.

References

Ichak Adizes. 1988. *Corporate lifecycles.* Englewood Cliffs , NJ : Prentice Hall.

Fritjof Capra. 2000. *The tao of physics.* Boston: Shambhala.

Lewis Carroll. 1871. *Through the looking glass (And what Alice found there).* London, UK: Macmillan.

Rich Karlgaard. 2005. Yin yang, big bang. *Forbes,* March 14. www.Forbes.com/Forbes/2005/0314/033_print.html!

Arnold J. Toynbee. 1992. *Change and habit.* Oxford, UK: One World Publications.

Lao Tzu. 1973. *Tao Te Ching.* Daniel Webster.

Ventana Research. 2008. *The time for performance management is now, not later.* www.ventanaresearch.com/research/category_new.aspx?id=1031

www.forbes.com/forbes/2005/0314/033_print.html

Chapter 4

Impact Framework

Alice laughed. "There's no use trying," she said: "one can't believe impossible things."

"I daresay you haven't much practice," said the Queen. "When I was your age, I always did it for half-an-hour a day. Why, sometimes I've believed as many as six impossible things before breakfast."

—**Lewis Carroll,** *Through the Looking Glass*

IMPACT Model

Lessons Learned

The assumption for organizational improvement was that organizations will set a focus on business reengineering, and on development of information systems that directly support company strategy, and management will be able to assume control and use it to their competitive advantage (Figure 4.1).

According to Peter Drucker, "We are entering a period of change: a shift from command and control organizations to information-based organizations of knowledge specialists. The typical large business 20 years hence will have fewer than half the levels of management of its counterpart today, and no more than one third the managers."*

---

* Peter Drucker, "The Coming of the New Organization," *Harvard Business Review*, January–February 1988.

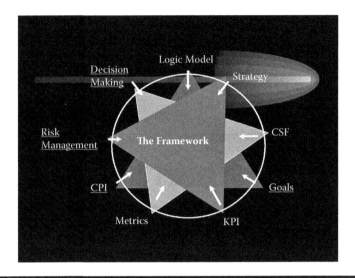

Figure 4.1 Impact framework includes critical success factors (CSF), key process indicators (KPI), and continuous process improvement (CPI).

A popular book, *Reengineering the Corporation*, written by Michael Hammer and James Champy, was published in 1993. And organizations were rushing into business process reengineering (BPR) to improve effectiveness and efficiency in order to achieve competitive advantage.

What was happening next is a big-time downsizing. In a lot of companies, middle managers were "reengineered." The middle management had two main job responsibilities: provide senior management with the information needed for decision making and implement internal policies and procedures that reflect directions and critical success factors set by senior management.

A big gap developed in between what was defined by the senior management in forms of goals and objectives and what was expressed in quantitative targets for achievement and actual measurable information from the operational level. Not much happened when a company changed strategy business processes (if defined); it stayed mostly the same.

In 1992, *Sloan Management Review* published a paper saying that "although many business process redesign initiatives start out amid a great fanfare and bold predictions of state-of-the-art performance improvements, lurking beneath the glare are often quite modest attempts to reduce operational cost in a single functional area, to improve product quality in a single product line, or downsize the business to reduce the firm's structure."

They continue: "The danger is simply that business process redesign may have little or no measurable impact on the firm's external market performance. To the extent that many companies still tend to use IT to automate existing processes rather than redesign them, investments in IT have yielded disappointing results."*

Many companies have abandoned their attempt to reengineer. They still blame their employees for the failure. Each and every time I'm hearing the same question: "How do you deal with the change? How do deal with resistance?" This convenient position is adapted on different levels of management.

Are we in search of a silver bullet methodology such as business process management (BPM), ITIL, CMMI, Agile, Six Sigma, etc., hoping that somebody else will do it for us?

Recently, the word *agility* became very popular in the business world. Every business, every corporation wants to be agile. Simple put, agility is the ability to rapidly adapt to change.

At the same time, there is a restriction. The restriction carries common sense that the "rate of progress should not exceed the rate of change." So, what has just been stated is a balancing act and points not to a simple implementation of up-to-date technology as a single step, as many vendors try to advocate, but to a journey. This journey starts with the questions: "How does my business perform? Do I know how it's going to perform tomorrow? How do I react to changes from the outside environment?" The outside environment provides many potential opportunities, problems, and threats that make any business forecasting and planning extremely difficult—a "crystal ball" like exercise.

One company, unexpectedly achieving a good fourth quarter in a short period of time, expanded their human capital by 40%, without realizing that additional revenue is not a trend, but a spike caused by effective sales effort and the ready-to-buy market condition. Eight months later, after realizing that the big expansion effort was the wrong move (the realization came from the balance sheet and a heated directors' meeting), the company made the decision to reduce human capital by a large percentage, causing a significant cost increase.

What Happened?

The company had all the needed state-of the-art tools and applications to support an intelligent decision, and trained MBAs from the best schools in a nation. The success of the fourth quarter did not suggest that the company readjust a corporate-wide strategy, which would prevent individual organizational growth at the expense of overall corporate performance. Company business analysts and sophisticated business intelligence (BI) applications could not help much to prevent such a fiasco for the simple reason that top-level strategic objectives were not aligned with bottom-level initiatives and operational performance.

---

* J.E. Short and N. Venkatraman, "Beyond Business Process Redesign: Redefining Baxter's Business Network," *Sloan Management Review*, Fall 1992.

There is a human tendency to discover a pattern in random data in support of a self-fulfilling prophecy. In professional sports, this is called the "hot hand" phenomenon. The hot hand phenomenon is the compelling, illusionary perception held by both fans and players that some players have "hot streaks" such that a successful shot is likely to be followed by another successful shot, while a failure is likely to be followed by another failure. University players were asked to place bets predicting the results of their next shot. Their bets showed strong evidence of a belief in the hot hand, but their performance offered no evidence for its validity.

Looking at this example, first what comes to mind is that a real-time system is needed that will alert management to problems and opportunities and empower them to react through quantitative information and company-wide collaboration. And this is exactly the purpose and function of the IMPACT.

The Foundation of the IMPACT

Organizations are challenged to constantly reshape their operations and improve performance, and to adapt quickly to new markets and opportunities. With new methodologies and frameworks such as BAM, BPM, BPI, Six Sigma, Lean, and executive dashboard, the real question becomes: How do I get started?

"Agility is the ability to both create and respond to change in order to profit in a turbulent business environment."* Traditional performance management decision making was based on organizational hierarchies. But when the companies changed organizational structures their performance management never changed. Because of that move, traditional key performance indicators (KPIs) are distorted. KPIs are mostly linked to the organizational strategy and not to operational decisions of line managers. Those measures do not have predictive capabilities and do not reflect changes until it is too late.

Arnold Toynbee, a late English historian, surveyed twenty-six civilizations that have risen and fallen into decline. In his study of history he sought the common weaknesses, external force, or failure of internal spark that drove those civilizations into decline, but he found none. For Toynbee there was no spark, no force to account for these phenomena, only the process of environmental challenge and response. He wrote that in a growing civilization the challenges are met with successful responses, which proceed to generate still different challenges and responses. If a challenge appears that is too great, or if the response is weak or inappropriate, then the process of decline is set into motion. This concept of challenge and response has a great deal of intuitive appeal as well as a certain unity at the microlevel—as a way explaining the longevity of individual enterprises.

In 1970, James R. Bright advocated something quite similar, which he called monitoring. His method called for more than simplistic scanning and accumulation

---

* Jim Highsmith, "Agile Software Development Ecosystems," (Addison-Wesley, 2002). 11.

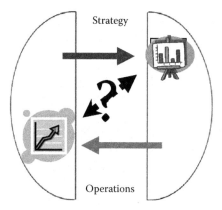

Figure 4.2   Balancing strategy and operations.

of data. Instead, he advocated consideration of alternative possibilities.* His advice was to:

> Search the environment for signals of the forerunners of significant change
>
> Assume that the signals are based on substance and identify potential consequences
>
> Determine which aspects of the environment should be observed and measured to verify the speed and direction of changes
>
> Report the information to management in a timely manner

The next requirement is that management uses this information to form an appropriate response.

Benjamin Tregoe noted that strategy is a framework within which you make the decisions that determine the nature and direction of your business (Figure 4.2).†
Process improvement is not a goal by itself. The International Organization for Standardization (ISO) defines process improvement as an "action taken to change an organization's processes so they meet the organization's business needs and achieve its business goal more effectively." Therefore, continuous process improvement is the means to achieve better business results by continuously improving the performance of the organizational processes.

Internal processes should reflect the strategy selected. Going back to the balance scorecard (BSC), Kaplan and Norton address two critical issues: the alignment of the processes with the strategic business goals and the identification and

---

* James R. Bright, "Evaluating Signals of Technological Change," *Harvard Business Review*, January–February 1970, p. 64.
† Benjamin Tregoe and John Zimmerman, *Top Management Strategy: What It Is and How It Works* (New York: Simon and Schuster, 1980).

application of measures to manage the performance of the business unit. When strategic and operational levels are not aligned, the organization suffers negative consequences, such as:

The corporate strategy is unknown or not used in the development project goals.
Financial indicators are the driver of the corporate decision making.
Measurements are implemented without a clear purpose.
Measurements are not connected to each other.

A recent KPMG study of U.S and European business and government executives revealed that one of the most common disappointments reported was the lack of data integrity and the inability of their system to produce meaningful information to support decision making. The study also discovered that BPM systems are not aligned with strategic business measures, are dependent on lagging and not leading indicators, are poorly integrated with internal and external information, and rely too heavily on financial measures. Some factors for failed BPM systems included measuring things that are easily measured versus what should be measured, data inaccuracy, measures that are too complicated, and users not understanding the system and its measures.[*]

This alignment has certain tasks:

Defines business in a way that internal staff can understand
Identifies customer needs, employee needs, and company needs and aligns them
Builds measures and process improvement capability
Connects employees' behavior to the mission of the company
Links teams and processes to the changing needs of the internal and external customers
Shapes business strategies using real-time customer information
Creates a focused and aligned culture

There are questions that are constantly asked by people involved in strategy and process improvement activities:

How do you align the organization top to bottom around shared goals?
How do you link shared goals across divisions or business units so they are aligned to the corporate strategy?
How do you ensure that your culture and incentive programs clearly align your people to the strategy?

---

[*] KPMG, *Achieving Measurable Performance Improvement in a Changing World: The Search for New Insights* (KPMG, 2001).

How do you ensure that the initiatives you undertake are clearly driven by your strategic priorities?

How do you ensure that your strategic plan is synchronized with your financial and operational plans?

Capra writes that dynamic unity of polar opposites can be illustrated with the simple example of a circular motion and its projection. Suppose we have a ball going around the circle. If this movement is projected on to a screen, it becomes an oscillation between two extreme points. The ball goes around the circle with a constant speed, but in projections it slows down as it reaches the edge, turns around, and then accelerates again only to slow down once more—and so on, in endless cycles. In any projection of that kind, the circular movement will appear as an oscillation between two opposite points, but in the movement itself, the opposites are unified and transcended (Figure 4.3).

Peter Drucker commented in one of his interviews, "The task of organizational leadership is to create an alignment of strength in ways that make a system weakness irrelevant." Does this mean that Drucker suggests that leading change is all about strengths? Does it mean that we have to create a change framework entirely based on any condition of change management by maintaining the strength of the organization? This framework should be able to maintain the level of organizational strength by adapting, learning, and engineering its performance.

Viewed as a whole, Figure 4.1 illustrates how strategy and operations can be aligned and interleaved to create a dynamic performance management asset. At

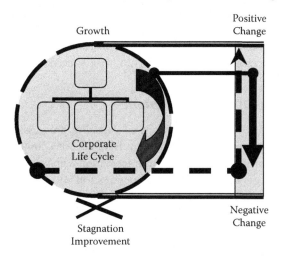

Figure 4.3   Opposites are unified and transcended.

the center of it all, of course, is company performance, which in a *strategy* environment is viewed from the four key perspectives: financial, customer, operational, and learning. BI is focused on company performance, particularly if guided by business-driven design and portfolio management methods.

Step 1: Strategy Mapping

Going to the top of Figure 4.1 and moving clockwise, step 1 of the performance management cycle starts with using the strategy method of strategy mapping to link company strategies to the core business processes via which the strategies are realized. This sets the stage for step 2, whereby the strategy strategic management framework is used to guide goal setting.

Step 2: Goal Setting

The goal-setting part of step 2 sets the stage for cascading objectives, measures, and targets throughout the organization. These can be simple hierarchical cascades or quite complex, cascading to cross-functional business processes based on different organizational roles. In any event, the objectives, measures, and targets need to be relevant and clearly tied to business processes that drive company performance. Each organizational level has its specific role with different performance measurements.

Step 3: Performance Measurement Framework Baseline

Step 3 establishes the performance measurement framework and baseline, which, when key process indicators are linked to the goals, ensures management attention to the business processes that contribute to strategic success.

Step 4: Performance Management

Performance measurement is the process of assessing progress toward achieving predefined goals. Performance measurement is an effective component of effective management. Performance measurement information helps to establish framework and influence changes in organizational processes and culture to:

Share results in the performance of goal achievement
Allocate and put priority on resources
Provide information about the need to change current policy or directions to meet predefined goals
Help establish agreed upon performance goals

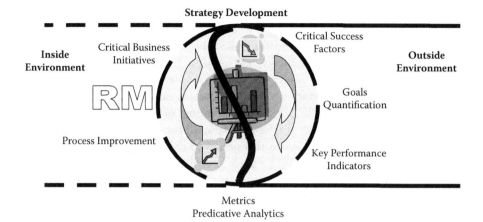

Figure 4.4 Connecting strategy and metric.

Often the publication of the metrics report triggers variance analysis, management reviews, and corrective action planning. In larger companies, the process of generating the measures, formatting the quantitative reports, and variance analysis/corrective action planning can be complex and manually intensive (Figure 4.4).

Moving back to an overall performance management perspective, we see that the strategy and operations are compatible and complementary tools that focus on company performance. If we drop Operations out of the equation, we see that the strategy is very suitable for establishing the strategic management framework and performance management baseline, and it can be used for timely performance measurement. But measurement alone is not enough. Managers have continually expressed the need for business information, analytical tools, and decision support so that they can improve the actual processes that drive the performance measurement numbers. And that is what operations is about. Performance management should operate and execute on all three levels: strategic, tactical, and operational.

Performance Management

Let's distinguish between performance management and performance measurements. First what does the word *management* mean? The word *manager* was derived from Italian (*maneggio*) and French (*manege*). The meaning of this word is "training, handling, and riding the horse." Guess who is the horse. In the past, management meant "command, control, set directions." It heavily relied on people's willingness to be managed. It was and is a very static approach—"taming of the horse."

The General Services Administration's (GSA) Office of Government-wide Policy developed a guide to help those who want to gain a further understanding of performance measurement, and for those who develop and use performance measures for information technology (IT) projects.* This guide sets out an analytical framework linking IT investment decisions to strategic objectives and business plans in federal organizations, and supplements existing OMB policies and procedures. The approach relies on the consistent use of performance measures to indicate potential problems. It emphasizes the need for an effective process when applying information technology in this period of reduced resources and greater demand for government services. This guide describes the major tasks to follow to measure the contribution of IT projects to an organization's goals and objectives. These same principles and tasks also apply when measuring mission performance.

Organizations succeed when their business units and support functions work together to achieve a common goal. This holds true for performance measurement, which entails more than just developing performance measures. It also includes establishing business strategies, defining projects that contribute to business strategies, and evaluating, using, and communicating the results to improve performance.

The GSA's defined steps are:

Step 1: Senior management translates vision and business strategies into actions at the operational level by creating a balanced scorecard for the organization. Business units and IT professionals contribute to the balanced scorecard by defining the information and IT capabilities that the organization needs to succeed. The IT professionals include managers, analysts, and specialists who plan or analyze requirements.

Principles of step 1 include:
Establish clear linkages
Define specific business goals and objectives
Secure senior management commitment and involvement
Identify stakeholders and customers
Nurture consensus

Steps 2 to 8 (except 4): IT professionals solicit feedback from business units to refine the information and capabilities defined in step 1: create a balanced scorecard for the IT function, develop performance measures, and communicate results. Together, IT professionals and business units establish baselines, and interpret and use results to improve performance. The IT professionals include managers, analysts, and specialists who plan, analyze, or deliver IT assets and services.

Step 4: IT professionals estimate the cost, value, and risk of IT projects to perform information economics calculations. Senior management and business unit

---

* General Services Administration Office of Government-wide Policy, *Eight Steps to Develop and Use Information Technology Performance Measures Effectively.*

managers define the evaluation factors and their associated weights to evaluate IT projects. Then they determine the value of each IT project and select the projects that provide the greatest value. The IT professionals include managers, analysts, and specialists who analyze the cost or benefits of IT solutions.

As important as strategic plans can be, they often are forgotten soon after they are prepared because they don't translate well into action. In most cases, business strategies reflect lofty objectives ("Be our customers' number one supplier"), which are nearly impossible to translate into day-to-day activities. Also, strategic plans typically focus three to five years into the future, in contrast with performance measures, which focus on ongoing operations. This difference in focus causes confusion, and sometimes conflict, for line managers and program managers

In *The Wizard of Oz*, the wizard tells Dorothy and her companions that before he can even begin to consider granting their wishes, they must undertake what he perceives to be a hopeless task—bringing him the wicked witch's broom. When they actually return with the broom, the wizard is quick to begin backpedaling on his end of the bargain. Enterprise performance improvement initiatives are often subjected to onerous analyses, microscopically detailed return on investment calculations, and lengthy development timelines and approval processes that must be completed before a new idea can be implemented, and in a lot of cases, existing initiatives continue to be funded, even if results are less than desirable.

In *The Fifth Discipline*, Peter Senge emphasizes the importance of a shared vision, where employees participate in the development of a corporate vision, and can then make decisions and take actions consistent with the directions set by senior leadership through the shared visioning process (Senge, 1990). In their research on consciousness, Edelman and Tononi identify the mechanism that provides unity to consciousness, thereby creating a continuous history of thought and a consistency of identity and action. This ability to maintain different parts of the brain in harmony and to pull them together in an organization is facilitated by constant and widespread communication.

Performance measurement is a structured process for developing measurable indicators that can be systematically tracked to assess progress in achieving goals, as well as to provide feedback and insight to management and leadership. Performance measures, implemented properly, drive greater accountability, visibility, and transparency. Not only do measures provide managers and executives with a tool to gauge organizational progress, but when well crafted and implemented, they can also inspire and motivate all employees, set direction for the organization, and encourage alignment from top to bottom.

Performance management is supposed to address the fundamental challenge of balancing strategic and operational knowledge and experience, and the problem analysis and actions intended to correct them. Organizations must focus on how to reduce rework and defuse the tense political environment. How do they do this? If you want to understand and clarify the problems, you have to measure. To

Figure 4.5   Where are the goals?

know what to measure, you have to start with the goals. Everything starts with the goals. The goals are usually somewhere in the organizational strategic plans (Figure 4.5).

Organizations are different, but they have a lot in common. To survive in an unforgiving business environment, they must find a right balance and develop the ability to draw knowledge from experience and use intelligence to derive their next course of action. Unfortunately, for most companies (small, medium, and big), imbalance is a rule. Businesses have to develop the ability how to use data and information resources to measure, balance, and manage performance. But this is only the part of the problems solution. The second part is how to connect it to the business success.

The successes are hidden in a triangle between strategies, critical success factors, and critical business initiatives. We need to understand how your business goals relate to your business processes. Measurement must be aligned with the organization's business goals to minimize the risk of not using the data gathered.

Goals are things you have plans about. Measurements help you answer: Are we on track? Are there risks? Are we getting to our goals? Each organization has different goals with different success criteria.

Business goals are often a function of where you sit: the IMPACT can be initiated at any organizational level, where goals can be readily identified.

The *program and project level* is primarily interested in (their goal) producing an end product that is on time, within the budget, and of acceptable quality. Hence, their success criteria are executing the plan and having a satisfied customer. The *business unit level* has a broader perspective and is interested in system or product line results. At the *organizational level* the goal is satisfying the organization's mission.

Since the goals are different at each level, the success criteria are also different. Each organizational level has its specific role with different performance measurements.

Since the goals and success criteria are different for the different organizational levels, the things that can be measured will also be different.

Also, the things that can be measured are also dependent upon the organizational level. The things that can be measured are directly dependent upon the roles. At the program and project level, you can measure to support the execution of the plan. At each organizational level there are specific things that can be measured that support the things that each level wants to know.

The approach that I find useful for the definition of performance management principles was developed by the U.S. Army:[*]

Principle 1: Performance driven: This principle deals with the key organizational drivers behind the change. All business process changes must be based on customer needs and business performance measurement. All business activities and processes that support them should be done for a reason. Measurement techniques such as balanced scorecards indicate whether we are acting consistently with organizational goals, which should be based on customer needs and traceable to key performance indicators (KPIs). This principle in no way says what the right measurement indicators should be. Every industry is different, and every organization has its own strategy for identifying which goals are achievable. Nonetheless, it is vital that each organization chooses wisely; the old adage "You get what you measure" is universal to all organizations.

Principle 2: Customer focused: This principle deals with the following questions: Why would your customer care about the change? Will the improvement initiative solve or improve an identified customer issue? Who are these customers?

Let's answer the last question first: a customer is any individual, organization, or institution that has a vested interest in or can influence the organization's performance in some way.

To analyze the gap between our current processes and what the customer's needs are in the future, we should consider two key factors. First, we should have a strong grasp of our customer's needs. Second, we should understand the state of our current relationships and a have view of what we want these relationships to be in the future. Gaps between these two states will drive our needs for change. The future state view will provide a set of evaluation criteria for change from the current reality, which then will be translated into balanced scorecard KPIs.

Principle 3: Traceable to the customer requirements and key business criteria: This principle speaks to the ability to trace change to a customer requirement; if you cannot trace an improvement to a specific customer requirement, then the viability of the improvement initiative needs to be questioned.

---

[*] www.army.mil.

The challenge is to build a traceable and actionable link to customer requirements and balance that with institutional and operational objectives. Conflicting business and political drivers can devastate a sound decision-making process. When those drivers are also misaligned with the organization's mission and culture, we cannot expect successful results. Change initiatives that waste millions and even billions of dollars can be found in almost all organizations and institutions of any size and complexity. Typically, the root cause is poor decision making, or poor interpretation of the organization's needs and customer expectations.

Principle 4: Segmented along business process lines to synchronize change: This principle deals with the importance of cross-functional integration and collaboration to ensure a sustainable change initiative. As more and more governmental agencies and commercial institutions move toward Web-enabled services, integration of products and services across an enterprise becomes more and more critical. Management structures with overly rigid organizational structures and boundaries that are too slow to respond will eventually become obsolete and nonresponsive to customer demands. Customer demand for Web-enabled services and seamless institutional response forces closer collaboration and integration between various organizational disciplines from front-end customer support functions to organizational enablers such as information technology and human resources departments. By segmenting the transformational initiatives along business process lines, we have a clear framework for organizing and prioritizing change and for measuring the impact of our efforts in terms that the business executives can understand.

Principle 5: Integrated with organizational change management: Change management initiatives are often used simply as ways of creating a document or developing the communication strategy for implementing a technology system. Clearly, this is a very limited view of change management. Instead, we must see change management as a vehicle for a more encompassing transformation. We must recognize that during initiatives such as implementing an ERP system we are not just impacting technology, data, or processes, we are also striving to identify champions and transform people into enthusiastic supporters and participants who will enable transformation initiatives. This is one reason we should encourage the analysis of existing organizational processes and capabilities. In addition to traditional change management tools, such as communication strategies, we must support changes with appropriate assignment of roles and responsibilities, organizational structures, empowerment, and most importantly, accountability.

During transition, the staff must feel that an appropriate level of trustworthy communication is happening. The main take-away is that staff affected by change should feel a sense of contribution as a result of their participation and should be positioned as the beneficiaries of the new process.

Principle 6: Conducted with a well-managed and time-boxed approach: This concept is not new and traditionally refers to program management. The program management discipline might appear on the surface to be simply managing program time and resources. If it is not aligned with the organization's culture and not integrated with change management components and not accepted by all levels of the organization, it will be a struggle to meet all program objectives and agreed upon stakeholder expectations. Managing complex transformational programs such as ERP implementation might be the toughest thing ever done. By sticking to a proven project management approach and methodology, program risk will be reduced and program goals and stakeholder expectations will be better managed.

Principle 7: Understood as a continuous process: A major distinguishing feature between continuous improvement process (CPI) and the wave of business process reengineering (BPR) efforts that proliferated in the early and mid-1990s is the approach to continuity of effort. BPR emphasized radical change of business processes and everything that touched them in the "big bang" approach. But it did little to uphold the notion of supporting the ongoing management of the implemented change or ongoing implementation of change. It assumed the solution would have stability in an unstable market with changing priorities. Perhaps for these reasons, as well as issues with people's natural tendency to resist change, most BPR programs failed to deliver their expected results.

We must recognize that in any given time, our stakeholders will have a set of requirements that are in flux and can be influenced by regulatory and market demands. If we accept the fact that change is an embedded part of business transformation, we should also recognize that building iterative processes in the overall business transformation is critical to the success of a CPI initiative.

The U.S. Army also defines eight phases of continuous process improvement. Table 4.1 lists the eight CPI phases and discusses their benefits and effect on the transformation program. Details for each phase and its associated tools and templates are provided under the CPI framework.

From a business perspective, performance management provides a mechanism to set targets (KPIs) for the different departments and function areas. An effective performance measurement system starts from the mission and vision of the organization and designs the KPIs for each unit or process from this overall corporate goal. In order to dynamically respond to a change, the goal and the KPI representing the performance toward the goal achievement have to be changed or modified. To continuously revise the business process and the low operational goals so that they are aligned with the new corporate goal is a serious undertaking for the senior- and mid-level management.

Table 4.1 CPI Phases and Their Benefits to a Successful Transformation Program

CPI Phases	Benefits	Effect on the Transformation Program
Define business drivers	Identifies business drivers and reason(s) for change early in the program	Identifies program champions and develops the foundation for organizational buy-in
Architect and align strategies	Aligns transformation program goals with the organization's business strategy	Ensures early alignment of the CPI initiative with the existing organizational strategy and capabilities
Develop vision	Identifies the key business drivers, organizational goals, and performance measures	Reduces the risk of initiating transformation programs without clearly defined performance measures
Current state understanding	Provides a clear map of the existing processes and identifies potential areas for improvement	Identifies root causes and reasons behind process bottlenecks early and the key features of future state processes
Future state design	Defines the renewed processes and identifies required organizational assets needed to enable continuous improvement	Confirms the business case and develops the foundation for developing the implementation road map
Roadmap development	Defines in detail the future state implementation road map, such as critical milestones and early wins	Reduces program management risks and identifies required steps to accomplish key milestones
Execution	Delivers the early and ongoing benefits of the transformation program	Delivers business objectives and secures organizational buy-in

An Eight-Step Framework to Execute Your Business Process Management Strategy

To succeed in today's unforgiving business environment, enterprises have to develop the ability to use operational data to measure, balance, and manage performance. However, business process management (BPM) practices are often deployed tentatively or inadequately. Those sporadic and uncoordinated efforts reflect the members of the executive team's ignorance of the strategic importance of performance management and a likely lack of consensus on priorities. Obtaining hard data that measure a wider array of business activities and outcomes is becoming increasingly complex and increasingly important to a business strategy. But it's also imperative that businesses connect this information to their business success.

Drive Strategy across All Levels of the Business

Various applications in the market help organizations manage the data pertaining to their strategic planning. For example, with the introduction of the SAP Strategic Enterprise Management (SAP SEM) application that comes standard with SAP ERP, SAP customers can link strategic planning and simulation with enterprise planning. This solution is a useful tool for enterprises in deriving the data for their next course of action. However, every company still needs an internal framework to act on this information: they use these findings to then align corporate goals with people, strategy and business initiatives, KPIs, and tasks. Companies that undertake this kind of strategic planning without a clearly defined, structured framework that defines KPIs and metrics from the bottom up will find it difficult to drive strategy down and across the organization.

Using BPM data in conjunction with a structured framework, enterprises can not only integrate strategic and operational information, but also align organizational strategy and operational goals. Small, medium, and large businesses alike—down to each organizational unit and even to the individual level—can understand the KPIs that they control and have responsibility for, and their relationship to the overall success of their organization. According to this framework, organizational strategy and goals should cascade from the top down—where each level of the organization derives its performance goals based on the strategic objective of the level above it.

A Clearer Approach to Improving Processes

After working with a number of customers who were struggling in the BPM area, I realized that they could benefit from a framework that would focus corporate management's ability to:

Align strategy with business operations in the hierarchy of organizations
Achieve common goals with well-defined success criteria
Monitor progress using standardized measures
Bridge the gap between high-level strategy requirements, technical issues, and
    operational risks

With these objectives in mind, I developed the Quantitative Business Performance Management (QBPM) framework. This framework offers an opportunity for management to better understand an organizational strategy by providing insight into how an organization interacts with its internal and external environment. The real issue is not that companies are having problems identifying where and how the operational efficiency can be improved. Rather, it is how to better manage the efficiency of the process or subprocess delivering value to a customer. This is why the issue of constantly analyzing organizational performance is getting more and more critical for survival in a global economy.

The QBPM methodology enables strategic decision making by using process-driven management scorecards and provides a structured framework for developing effective metrics and KPIs. The QBPM framework allows organizations to consistently monitor their progress to maturity, and helps them prioritize process improvement efforts by identifying and focusing on the activities with the highest impact on the bottom line.

QBPM is all about creating a framework and an actionable effort aimed at configuring, coordinating, and aligning business processes to achieve the goals of the organization. Following the QBPM methodology, enterprises adopt a corporate philosophy that addresses the measurement of an organization, allows feedback, and facilitates communication between all management levels.

Executing the Eight Simple Steps

The QBPM framework is a step-by-step methodology (see Figure 4.6) that allows enterprises to use this quantitative information and improve management control over the execution and prioritization of business strategy. The process follows these clearly delineated steps:

1. Develop and refine an overall strategy. To know what to measure strategically, you have to start with the mission or vision—the overarching goal for the growth of the business as a whole. Every business unit's strategy and goals have to be aligned with overall company strategy, but with its own mission and success criteria. Begin by stating a clear company-wide strategy with quantifiable targets for each level of the organization—every functional department and its key processes should have a strategy and quantifiable targets that directly relate to the overall strategy. An example of a company-wide target would be to "increase revenue."

2. Identify critical success factors. Critical success factors (CSFs) are the elements or activities necessary for ensuring a successful business. Once a company identifies its CSFs, it can set out to design strategies around them (or decide whether it can build the requirements necessary to meet them). To go along with the "increase revenue" target, an example of a CSF would be "sales management involvement and support."

3. Define and quantify strategic business goals. Strategic goals are operational requirements from which an organization can derive more detailed goals and

Figure 4.6   The eight components of the QBPM framework.

activities for achieving its vision. They lay the foundation for this planning and help outline the approach. Companies need to understand how their business goals relate to their business processes. Following the example, a strategic goal would be "increase sales in the overseas divisions."

Because these strategic goals are purposely at a high level of abstraction, it is necessary to derive subgoals. For the most part, a successful subgoal articulates a quantitative component and possibly an element of timing. for example, "increase sales by 15% in the next fiscal year." In order to truly benefit from this framework, the organization should prioritize these subgoals and develop a meaningful and efficient strategy for achieving them, rather than trying to achieve every one independently of the others and at random.

There are five principles to focus and align every process and system within an organization to match its overall strategy:

a. Translate the strategy into operational terms. Everybody must understand the strategy of the organization so it's presented in a cause-and-effect linkage that reveals how the strategy will be implemented.

b. Align the organization to strategy—to create synergy within the organizational. The activities of the individual functional divisions must be aligned and integrated.

c. Strategy is a part of everyone's job. Everybody should be aware of how he or she contributes to the overall strategy.

d. Strategy is a continual process. Organizations must be able to adapt their strategies as external changes happen or the existing strategy matures. Everyone must be linked to the strategy environment to create a collaborative environment and open communications.

e. Educate and mobilize leadership for change. Every member of the executive team must realize that the change is a good idea and keep the strategy transparent—in front of the people.

In this example of a strategic goal, "increase customer satisfaction to get a bigger market share," there are dependencies within the goal statement itself, which makes the statement seem like two distinct goals. This is often the case: one strategic goal statement combines concepts from more than one goal. Here, the company aims to increase customer satisfaction. But the second part is also a goal that has a quantitative expression of achievement: "to get a bigger market share."

Subgoals are like functional requirements, which an organization must plan and implement to satisfy not only its subgoals, but its strategic goals as well. Subgoals stem from strategic goals and often articulate more specific elements, such as timing. For example, "increase market share by 15% in the next fiscal year" is a subgoal that could possibly come from the above stated overarching strategic goal.

4. Define KPIs. After companies define strategic goals, they need to define KPIs to support them to show how individuals are performing—whether they are achieving the goals or deviating from them. KPIs help to allocate and put priorities on resources and provide information about the need to change current policies or directions to meet predefined goals. KPIs, usually defined as a measure or combination of measures that provides insight into a process, project, or product, may be classified mainly in one of three ways:

Success: Determines whether the goals are met.

Progress: Tracks the progress and execution of the defined tasks.

Analysis: Assists in analyzing the output of each task.

For instance, "sales frequency" would be an appropriate KPI for the example.

5. Establish metrics. The term *metrics* means a quantitative measure of the degree to which a system, component, or process is a given attribute. Metrics provide quantitative insight into KPIs, and they result from a continuous measurement process throughout all steps of the QBPM framework. Organizations must align metrics with their business goals to minimize the risk of not using the data gathered. Measurements help you answer questions like: Are we on track? Are there risks? Are we getting to our goals? "Sales growth" is an example of a metric that would give insight into the "sales frequency" KPI.

6. Continuously improve processes. Improve and fix only the parts of the process that are influencing or contributing to goal deviation. To accomplish this, organizations can apply different methodologies, such as Six Sigma or Lean Sigma. Organizations must take great care in selecting which processes to improve, keeping in mind that the improvement project should be focused and support CSFs. What are the critical success factors? These are things

that your organization must do right if you expect to survive in the future. These critical areas require constant attention on the part of management. According to John F. Rockart in the *Harvard Business Review*, "Critical success factors for any business are the limited number of areas in which results, if they are satisfactory, will ensure successful competitive performance for the organization." Measurements should track performance in each critical success area. Critical success factors are both internal and external. In order to identify critical success factors, we have to go through a strategic planning process. As a result, a well-defined set of critical success factors will serve as a foundation for the performance measurement system. Critical success factors are important links between strategic plans and the performance measurement system.

7. Prioritize and manage enterprise risk. You must manage risks associated with failing on CSFs and identified strategic goals. Risk management is the practice of systematically selecting cost-effective approaches to minimize the probabilities of not meeting predefined goals. By following the previous framework steps, companies can prioritize risk based on the quantitative information already at hand.

8. Make scorecard-based decisions. A scorecard enables a company to translate its mission and strategy into a coherent set of forward-looking performance measures that can be automated, linked at all levels of the organization, and tied to the company's business drivers. This method of measuring performance assesses progress toward achieving predefined, specific, and measurable goals and is an important component for efficient management.

Each organizational level has its specific role with different performance measurements. A balanced scorecard links KPIs to individual goals, and this mapping ensures management attention to the business processes that contribute to strategic success. With a scorecard, efforts involving these business processes will no longer be rigid and disconnected. Applying a balanced scorecard to a QBPM framework can significantly affect how value flows through the organization.

Core versus Enabling Processes

Business Process Goals

The goal(s) of any organization is driven by the strategy of the organization. Commonly accepted competitive factors include:

Quality
Delivery lead time
Time to market
Delivery reliability

Design flexibility
Volume flexibility
Cost/price
Innovation
Trustworthiness

Processes are either core processes or enabling processes. Core processes directly relate to generating revenue, providing products or services to a revenue-generating customer, or creating a strategic advantage for the company. Core processes include financial and operational planning, consolidation and reporting, modeling, analysis, and monitoring of KPIs linked to organizational strategy. Typically, there are only four to six core processes in a company (e.g., sales and marketing, manufacturing/fulfillment, design engineering, order entry and processing), and they are made up of various major processes and subprocesses.

Enabling processes do not touch or directly affect the external customer. They exist to enable and support the execution of the core processes. A core process could not sustain itself without the support and services the enabling processes provide. Examples of typical enabling processes are information technology, human resources, finance, legal, and documentation.

A Closer Look at the Scorecard

Perhaps the most widely used piece of the IMPACT framework is the scorecard, which has been around for more than fifteen years and has found widespread adoption in Fortune 1000 companies. The information the scorecard provides helps to establish changes in organizational processes and culture. A balanced scorecard benefits a company in the following ways:

Communicates a clear and accepted strategic vision that is tied to the CSFs and goals
Permits departments and individuals to make decisions based on KPIs
Ensures data integrity, as companies can collect the right information to monitor progress toward their goals
Helps management establish agreed upon performance goals and shares results of goal achievement
Allocates and puts priority on resources
Provides information about the need to change current policy or directions to meet predefined goals

Two tenets of business process management are to respond quickly and decisively to changes in the business environment and to know you are working on the right set of activities. It is essential for organizations to immediately respond to, reprioritize, and shift goals and targets as needed—not when some schedule says they should. Static reviews, whether annual, quarterly, or even monthly, do not reflect the real pace of business and will not enable companies to act quickly. Using a balanced scorecard, companies can respond with both agility and the certainty that their actions and decisions are the right ones, which lessens the likelihood that they will underperform or be outdone by their competitors.

Performance Measurements

Performance measures provide the means to assess effectiveness and efficiency. Effectiveness is doing the right things; efficiency is doing things by employing the best use of available resources. Performance measures are not static. You have to review and revise strategies in relation to strategies and business cycles.

> What is the output of our activities?
> How will we know if we met customer requirements?
> How will we know if we met stakeholder requirements?
> How will the system be used?
> For what purpose will the system be used?
> What information will be produced, shared, or exchanged?
> Who will use the results?
> For what purpose will the results be used?
> Why do the output and results matter?
> How do the results contribute to the critical success factors?

Measurement is an iterative process. It focuses an organization on what matters most, which in turn results in higher performance. Developing performance measures communicates an organization's objectives and aligns activities to achieve them. This is accomplished over time by communicating assumptions about the objectives and the organization and building consensus with associates.

A combination of output and outcome measures provides an effective assessment. Output measures record whether or not what was done was done correctly and if the products or services were provided as intended. Outcome measures assess whether the completed work contributed to the organization's accomplishments.

Outcome measures have more value than output measures. Outcomes can only be measured upon completion of a project. Measuring intermediate outcomes, if possible, provides an assessment before completion of a project. For example, by implementing a nationwide system in stages, an agency could assess the performance in one region of the country before implementing the system in other areas.

Results, particularly outcomes, rarely provide meaningful information by themselves. Results must be examined in the context of the objectives, environment, and external factors. Therefore, after collecting the results, organizations should conduct measurement reviews to determine how well the indicators worked and how the results contribute to objectives. The purpose of this step is to improve the measures for the next measurement cycle, to look for ways to improve the performance and effectiveness of IT within agencies, and to make meaningful conclusions from the results.

The balanced scorecard (BSC) is a framework that helps organizations translate business strategies into action. Originally developed for private industry, the BSC balances short- and long-term objectives. Private industry routinely uses financial measures to assess performance, although financial measures focus only on the short term, particularly the results of the last year or quarter. The BSC supplements financial measures with measures from three perspectives: customer, internal business, and innovation and learning.

The customer perspective examines how customers see the organization. The internal business perspective examines the activities, processes, and programs at which the organization must excel. The innovation and learning perspective, also referenced as the growth perspective, examines ways the organization can continue to improve and create value by looking at processes, procedures, and access to information to achieve the business strategies.

The BSC provides organizations with a comprehensive view of the business and focuses management on the handful of measures that are the most critical. However, the BSC is more than a collection of measures. If prepared properly, the BSC contains a unity of purpose that ensures measures are directed to achieving a unified strategy. "Every measure selected for a BSC should be an element in a chain of cause-and-effect relationships, linkages, that communicates the meaning of the business unit's strategy to the organization" (Figure 4.7).* For example, do process improvements increase internal business efficiency and effectiveness? Do internal business improvements translate into improved customer service?

Each project employs people, purchased inputs, and some forms of technology. These constitute the inputs. A project transforms the inputs into products or services (outputs) for use by customers. Customers can be taxpayers, other government agencies, or internal agency personnel who receive or use the products and services. The outcomes are the effects of the output on the customers. Impacts are the long-term effect of the outcomes. The cloud around the impacts indicates that the impacts are difficult to discern. Semantically, it is difficult to distinguish between long-term outcomes and impacts.

The arrows in Figure 4.8 represent cause-and-effect relationships and should be read as "lead to." The thickness indicates the strength of the cause-and-effect relationships. There is a direct relationship between the level of input and the level

---

* Robert S. Kaplan and David P. Norton, *The Balanced Scorecard: Translating Strategy into Action*, p. 31.

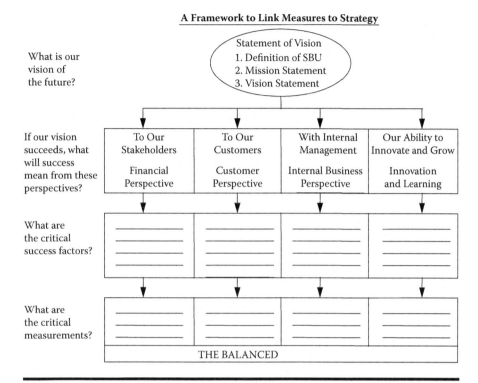

A Framework to Link Measures to Strategy

What is our vision of the future?

Statement of Vision
1. Definition of SBU
2. Mission Statement
3. Vision Statement

If our vision succeeds, what will success mean from these perspectives?

| To Our Stakeholders | To Our Customers | With Internal Management | Our Ability to Innovate and Grow |
| Financial Perspective | Customer Perspective | Internal Business Perspective | Innovation and Learning |

What are the critical success factors?

What are the critical measurements?

THE BALANCED

Figure 4.7 The Balanced Scorecard. (Adapted from Robert S. Kaplan and David P. Norton, "Putting the Balanced Scorecard to Work," *Harvard Business Review*, September–October 1993, p. 139.)

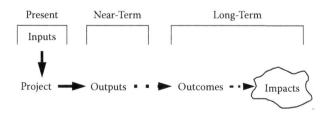

The Ideal Flow of Results

Present   Near-Term   Long-Term

Inputs

Project → Outputs ■ ■ ► Outcomes - - ► Impacts

Figure 4.8 The ideal flow of results.

of outputs. Outputs lead to outcomes, but the relationship is less direct than inputs to outputs. Outcomes lead to impacts, but the relationship is often negligible, if existent, and difficult to determine. An ideal flow occurs when a relationship exists between inputs and impacts.

In most cases, the balanced scorecard is broken down into four perspectives:

Financial: The strategy for growth, profitability, and risk from the shareholder perspective.

Customer: The strategy for creating value and differentiation from the customer perspective.

Internal business: The strategic priorities for various business processes that create customer and shareholder satisfaction.

Learning and growth: The priorities to create a climate that supports organizational change, innovation, and growth.

A balance of measures across these four perspectives is what defines the balanced scorecard. However, the measures that make up a scorecard do not exist in isolation from each other. They relate to a set of goals derived from the CSFs. To sum it up in the simplest terms, you create a balanced scorecard as follows: The company clarifies its overall mission statement. From this, each organizational unit derives a set of strategic goals and subgoals. The business manager tasked with generating the scorecard then maps the subgoals to each quadrant, defining the successful KPIs and metrics for each.

Once the requirements for the scorecard are defined by business management, the scorecards are implemented as part of the enterprise executive reporting suite, which is based on data reported directly from SAP Business Warehouse, CRM (customer relationship management) application, and other available sources of operational data, and are considered an integral part of company's business intelligence reporting.

Over the past decade, organizations have adopted the balanced scorecard as a key framework for managing their businesses. This concept has spread through businesses and consulting communities at the speed of light. This concept instantly appealed to CEOs. It was easy to comprehend because on one sheet of paper it was possible to capture not only financial goals, but also the nonfinancial drivers for their achievement. No longer will the operational side of the business be disconnected from the financial measures that stockholders used to judge the performance. What CEO would fail is to commit to the creation and management of this balanced scorecard? Given that lack of management commitment has repeatedly been identified as the single most important factor in explaining the failure of organizational change initiatives.

Arthur Schneiderman offers his view on why most balanced scorecards fail:

1. The independent (nonfinancial) variables on scorecards are incorrectly identified as primary drivers of future stakeholder satisfaction.
2. The metrics are poorly defined.

3. Improvement goals are negotiated rather than based on stakeholder requirements, fundamental process limits, and improvement process capabilities.
4. There is no deployment system that breaks the high-level goals down into the subprocess level, where the actual improvement activities reside.
5. A state-of-the-art improvement system is not used.
6. There is not and cannot be a quantitative linkage between nonfinancial and expected financial results.

More broadly, performance measurement is only one part of the performance management cycle.

Unfortunately, these measures—and the BSC in general—do not provide the business information, analytical tools, and structured decision support that is needed to actually improve business performance in relation to specified targets. For that, we need a unified framework.

Do You Accept the Challenge?

For companies to survive in the global economy and ensure they are delivering the best possible value to their customers, they must look to improve their business process management practices. Not only must companies develop comprehensive goal-reaching strategies that address every level of the organization from the bottom up, but they must also constantly monitor and alter each goal as changes or problems arise. While it's hard enough just to identify ways to improve operational efficiency, the greatest challenge may be to vigilantly keep track of all of the company's goals once they are determined.

Management needs more insight into how the organization interacts with its internal and external environment, and the only way to gain that insight is to better manage business processes. Once business process strategies align with a hierarchical set of goals, companies will finally be on their way to operational excellence (Figure 4.9).

This quantitative framework offers an opportunity to management to better understand an organizational strategy by providing insight into how an organization interacts with its internal and external environment. The real issue is not that companies are having problems identifying where and how the operational efficiency can be improved in support of business drivers and critical success factors. Rather, the real issue is how to better manage the efficiency of the process or subprocess delivering value to a customer. This is why the issue of constantly analyzing the organizational performance is becoming more and more critical for survival in a global economy.

In 2008 Ventana Research published a paper called "The Time for Performance Management Is Now, Not Later." In this paper they said that two tenets of performance management are to respond quickly and decisively to changes in the business environment, and to know you are working in a right set of activities.

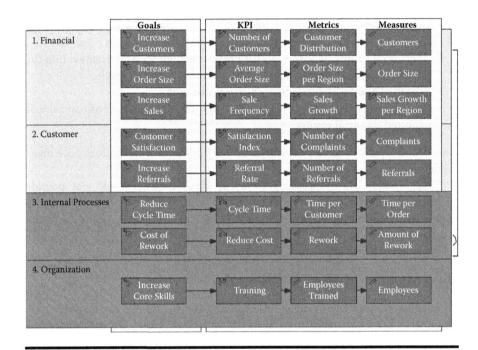

Figure 4.9 The alignment of goals and process strategy.

Immediate responsiveness is essential; organizations should be able to reprioritize and shift goals and targets as needed, not when some schedule says they should. Static reviews, whether annual, quarterly, or even monthly, do not reflect the real pace of business and will not enable you to act quickly. If you cannot respond with both agility and the certainty that your actions and decisions are the right ones, you likely will underperform or be outdone by the competition. Ventana says that their research shows that performance management processes are deployed tentatively or inadequately. Those sporadic efforts reflect the failure to realize the strategic importance of performance management and likely also lack of consensus on priorities among members of the executive team. One-third of the organizations react to change in an uncoordinated fashion. Ventana believes that organizations must act to deploy performance management in order to avoid failure and to deliver expected results. The need to manage performance is a reality when companies fail to hit their financial and operational targets.

Applying this methodology brings a handful of core concepts to achieve results within a simple, repeatable process:

Define: The initial focus of the effort comes from a concise description of the problem—what and how existing conditions impose a negative impact on current operations or limit opportunities to optimize resources. A problem must be understood in context with strategic objectives and business goals.

Measure: While seemingly an obvious step, selecting the most appropriate metric for performance takes careful deliberation. The target metrics must accurately reflect key performance indicators. The absolute numbers are less important than the trend uncovered. Continuous improvement is only evident by demonstrating a positive trend against an established baseline.

Analyze: When a business problem is understood in light of strategic goals, the best analysis reflects performance toward strategy. Then the analysis must support decisions and validate effectiveness.

Improve: When validated and meaningful analysis is reported to business leadership regularly, the opportunities to improve quality and optimize resources become increasingly obvious. This leads to a reliable process for sustaining and continuing the process of improvement.

Control: The analysis tools mentioned above form a reliable mechanism for monitoring performance. As such, these become a means to ensure activities and products stay within the limits of acceptability—performance boundaries. Essentially, asserting control over business processes and monitoring their benefits becomes a reliable, repeatable process to maintain control over progress while continuing improvements.

References

Fritjof Capra. 2000. *The tao of physics*. Boston: Shambhala.

Lewis Carroll. 1871. *Through the looking glass (and what Alice found there)*. London, UK: Macmillan & Co.

Gerald Edelman and Giulio Tononi. 2001. *A universe of consciousness: How matter becomes imagination*. New York: Basic Books.

Rich Karlgaard. 2004. Peter Drucker on leadership. *Forbes*. www.forbes.com/2004/11/19/cz_rk_1119drucker.html

John Rockart. 1979. Chief executives define their own data needs, *Harvard Business Review*. (2), 81–93

Arthur Schneiderman. 1999. Why balanced scorecard failed, *Journal of Strategic performance Measurement*, January.

Peter Senge. 1994. *The fifth discipline*. New York: Doubleday Business.

www.estrategy.gov/documents/eight_steps_to_develop_use_IT.doc

www.ventanaresearch.com/.../OperationalPerformance.html

Chapter 5

Business: The Value Planning Domain

"Would you tell me, please, which way I ought to go from here?"

"That depends a good deal on where you want to get to," said the Cat.

"I don't much care where … ," said Alice.

"Then it doesn't matter which way you go," said the Cat.

"… so long as I get SOMEWHERE," Alice added as an explanation.

"Oh, you're sure to do that," said the Cat, "if you only walk long enough."

—Lewis Carroll (1865)

The Logic Model

The logic model is a framework for planning, managing, measuring, and evaluating (Figure 5.1). Using a goal-measure approach, it connects activities and outcomes-based results.

A common problem is that activities and strategies often do not lead to the desired outcomes. Check your mission statements. Do they make sense and lead to the outcomes you want to achieve? A logic model makes the connections explicit.

The logic model is not new. It was first introduced by the Kellogg Foundation in the 1960s and got a new life because it helps to focus for what matters—outcomes—and allows the making of direct connections to continuous improvement. It was developed as an approach to develop performance measures in government

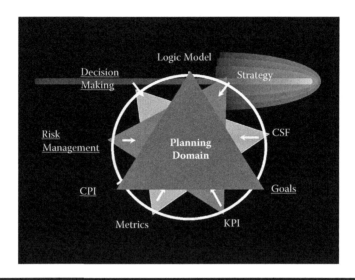

Figure 5.1 Business: the value planning domain—logic model, goals, and continuous process improvement.

and public sectors. It has been used for years by a number of public and private foundations, as well as federal, state, and local agencies.

The logic model helps to make our assumptions more explicit, more obvious. The assumptions are the part of our paradigm. The main idea behind the development of the model was to develop a framework that will be able to describe the relationships between investments, activities, and results and provide a common approach for integrating planning, implementation, evaluation, and reporting.

Osborne and Gaebler in 1992 identify these points:[*]

What gets measured gets done.
If you don't measure results, you can't tell success from failure.
If you can't see success, you can't reward it.
If you can't reward success, you're probably rewarding failure.
If you can't see success, you can't learn from it.
If you can't recognize failure, you can't correct it.
If you can demonstrate results, you can win public support.

What Is the Logic Model?

Any successful organization should have a clear understanding of its mission, vision, values, goals, and strategies to survive.

---

[*] David Osborne and Ted Gaebler, *Reinventing Government* (1992).

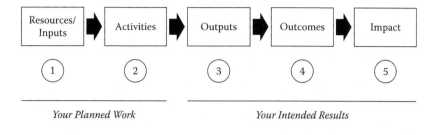

Figure 5.2 The basic logic model.

The W.K. Kellogg Foundation defines *logic model* as a systematic and visual way to present and share understanding of the relationships among the resources you have and the activities you plan to do, and the changes or results you hope to achieve.

The most basic logic model (Figure 5.2) is a picture of how we believe our organizational processes should work to deliver value to the customer. It describes the sequence of activities and how these activities are linked to the results we expect to achieve.[*]

The basic components of the logic model are defined below. Planned work describes the resources needed to implement what it is intended to do.

1. Resources include the human, financial, and organizational resources that are available or needed to do work. They are also referred to as inputs. Resources are the time, money, human resources, office space, utilities, equipment, supplies, management, support, etc., needed to accomplish what you plan. If resources are not available and cannot be obtained, the organization should rethink objectives and activities and modify them to be more realistic.
2. Activities are what you do with resources. Activities are the processes, tools, events, technology, and actions that are part of implementation. They are what you spend your time doing to achieve desired outcomes, produce necessary outputs, or obtain resources. Intended results include all of the desired results, such as outputs, outcomes, and impact.
3. Outputs are the direct product of the activities. They are physical products resulting from activities needed to achieve the desired outcomes.
4. Outcomes are the specific changes in process participants' behavior, knowledge, skills, status, and level of functioning. Short-term outcomes should be attainable within one to three years, while longer-term outcomes should be achievable within a four- to six-year time frame. The logical progression from short-term to long-term outcomes should be reflected in impact, occurring within about seven to ten years.

---

[*] W.K. Kellogg Foundation, *Logic Model Development Guide* (1998).

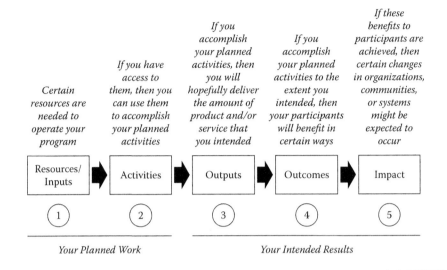

Figure 5.3 How to read a logic model.

Long-term outcomes describe the intended effect of the initiatives in the issues. They might be different in nature, such as social, economic, environmental, or individual.

Midterm outcomes describe expected changes in the environment or organizational behavior based on the continuation of the initiative.

Short-term outcomes describe the expected immediate effect of a program or project.

5. Impact is the fundamental intended or unintended change occurring in organizations, communities, or systems as a result of process activities, within seven to ten years.

When read from left to right, logic models describe transformation over a period of time, from planning through results (Figure 5.3). A logic model is a graphic representation of process transformation that shows the logical relationships between the following:

The resources that go into the program—inputs
The activities the program undertakes—outputs
The changes or benefits that result—outcomes

A series of if-then relationships connect the components of the logic model: if resources are available, then activities can be implemented; if activities are implemented successfully, then certain outputs and outcomes can be expected

Figure 5.4   Inputs and outcomes.

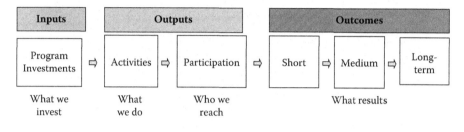

Figure 5.5   Connect inputs to outcomes.

(Figure 5.4). The strength of the logic model is in causal links, which are expressed in if-then statements.*

The logic model serves as a valuable tool for planning and management (Figure 5.5). It helps to clarify where we are and where we want to be. It connects the dots between resources, activities, and outcomes and can serve as a basis to develop a more detailed management plan. The outcomes drive activities.

The process logic model is defined as a picture of how your organization does its work—the theory and assumptions underlying the process (Figure 5.6). A process logic model links outcomes (both short and long term) with the goals and activities.

The most basic logic model is a picture of how you believe your process will work. It uses words, pictures, or both to describe the sequence of activities thought to bring about change, and how these activities are linked to the results the process is expected to achieve. Logic models link projected outcomes with activities, outputs, and inputs (or resources).

The purpose of a logic model is to provide stakeholders with a road map describing the sequence of related events connecting the need for the planned process with the process's desired results. Mapping a proposed process helps you visualize and understand how human and financial investments can contribute to achieving your intended program goals and can lead to program improvements.

The flow of the logic model starts with inputs and works through to a final outcome or impact (Figure 5.7).

Defining the situation is a critical first step in logic model development because you have to think outside the logic model box (Figures 5.8 and 5.9).

---

* http://www.usablellc.net/Logic%20Model%20(Online)/Presentation_Files/index.html.

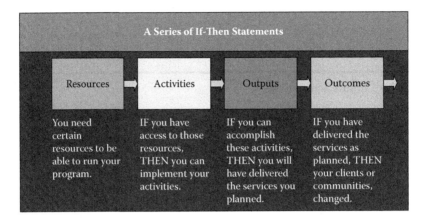

Figure 5.6 Examples of IF-Then statements.

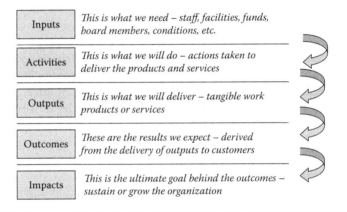

Figure 5.7 The flow of the logic model.

Situation Analysis and Problem Definition

The situation statement is important because it gives us an opportunity to understand the relevancy of the strategy we are trying to develop. At the same time, it is much easier to improve a situation after good analysis and understanding of the present problems and potential benefits.

Businessdictionary.com gives a definition of situation analysis:

> Systematic collection and evaluation of past, present, economical, political, social, and economical data. It is aimed at (1) identification of internal and external forces that may influence the organization's performance and choice of strategies, and (2) assessment of the organization's current and future strengths, weaknesses, opportunities, and strengths.

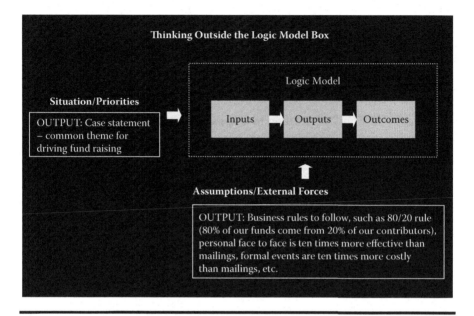

Figure 5.8 Outcomes and impacts should be SMART: specific, measurable, action oriented, realistic, and timed.

Resources	Activities	Outputs	Short- and Long-Term Outcomes	Impact
In order to accomplish our set of activities, we will need the following:	In order to address our problem or asset, we will conduct the following activities:	We expect that once completed or under way, these activities will produce the following evidence of service delivery:	We expect that if completed or ongoing, these activities will lead to the following changes in 1–3 then 4–6 years:	We expect that if completed, these activities will lead to the following changes in 7–10 years:

Figure 5.9 Position references toward success.

According to Matt Evans, once you have organized the process, the next step in the process is to assess your current situation. The organization needs to take a hard look at itself: "Where are we going? Where are we now? What are our choices?" In order to assess your current situation, you will need to collect information so that everyone understands the current situation. This will involve a review of past history, a critique of the current mission statement, and analysis of organizational strengths, weaknesses, opportunities, and threats. You also need to understand the external environment—current competition, customer trends, technology trends, demographic changes, etc. Information can be collected through surveys, questionnaires, interviews, and other analytical techniques. The planning team will conduct situational analysis by following a series of steps, such as the following:

> Collect background information to assess the situation. Start with a history of the organization, current mission, significant changes, stages of growth, etc. Have someone give a presentation on the history of the organization. Reach consensus on how successful the organization has been in the past few years.
>
> Assess the strengths and weaknesses of the organization. Confine your list to the most significant strengths and weaknesses. Reach agreement on a good list. This list will help in the development of strategic objectives.
>
> Next, develop a list of significant opportunities and threats facing the organization's future. You will need to gather information about external forces—customers, competition, social trends, technology, political, etc. If the planning team comes up with a long list, ask everyone to list the most significant eight and reach consensus on a list of eight opportunities and threats.

Now that you have identified strengths, weaknesses, opportunities, and threats, you need to review the mission statement. Does it fit? Should it be broader or more narrowly focused? A good mission statement should capture the essence of why your organization exists. A good mission statement includes the following characteristics:

> Provides overall direction and vision for the organization
> Conveys an image of success for addressing the future
> Defines the competitive boundaries of the organization
> Usually is expressed in relation to marketplace served and products/services
> Avoids being too specific so as to allow room for change

At the heart of situational analysis is the need to better understand what is going on and to properly account for what is happening. Before we proceed to develop a strategic plan for dealing with these critical issues, it is imperative that we find some degree of overlap or matching with:

> What you are trying to accomplish (mission)
> What you are capable of doing (strengths and weaknesses)
> What is required and possible (opportunities and threats)

If there is no overlap between these three elements of strategic planning, then you should not proceed to develop a formal strategic plan.

There are many methodologies developed over the years to help describe the situation and solve problems. Unfortunately, they focus only on the solution in a short period of time—working mostly on situational outputs and not concentrating on the outcomes and potential impact of the resolved problem:

> What problematic condition exists that demands a potential strategy correction?
> Why does it exist?
> For whom does it exist?
> Who has a stake in the problem?
> What can be changed?

If incorrectly understood and diagnosed, everything that flows from the questions will be wrong.

> Factors affecting problems: protective factors and risk factors
> Review research, evidence, knowledge base
> Traps:
> > Assuming we know cause; symptoms versus root causes.
> > Framing a problem as a need where need is actually a program or service. This precludes a discussion of the nature of the problem: What is the problem? Whose problem? And it leads one to value provision of the service as the result—is the service provided or not?

This is why the development of a problem statement and a statement of objectives is extremely important.

> The need to solve problems is as old as the human civilization. From the earliest years of history to the present times, we have been faced with a number of issues, which require resolution, on a daily basis. There are two main reasons for problem to be solved: (1) something around us is not to our liking, and thus we need to do something to improve this situation to conform to our beliefs; and (2) something potentially useful exists independent from our observations and perception, and thus we need to discover this phenomenon and put it to use.[*]

In order to write a meaningful problem statement and objective statement, one should explain what needs to change and few questions should be answered:

> Which processes that I work in are the key to the success of the organization, the customer, and are in need of improvement?
> Who is affected by the problem?
> What specific problem can I solve to improve the performance of this process or my company?

---

[*] Mark G. Barkan Concept Catalists, Inc.

What is the current baseline level of performance that quantifies this problem or process performance?

By how much and by when do I want to improve the performance—what is my objective?

How much money would I save if I improved the process performance to the level stated in the objective statement?

If I make an improvement, which of the company's goals and objectives does it support?

Problems without proper definition are elusive and slippery. They tend to change day by day as circumstances affect your and the organization's opinions and attitudes about them. There will be many ideas and opinions about what the problem really is, how bad it is, what processes are associated with it, who is involved, how much should be improved, and so on. Such an environment creates ambiguity or uncertainty about the problem. When uncertainty exists, it is difficult, at best, to get a focused effort to resolve the problem.

How to Build a Logic Model

Before building a logic model, the following questions should be asked:*

What is a current situation that we intend to impact?

What will it look like when we achieve the desired situation or outcome?

What behaviors need to change for that outcome to be achieved?

What knowledge or skills do people need before the behavior will change?

What activities need to be performed to cause the necessary learning?

What resources will be required to achieve the desired outcome?

Before we begin working on a project or any initiative, it will be good to decide what kind of impact we want to achieve, and only then how to achieve it. There are a few questions to ask:

What are the desired or expected outcomes as a result of our planned effort?

What are the steps in the mid and short term that demonstrate you are making progress toward that long-term outcome?

What activities and information are needed to move the issue from its present state to the desired state (state of the expected impact)?

What will be needed to achieve the desired impact?

What is available?

---

* Paul F. McCawley, *The Logic Model for Planning and Evaluation* (University of Idaho Extension).

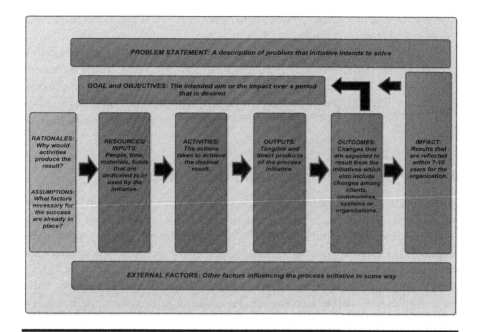

Figure 5.10   A logic model.

With outcomes developed, the way to measure them is easier identify. I'm referring to the performance measures that will show whether you meet objectives. Therefore, the performance measures should be selected from all levels of outputs and outcomes.

Set performance targets at the highest level—final outcomes.
Define the outputs needed to create the targeted outcomes.
Develop a plan of activities and resources required for generating the outputs.

A logic model is a framework and a process for planning to bridge the gap between where you are and where you want to be. It provides structure for understanding the situation that drives the need of the initiative, the desired end state, and how resources are linked to planned activities in order to achieve the desired results (Figure 5.10).

Why Use the Logic Model?

It is a clean process for capturing cause-effect relationships, covering the life cycle of the fundraising program.
It is easy to follow and understand, from left to right.
It drills down to the activity level, where execution takes place.

It forces proactive planning and adjustments before you reach the end of the fundraising campaign.

It leads us to develop indicators for outputs and outcomes. But those indicators should be derived directly from identified strategic needs. Those indicators should represent a baseline on how the organization brings value to the customer. The indicators should be linked to the goals and metrics in value-adding activities and elimination of waste.

A Value Stream Focus within the Enterprise

In spring 2007 I came across an article in the *Washington Post*: "Pearls before Breakfast." This article described an experiment conducted at L'Enfant Plaza early in the morning during the rush hour. The main attraction was supposed to be Joshua Bell, a famous virtuoso violinist. Usually, the tickets to his concerts are extremely expensive or even impossible to buy. Bell was playing at the Plaza's famous pieces at 7:30 a.m. as a street musician. Very few people stopped. Even fewer people threw money into the hat. He collected a few dollars, but much less than he expected. Why?

Everything was set right: busy place (people on their way to work—most of them government employees) and a famous violinist (celebrity, classical music). The value and value delivery were obvious. So, what went wrong? Content? Perception? Place? People priorities? All of the above?

The answer probably is all of the above. We need a lot of supporting activities to deliver the value. Without them, the value is not recognized or appreciated.

A value stream is all of the actions (both value added and non-value added) currently required to deliver a product or a service. It is the work activity and information flow occurring as raw material or information becomes a product/service that is delivered to a customer. It is the flow of paper and information from its origin or initial request, to the desired service or action, to its final delivery to the user or customer. It is the entire flow, from door to door. It can comprise several key process areas that together achieve the deliverable.

Using a value stream perspective means working on the big picture, not just individual process steps to find individual opportunities to optimize the whole. For any given product or service, a value stream spans all of the processes, from the delivery of supplied parts, material, and information, to the delivery and receipt by the user or customer. It is an analysis that helps you to see and understand the flow of materials, documents, and information as a product or service flows through all of the processes, from the customer back to the supplier.

With products and services, we tend to think mostly of the flow of materials that achieve the required deliverables. It is important to know the information flow also. Information tells each process step what to do next and what to produce. The goal is to understand how information flows so every discrete process will do only what is needed when it is needed. We must define the workflow, then look at how the workflow is managed using various forms of information and communication. For the purposes of this class, we will focus only on the workflow, and just briefly cover information flow.

Successfully applying CPI requires a comprehensive value stream focus within the transformed enterprise. Enterprise creates myriad nodes, interfaces, activities, and other "touch points" that may need to be considered as parts of a specific value stream—the cross-functional enterprise-wide process—that may contribute to the improved process and support activity.

This is where process management can make a significant difference. Process management is all about creating a framework and an actionable effort aimed at configuring, coordinating, and aligning both core and enabling business processes to achieve the goals of the organization. Process management creates the insight to see how value flows across the various stovepipes or functional organizations of the company. Key inputs and outputs of these value-creating and -supporting processes are identified, and their performance or capability is characterized. The organization can see how outputs of one process become inputs to another process until, finally, an output to an external customer is made.

Process and Continuous Process Improvement

Anthony Jay in his book *Management and Machiavelli* tells a story about the Royal Artillery giving a demonstration to some visiting Europeans on Salisbury Plain in the 1950s. The visitors were most impressed with the speed and precision of the light artillery crew, but one of them asked what was the duty of a soldier who stood at attention throughout the whole demonstration.

"He is number six," the adjutant explained.

"I too can count. But why he is here?"

"That is his job. Number six stands at attention throughout."

"But why then do you not to have five?"

No one knew. It took a great deal of research through old training manuals, but finally they discovered his duty. He was the one who held the horses.

The underlying theory of process improvement and innovation has been around a long time. Basically, a process represents some activity that adds value. Each process has inputs, the value-added activity, and an output. The benefit derived from the output is dependent on (1) consistency in form and content of the input and (2) validation that a process activity actually adds value. Any input or activity without value is, by definition, waste.

There is no question whether process improvement must be used. The only question is how much and how fast the improvements should be. There is no specific answer. The general answer is that continuous process improvement combined with new technologies is needed. Pearce and Robinson suggest the following approach for strategic management process:

1. Formulate or revise your company mission. Include statements about your purpose, vision, philosophy, and goals.
2. Develop your profile and assess internal strength and weaknesses and capabilities.
3. Evaluate your firm's external environment.
4. Examine your options. This is done by matching your external strength and capabilities with external factors.
5. Identify the most desirable options in keeping with your mission.

Now it's time for your long-range goals and strategies that will achieve the long-term objectives:

6. Develop short-term objectives and strategies that are in keeping or compatible with your long-term goals and strategies.
7. Implement your strategic choices. Focus on your budget, resources, tasks, staffing, control, directing, technologies, and structure.
8. Evaluate or check the success of the process base on a measuring system that was instituted for monitoring purposes.

CPI is an enabler to achieve the goals of the enterprise. The main concept of the CPI as part of the framework is to improve response time to the challenge and support decision-making agility. The objective is to align the organization and its processes to shorten the cycle time without adversely affecting the reliability and cost of the good or service. Cycle time improvement can be focused on any process to reduce the time and resources involved. An important CPI-related concept is the expansion of thinking beyond a focus on direct labor alone to looking at the larger picture of all utilized labor resources, including direct, indirect, and other supporting stakeholder efforts. At the same time, experienced CPI practitioners know that simply attempting to speed up a process with the objective of reducing cycle time is to run the risk of compromising quality, thereby degrading reliability. CPI balances the need for speed with the need for reliability.

Effectiveness and efficiency can often be improved at little cost. However, high-leverage and sustainable organizational improvements are likely to require substantial investment. CPI practitioners must consider the costs and benefits of process improvements before undertaking them.

CPI efforts should consider the anticipated improvement in the context of improved productivity lowering total cost to deliver the targeted required value to the customer within the entire value streams at multiple levels under study. Experience in both the public and private sectors indicates that the following conditions are required to ensure effective CPI implementation:

1. Strategically aligned outcome-focused goals based on the voice of the customer are identified to drive real customer value through the operations of the organization.
2. A thorough problem-solving structure—for example, definition, measurement, analysis, improvement, and control (DMAIC)—within a logical, methodical CPI plan of action exists for all projects and other initiatives that are related to organizational objectives and priorities.
3. Strong and continuously visible leadership commitment and involvement from the very top of the organization stresses and supports a CPI culture of innovation and teamwork.

The CPI cycle is supported by KPI-based Process Improvement (KAPI).

The emphasis of KAPI is on the infinitely repeating nature of decision making in support of principles of the framework and continuous improvement. Both principles are based on the concept that the process is never done.

Step 1: Validate the problem using KPI.
Step 2: Develop a problem statement.
Step 3: Set improvement objectives in support of goals.
Step 4: Determine gaps in the value stream delivery process.
Step 5: Apply applicable methodology and toolboxes for analysis.
Step 6: Improve the value stream process.
Step 7: Standardize successful processes.
Step 8: Go back to step 1.

Consistent application of the eight-step problem-solving process will provide a concise and common format for presentation of data, problem-solving facts, and information. This will ease benchmarking and sharing of best practices when similar problems arise in other areas. The common structure provides a common language that will more easily translate into a common understanding.

Every activity performed within the organization is part of the process. So, any improvement that an organization is trying to achieve is process improvement related. When we focus on process improvement, we have to understand how it is going to improve the value it delivers to the customer.

The value stream defines overall flow and interaction between the various people and organizations that comprise the value stream. The goal is to understand how information flows so every discrete process will do only what is needed when it is needed.

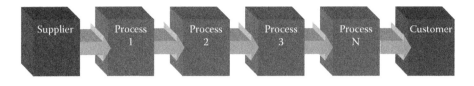

Figure 5.11 Delivering value to the customer.

We must define the workflow, then look at how the workflow is managed using various forms of information and communication. For the purposes of this chapter, we will focus only on the workflow, and just briefly cover information flow (Figure 5.11).

Each process, i.e., a key process from your workplace project, is linked together to form the total value stream of a given product or service. Value stream mapping can be thought of as being done at the key process level. By thinking about linking the key processes together, you will be interested in the performance from the key process level.

Always start at the "shipping" end in your facility and work upstream. This way, you will first see the processes linked most closely with the customer and will better understand the impact of upstream processes. Begin with a quick walk along the entire door-to-door work stream to get a feel for what activities, resources, inventories, and other noticeably important things are occurring. Remember, you are acting like you are the product or service that is being produced for a customer.

The main concept of the CPI as part of the framework is to improve response time to the challenge and support decision-making agility. The objective is to align the organization and its processes to shorten the cycle time without adversely affecting the reliability and cost of the good or service. Cycle-time improvement can be focused on any process to reduce the time and resources involved. An important CPI-related concept is the expansion of thinking beyond a focus on direct labor alone, to looking at the larger picture of all utilized labor resources, including direct, indirect, and other supporting stakeholder efforts.

The five CPI critical success factors are based primarily on leadership effectiveness, clear performance measurement goals, and well-designed change management plans.

1. Strong executive leadership and alignment
   - Executives and program champions must communicate the reason(s) behind the transformation program and establish a sense of urgency.
   - Executive leadership and support must be visible early in the transformation program and be reinforced throughout.
   - Executive leadership must clearly define program objectives.
2. Clear and measurable goals
   - Goals of the transformation program must be in line with the organization's strategy, and they must be measurable.
   - Executive leadership and support must clearly define the criteria for measuring progress toward program objectives.

3. Actionable business case and performance measures
   - Program benefits and returns on investment must be clearly defined and approved by the key stakeholders.
   - Organizational and individual performance measures must be aligned to the objectives of the transformation program.
4. Clearly defined roles and responsibilities
   - Key stakeholders, internal and external, must be identified early in the program.
   - Roles and responsibilities need to be clearly defined.
5. Well-designed execution and continuous improvement plan
   - Change management should be part of the program.
   - The execution strategy and implementation plan must be well defined and clear to all stakeholders.
   - Program milestones must be designed to deliver program goals and objectives.
   - Impacted individuals need to be trained and ready for their new assignments.

Step 1: Validate the Problem Using KPI

This phase is the most critical to the overall decision-making process. The KPI presents data that should be continuously monitored and analyzed.

By constantly applying the KAPI-based eight-step process, management can understand how they and their organizations solve problems and make decisions.

Step 2: Develop a Problem Statement

The critical first step to effective problem solving clearly understands the problem. Any problem-solving effort that begins with "We all know what the problem is. So what are we going to do about it?" is doomed to failure before it begins.

At this point, you've identified what needs to be improved, you know which processes are involved in creating your problem, and you have determined your current level of performance. With this knowledge you can be make a reasonable estimate of how this problem impacts the organization and how much money you could save if you made some level of improvement—a best estimate. At this point don't worry about being precise in your dollar estimate. If it could save tens of thousands, don't worry about the thousands, and if it can save thousands of dollars, don't worry about the hundreds; you will have a chance to fine-tune the number later, when you have further characterized the process.

Next, consolidate all that you have learned up to this point into a problem statement. The problem statement serves several purposes. A problem statement significantly clarifies the current situation by knowing specifically what you need to improve, what the level of the problem is, where it is occurring, and the financial impact of the problem. It also serves as a great communications tool helping to get buy-in and support from others. When problem statements are well written, people readily grasp and understand what it is that you are trying to solve.

The best way to learn how to write a good problem statement is to study poorly written statements first. As you review these statements, remember the following format of what needs to be in a problem statement: *What* is wrong? *Where* and *when* is it occurring? What is the *baseline* magnitude at which it is occurring? What is it *costing* me?

You must take caution to avoid underwriting a problem statement. Your natural tendency is to write a problem statement too simplistically because you are already familiar with the problem. You must remember that if you are to enlist support and resources to solve your problem, others will have to understand the context and the significance in order to support you.

The problem statement cannot include any speculation about the cause of the problem or what actions will be taken to solve the problem. It's important that you don't attempt to solve the problem or bias the solution at this stage. The data and the Six Sigma methodology will find the true causes and solutions to the problem.

You now know where you are coming from. You have determined that you have a viable problem, one worthy of being worked, and you have the ability to convince others that you have a problem worthy of attacking. You know specifically what must be improved to make life better for you and others. Now the question is: How much improvement do you need or how much improvement can you make? You are ready to create the objective statement for the project, so that you know where you are going.

Which Problems First?

There are five Lean tools that can assist the Air Force leader in deciding which problems should be tackled.

1. Strategic alignment and deployment (SA&D): Provides a framework for ensuring resources and activities are linked to the key strategies, directives, and goals of the organization. Any individual problem-solving effort can have a greater impact if it is coordinated with the rest of the organization.
2. Strengths, weaknesses, opportunities, and threats (SWOT) analysis: Provides an objective means to identify areas of need for problem-solving efforts.
3. Voice of the customer (VOC): Only one entity can define value, and that is the customer. Understanding who the customer is and what their needs are is a prerequisite to understanding whether or not those needs are being met.
4. Value stream mapping (VSM): Overview of the process at any level to determine areas of needed focus.
5. Go and see: Determine problems with data. Actually walking the process or problem area provides firsthand data rather than secondhand opinions.

When deciding where to deploy limited problem-solving assets, the Air Force leader should be guided by four questions:

1. Would solving this problem directly contribute to my organization's strategic goals (SA&D)?
2. Would solving this problem directly address an organizational level weakness (SWOT)?
3. Has this problem been identified as a barrier to transforming my organization from its current state to the needed future state (VOC and VSM)?
4. What opportunities were identified or observed by the process or problem "walk," and do these opportunities align with the first three questions?

How to Craft a Problem Statement

A good problem statement is the first step to an effective solution. A good problem statement is:

Written down: Usually one paragraph and always less than one page. More than one paragraph may be a sign of combining more than one problem in a single problem statement.

Factual: All the descriptive terms should be precise, without emotion and without names.

Agreed to by all parties: Lack of consensus at this stage indicates the problem is still unclear.

A good problem statement should include:

What is the problem? Often two or three words (a noun and a verb) are enough.

Where did the problem happen?

When did the problem happen?

What is the significance of the problem? Many problems exist; some are more critical than others. When tackling any problem we should ask themselves: "How will the solution of this problem contribute to the critical success factor supporting the strategic goals of the organization?"

Step 3: Set Improvement Objectives in Support of Goals

Next, you consolidate all that you have learned up to this point into a problem statement. The problem statement serves several purposes. A problem statement significantly clarifies the current situation by knowing specifically what you need to improve, what the level of the problem is, where it is occurring, and the financial impact of the problem. It also serves as a great communications tool, helping to get buy-in and support from others. When problem statements are well written, people readily grasp and understand what it is that you are trying to solve.

The objective statement should directly address the information in the problem statement. Just like the problem statement, the objective statement is expected to contain certain elements in order for it to be effective. A good objective statement will contain all of the following elements: improve some metric, from some baseline, to some goal, in some amount of time, with some impact against some corporate goal or objective.

The objective statement should directly address the information in the problem statement. Just like the problem statement, the objective statement is expected to contain certain elements in order for it to be effective. As you review these statements, remember the following format of what needs to be in an objective statement: improve some *metric* from some *baseline* level to some *goal*, by some *time frame*, to achieve some *benefit* and improve upon some *corporate goal* or *objective*.

Remember the baseline performance you established in the problem statement? Once you have determined your goal in terms of the amount of improvement, you can now understand the gap that must be closed. Now you can really talk about the impact your improvement project will have on the work that is done in this process and the effect on the customer. You are also in a position to better estimate the financial benefits of the improvement.

It's always good to link an improvement project to the key goals and objectives of the organization, as we have previously discussed in this module. Aside from the common sense of doing this, this is a good way to roll up the number of projects and their benefits as they relate to achieving the company's goals and objectives. In some corporations, Six Sigma has created the ability to quantitatively link effort to strategy for the first time. Objective statements tell us where we are going or where we need to go. It is important to write a good objective statement to keep yourself and your team aligned on the opportunity and the needs of the organization. Before you practice writing an objective statement, we need to provide some guidance on how to track the performance of the selected Y.

Step 4: Determine Gaps in Value Stream Delivery Process

There are two Lean tools that can assist in understanding what data are needed and the story they are trying to tell.

1. Performance gap analysis: What is the difference between the level of performance seen today and the level of performance identified as needed tomorrow?
2. Bottleneck analysis (or constraint analysis): Which steps in the process are inhibiting the flow of the entire process. Sometimes referred to as the weakest link, or the slowest step, this analysis is defined by the theory of constraints.

When gathering and analyzing problem data, airmen should be guided by five questions:

1. Does the problem require more analysis, or does leadership have enough information to execute a solution?
2. If more information is needed:
   - What measures are available today?
   - Do these measures align with the customer-driven key performance indicators (KPIs)?
   - Is there a gap between the data available and the data required? That is, does the data needed not exist today, thus requiring a new measurement system?
3. What is the gap between current performance and the customer's requirements?
4. Does the data point to any specific areas of root cause?
5. Does the data indicate a bottleneck/constraint?

Step 5: Apply Applicable Methodology and Toolboxes for Analysis

Improvement targets must be set on two levels simultaneously: the strategic and the tactical.

Strategic Vision

Value stream mapping (VSM) is the primary Lean tool for defining the current state, the ideal state, and the practically achievable future state. A vision is a view into the future that succinctly describes how the organization will conduct business. It implies a gap between the current state and a better future state. A future state can be defined as "better" only when it supports effective fulfillment of the organization's mission.

1. Common vision(s) and goals foster teamwork, interdepartmental cooperation, and alignment between goals, metrics, and actions.
2. Focus on reducing constraints to achieve better utilization of resources and capabilities.
3. Continue acceleration of improvement efforts.
4. Build a better foundation for fact-based analysis and decision making.
5. Expand your perspective on the entire (end-to-end) value stream.

Tactical Targets

Tactical targets define the performance levels required to make the vision a reality. Targets should be challenging but achievable and have B-SMART characteristics:

Balanced: Ensure goals are balanced across the multiple fronts of organizational output and multiple targets.

Specific: Have desirable outputs that are based on subject matter expert knowledge and experience and are applicable to the process improvement activity.

Measurable: Include time frames and have data that are obtainable from specific sources.

Attainable: Resources are available; may have some risk, but success is possible.

Results focused: Link to the mission, vision, and goals and are meaningful to the user.

Timely: Provide step-by-step views versus giant leaps and are measurable at interim milestones.

All too often management find themselves addressing problems that have been "solved" many times before. This is usually due to problem-solving efforts being directed at the symptoms of a problem rather than at the root cause of the problem. If an aircraft is constantly breaking down and becoming non-mission capable, should the goal be to reduce the aircraft usage, improve repair cycle time, improve the quality of replacement parts, improve the aircraft design, or improve the aircraft design process? Clearly, each step becomes increasingly difficult, but each step also has a greater impact in preventing the recurrence of the problem. Root cause analysis is a trade-off between digging as deeply as possible and finding the deepest point that is still within the team's sphere of influence.

CPI Management Tools

LEAN

Lean is really a mindset—a way of viewing the world. Lean is about focus, smooth process flows, doing only those activities that add value (as the customer defines value), and removing waste (eliminating all other activities that don't add value). Lean can be simplified as removing wastes (those activities and processes that don't add to a product's value). Value is defined by the customer.

The essence of Lean is to concentrate effort on removing waste while improving process flow to achieve speed and agility at lower cost. The focus of Lean is to increase the percentage of value-added work performed by a company. Lean recognizes that most businesses spend a relatively small portion of their energies on the true delivery of value to a customer. While all companies are busy, it is estimated for some companies that as little as 10% of their time is spent on value-added work, meaning as much as 90% of time is allocated to non-value-added activities, or waste.

Forms of waste include wasted capital (inventory), wasted material (scrap), wasted time (cycle time), wasted human effort (inefficiency, rework), and wasted energy (energy inefficiency). Lean is a prescriptive methodology for relatively fast improvements across a variety of processes, from administrative to manufacturing applications. Lean enables your company to identify waste where it exists. It also provides the tools to make improvements on the spot.

Lean focuses on the value stream, the sequence of activities and work required to produce a product or to provide a service. It is similar to a linear process flow map, but it contains its own unique symbols and data. The Lean method is based on understanding how the value stream is organized, how work is performed, which work is value added versus non-value added, and what happens to products and services and information as they flow through the value stream. Lean identifies and eliminates the barriers to efficient flow through simple, effective tools.

Lean removes many forms of waste so that Six Sigma can focus on eliminating variability. Variation leads to defects, which is a major source of waste. Six Sigma is a method to make processes more capable through the reduction of variation. Thus, there is symbiotic relationship between the two methodologies.

Lean principles include:

1. Specify what creates value from the customer's perspective.
2. Identify all the steps along the process chain.
3. Make all the processes flow.
4. Produce only what is "pulled" by the customer.
5. Strive for perfection by continually removing wastes.

Many steps have been added over time to a process: internal accounting, supervisory controls, compensation for a poor worker, specifics for an individual worker's personality, communication, and record keeping. All of these added steps have been deemed significant and important over time by management or workers, but in reality have nothing to do with the actual requirements of value identified by the customer. In many cases, if customers actually knew about the added steps, they would not agree to pay for those added steps; therefore, they are really wastes in the process. In many cases, these hidden steps are hidden costs that an organization's leadership has been unable or unwilling to recognize (cost of delay time, cost of rework, cost of additional labor, cost of storage).

Every aspect of an organization has the potential for huge amounts of waste. The correct application of Lean tools and techniques allows leaders to peel away layer after layer of waste. Like peeling an onion, even after taking away the biggest outer layers, there are always layers of waste underneath.

Unfortunately, in many cases, there is strong resistance, and organizational culture and beliefs that certain procedures and protocols are necessary, required for good order and discipline, promotion and competitiveness, or quality of life. Lean is a mental approach, a journey of continuous improvement rather than a destination. There is no endpoint—only the endless journey of continuously eliminating waste.

5S

The term *5S* derives from the Japanese words for five practices leading to a clean and manageable work area. The five Ss are:

Seiri: To separate needed tools, parts, and instructions from unneeded materials and to remove the latter.
Seiton: To neatly arrange and identify parts and tools for ease of use.
Seiso: To conduct a cleanup campaign.
Seiketsu: To conduct *seiri*, *seiton*, and *seiso* at frequent, indeed daily, intervals to maintain a workplace in perfect condition.
Shitsuke: To form the habit of always following the first four Ss.

Simply put, 5S means the workplace is clean; there is a place for everything and everything is in its place. The 5S will create a workplace that is suitable for and will stimulate high-quality and high-productivity work. Additionally, it will make the workplace more comfortable and a place that you can be proud of.

Developed in Japan, this method assumes no effective and quality job can be done without a clean and safe environment and without behavioral rules.

The five Ss allow you to set up a well-adapted and functional work environment, ruled by simple yet effective rules. 5S deployment is done in a logical and progressive way. The three first Ss are workplace actions, while the last two are sustaining and progress actions.

It is recommended to start implementing 5S in a well-chosen pilot workspace or pilot process, and spread to the others step by step.

5S and Its Environment

The flows in product development are of information rather than physical materials. Therefore, we would expect to find wastes associated with the information flows, analogous to the seven wastes identified in the factory (Table 5.1). Therefore, the best practices are to quickly reduce information wastes and clear bottlenecks to flow.

Goals

Effectiveness in achieving goals and objectives has replaced efficiency as the most effective business priority.

As historian Arnold Toynbee once said, "It is a paradoxical but profoundly true and important principle of life that the most likely way to reach a goal is to be aiming not at the goal itself but at some more ambitious goal beyond it."

Table 5.1 Table Information Wastes

Types of Information Waste	Examples	Causes
Waiting Idle time to unavailable information	People waiting for information	Lack of access Untimely updating of databases Multiple approvals Poorly designed or executed process to provide information
	Information waiting for people	Information created too soon may be obsolete by the time it is used
Inventory Information that is unused or is a "work in progress"	Too much information	Poor understanding of user needs
	Multiple/ redundant sources	Tendency for everybody to maintain his or her own files
	Outdated/obsolete information	Lack of version control. Lack of disciplined system for updating new and purging old information Inadequate archiving standards or practices
	"Just in case" information	Collection, processing, and storage of every element of data that process participants can think of, whether or not specific end use has been identified
Excessive processing Information processing beyond requirements	Excessive/custom formatting	Lack of standardization
	Numerous, fragmented reports	Poor output design Lack of understanding of the needs of the user of process output
	Unnecessary serial processing	Poor system design Lack of understanding of concurrent processing capabilities
	Excessive approval for information release	Stovepipe, command and control mentality Turf protection

Table 5.1 (continued)   Table Information Wastes

Types of Information Waste	Examples	Causes
Overproduction Producing, distributing more information than needed	Unnecessary detail and accuracy	Tendency to overdesign More detail than necessary in early design
	Pushing, not pulling data, information	Uncontrolled process
	Overdissemination	Poor understanding of each participant's needs Send information to everyone rather than to meet specific needs
Transportation Unnecessary movement of information between people, organizations, or systems	Information handled by multiple people before arriving at user	Lack of direct access due to IT system limits, organizational inefficiencies, knowledge hoarding, security issues
	Information hunting	Lack of clear information flow paths, failure of process to produce information needed
	Data reformatting or reentry	Incompatible information types Incompatible software systems or tools Lack of availability, knowledge, or training in conversion and linking systems
	Switching computers to access information	Software/hardware incompatibilities IS support
Unnecessary motion Unnecessary human movement (physical or user movement between tools or system)	Walking to information, retrieving printed materials	Lack of distributed, direct access Lack of online access Lack of digital versions or heritage information

Table 5.1 (continued)   Table Information Wastes

Types of Information Waste	Examples	Causes
	Excessive keyboard, mouse operations	Lack of training
		Poorly designed user interfaces
		Incompatible software suites
		Too much information to sort through
	Poor physical arrangement of the organization	Team members not colocated
		Organization structure inhibits formation of right teams
Defects Erroneous data, information, reports	Errors in data reporting/entries	Human error
		Poorly designed input templates
	Errors in information provided to customers	Lack of disciplined reviews, tests, verification
	Information does not make sense to user	Raw data delivered when user needs delivered information, recommendations, or decisions

Source: Product Development Value Stream Manual, LAI.

If we have goals, do we know what are they and what to do with them? What is the purpose of setting a goal? Goals should serve as a frame for all elements of the logic model. They should reflect organizational priorities and help you define a clear direction for future action.

Goals should include the intended results and specify the target outcomes.

What is the difference between goal commitment and goal acceptance? *Goal acceptance* is defined as "an attitude reflecting the reasonableness and personal acceptability of an assigned goal," and *goal commitment* as "the determination to achieve a goal, and the willingness to put forth effort to attain a goal" (Renn et al. 107–8). They declared the seven-point, three-anchor rating scale, twelve-item questionnaire useful for further reliability and validity after clarifying earlier varied results.

Goals are set on a number of different levels: First, you create a "big picture" of what you want to do with your life, and what large-scale goals you want to achieve. Second, you break these down into smaller and smaller targets that you must hit so that you reach your lifetime goals. Finally, once you have your plan, start working to achieve it.

Set performance goals, not outcome goals: You should take care to set goals over which you have as much control as possible. There is nothing more dispiriting than failing to achieve a personal goal for reasons beyond your control. In business, these could be bad business environments or unexpected effects of government policy. In sports, for example, these reasons could include poor judgment, bad weather, injury, or just plain bad luck. If you base your goals on personal performance, then you can keep control over the achievement of your goals and draw satisfaction from them.

Keep operational goals small: Keep the low-level goals you are working toward small and achievable. If a goal is too large, then it can seem that you are not making progress toward it. Keeping goals small and incremental gives more opportunities for reward. Derive today's goals from larger ones.

I remember reading an article in *Inc.* magazine (John Case, June 1995). The author was writing about a long-forgotten term and management method called open-book management. I reread the article in 2007, and the issues are still valid today. He was writing that the best-known managerial methods have a pretty spotty record. The good example would be quality efforts. Quality efforts are going to improve quality, but necessarily they improve business. He wrote about one company—a maker of scientific equipment. Employees got so obsessed with quality-related measures that they quit returning customers' phone calls. "All of the quality-based charts went up and to the right, but everything else went down."

Another example that is very typical is management's obsession with the idea that they have to do something to improve organizational performance by deploying the methodology/model. One company spent close to $1 million to implement CMMI (Capability Maturity Model Integrated) level 2, trying to improve marketing image and fighting the problem of quality cost.

A manager needs information about projects to be able to make decisions, plan and schedule, and allocate resources for the different activities. Sources of information are documents produced during the development and direct contact with the developers. However, these sources are not sufficient, and the manager must rely on experience and estimations. It would be better to know instead of estimating, but when this is not possible, the approach has to be to make as good estimations as possible. To be able to make good estimations, the manager needs to have in-depth information about the organization and the staff. Also, there is a need for validation of the estimations. The underlying problem for a manager is that it is very difficult to control something that one has little knowledge about.

Now we have goals—what are we going to do with them? Application of goal setting also proves useful in organizations. David Terpstra and Elizabeth Rozell's article points out that approximately 50% of large organizations with management by objective (MBO) programs use goal-setting principles. MBO, while similar to goal-setting theory, regards participation as a strong component of setting goals. In general, a positive correlation between the use of goal setting and profitability proved helpful. Terpstra and Rozell's research results indicate that 61% of responding organizations used goal setting as a means to increase performance, and these organizations exhibited statistically significant higher levels of annual profit and profit growth. Terpstra and Rozell concluded:

> Goal setting constitutes a simple, but potentially powerful means of increasing organizational effectiveness. Previous research has found that goal setting enhances employee performance and productivity. The current study also suggests that the use of goal setting may have an impact on businesses' bottom line.[*]

Sun Tzu, the early authority on warfare strategy, believed that the moral strength and intellectual faculty of humans were decisive in war, and if applied properly war could be waged with certain success. This intellectual faculty consists of a combination of past experience, intuition, judgment, common sense, and the ability to comprehend complex situations within the context of immediate goals and objectives. In short, to deal with rapidly changing, complex, nonlinear, uncertain situations, one must be able to see beyond images, hear beyond words, and sense beyond appearances. This is a blending of the cognitive capabilities of observing and perceiving a situation, the cognitive processing that must occur to understand the external world and make maximum use of our intuition and experiences, and the faculty for creating deep knowledge and acting on that knowledge.

This construct of knowing can be elevated to the organizational level by using and combining the insights and experiences of individuals through dialogue and collaboration within teams, groups, and communities. Such efforts will significantly improve the quality of understanding and responsiveness of actions of the organization. It also greatly expands the scope of complex situations that can be handled through knowing because of the greater resources brought to bear—all of this significantly supported by interoperability and ubiquity.

Organizational knowing is an aspect of organizational intelligence, the capacity of an organization as a whole to gather information, innovate and generate knowledge, and act effectively. This capacity is the foundation for effective response in a fast-changing and complex world. Support capabilities of organizational knowing include organizational learning, knowledge centricity, common values and language, coherent vision, openness of communications, and effective collaboration.

---

[*] David Terpstra and Elizabeth Rozell, "The Relationship of Goal Setting to Organizational Profitability," *Group & Organizational Management*, September 1994, p. 285.

What are the critical success factors we use for a strategic plan? Somewhere in our plans there should be a set of objectives. The first test is: Are they specific? Are they outcome focused? Do they say where we want to be? Our plan will also have some actions, or perhaps strategies, depending on your jargon. The things that are supposed to make the plan happen—are they specific with a deadline? Will we clearly know if this action has been achieved? If the actions aren't specific, it is very difficult to determine the resources, money, or people necessary to make it happen.

Are the actions actually achievable? There is little point in putting in place a strategy or action that everybody knows really can't be achieved. It's fine to have objectives that may seem very difficult, but it is pointless to have an action that is the first step in achieving that objective that is also unachievable.

Our plan also needs to incorporate some performance or success measures. Are they really performance measures, not a busyness measure? For example, do they relate to achievement relative to a target rather than simply turnover? They should preferably be outcome (or even output) measures, rather than input.

Why start with goals? Because measurement can influence behavior. How do we define the goal? "We run the company by questions, not by answers," said Eric Schmidt, the CEO of Google.

The Goal Question Metric (GQM) paradigm was developed in 1984 at the University of Maryland in response to the need for a goal-oriented approach that would support the measurement of processes and products in the software engineering domain. The GQM paradigm (sometimes called the GQM approach) supports a top-down approach to defining the goals behind measuring software processes and products, and using these goals to decide precisely what to measure (choosing metrics). The GQM paradigm additionally supports a bottom-up approach to interpreting data based on the previously defined goals and questions. If viewed narrowly, the GQM paradigm may be seen as purely an approach for choosing metrics. However, we encourage a broader view of the GQM paradigm as a means for defining the measurement view of a software project. In other words, the analysis and evaluation of processes and products from all activities and phases of a software engineering project may be planned and performed with help of the GQM paradigm.

Principles behind GQM

A principle, as used here, is a fundamental idea or doctrine. The idea behind these principles is that each must hold; i.e., if one does not, then the program is not in conformance with the dictates of the GQM paradigm. The GQM paradigm is based on the idea that measurement should be goal oriented; i.e., all data collection should be based on a rationale that is explicitly documented. This approach offers several advantages. First, it helps in the identification of useful and relevant metrics. Second, the goals provide a context for the analysis and interpretation of collected data. Third, an explicit rationale explaining the refinement of goals into metrics enables an assessment of the validity of the conclusions that were drawn. Finally, because the software development personnel helped define the rationale for data collection, and know that the data will be used for their own purposes, they offer less resistance against a measurement program than they would if they feared the data might be used against them. To yield these advantages, GQM-based measurement programs should be planned and performed according to the following principles:

1. The analysis task to be performed must be specified precisely and explicitly using a detailed measurement goal.
2. Metrics must be derived in a top-down fashion based on goals and questions. A structure of goals and questions may not be retrofitted onto an existing set of metrics.
3. Each metric must have an underlying rationale that is explicitly documented. This rationale is embodied in the series of questions via which a metric is derived from a goal. The rationale is used for justifying data collection and for guiding data analysis and interpretation.
4. The data that are gathered for the metrics must be interpreted in a bottom-up fashion using the GQM goal and questions. This supports interpreting the data subject to the limitations and assumptions behind the rationale for each metric.
5. The people from whose viewpoint (i.e., perspective) the measurement goal is formulated must be deeply involved in the definition and interpretation of the measurement goal. Not only will they supply the data, but they are also the real experts with respect to the analysis and interpretation tasks.

Goals should address:

■ Customer satisfaction
■ Productivity
■ Innovation
■ Resource conservation
■ Management development and performance
■ Employee development and performance
■ Public responsibility

GQM is a top-down approach to establish a goal-driven measurement system for software development, in that the team starts with organizational goals, defines measurement goals, poses questions to address the goals, and identifies metrics that provide answers to the questions. GQM defines a measurement model on three levels, as illustrated in Figure 5.12.

GQM begins by identifying measurement goals (conceptual level) that support (are aligned with) business goals. The team (project managers, development team, customers, or other stakeholders) then poses questions (operational level) to further

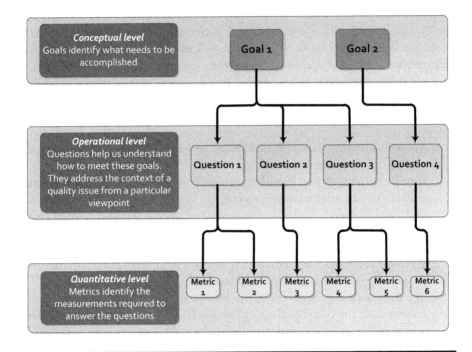

Figure 5.12 Connecting goals and metrics.

clarify and refine the goals as well as capture the variation of understanding of the goals that exists among the stakeholders with respect to their notions of quality and the environment that will impact goal attainment. The team then identifies metrics that will provide answers to the questions (quantitative level). What distinguishes GQM from other measurement paradigms is the hierarchical tree structure used to maintain the relationships among goals, questions, and metrics.

Once appropriate metrics are identified, the last three steps of the GQM process address how to implement the metrics program in a way that ensures the focus will remain on goal attainment. Basili and other GQM experts stress the importance of planning data collection mechanisms and planning how the resulting measurement data should to be organized and presented in order to maximize their value to the stakeholders who will interpret the results in relation to the goals. The literature notes that when measurement programs fail, the primary cause of failure is often a lack of attention to how the measurement results will be used.

GQM can be applied at the strategic level of an organization, or the project level, or at both levels concurrently. When applied at the strategic level, the measurement data consist of results from targeted pilot projects providing feedback to strategic-level planners for decision making relative to product and process strategies.

Organizations often use a phased approach for implementing GQM that integrates GQM-related activities (derived from Basili's GQM process) with project planning and management activities. The phases are GQM planning, definition, data collection, and interpretation. A more extensive explanation of the phased approach, and how it relates to Basili's six-step process, is provided in the body of this document.

This part (the first three steps) of Basili's GQM process, often called the definition phase of GQM, provides the process structure for migrating from concepts to meaningful metrics that, when implemented, quantify the goals and provide meaningful data for decision making. *Goals* identify what we want to accomplish; *questions*, when answered, tell us whether we are meeting the goals or help us understand how to interpret them; and the *metrics* identify the measurements that are needed to answer the questions and quantify the goal.

The mapping among goals, questions, and metrics is not one to one. A single measurement goal may apply to multiple business goals and vice versa; for each goal, there can be several questions, and the same question can be linked to multiple goals as appropriate. For each question, there can be multiple metrics, and some metrics may be applicable to more than one question. Adherence to, and preservation of, this hierarchical structure helps ensure that the measurement program focuses on the right metrics and that we avoid extra work associated with collecting metrics that are not really needed.

The remaining steps of Basili's GQM process (relating to data collection and analysis for decision making and future recommendations) are actionable only when the appropriate definition of metrics has occurred. A goal-driven metric definition, using the goal-question-metric process, is what separates GQM from other measurement methodologies. Thus, this document emphasizes the initial steps of Basili's GQM process because they provide the foundation for the remaining steps of the process.

A primary tenet of GQM, not usually evident in illustrations of the GQM paradigm, is that stakeholders need to be involved throughout the process in order for it to be successful. Basili advocates for planning the implementation of GQM to ensure that those with a stake in any part of the process actually participate to ascertain their knowledge is considered, understand their contribution (role) in the process, and promote their buy-in and acceptance of the measurement program. Those who implement GQM may use a variety of approaches to ensure the appropriate level of participation. The key message is that the measurement program should be planned and implemented from within the organization or project, rather than be outsourced. However, the experts agree that it is helpful to have a consultant (GQM expert) work with the team or organization in the initial stages to ensure that the principles of GQM are implemented, and to transition those principles to key people within the organization.

GQM Process Details

This section provides details about each of the six steps of Basili's GQM process.

Step 1: Establishing Goals

Sometimes, it is difficult to distinguish between a business goal and a measurement goal; they may not always be mutually exclusive. What is important is that the driving goals originate from the group or organization that is responsible for the broader scope of a software initiative, the business environment in which the initiative occurs, rather than from within a particular project. It is not important whether the business goals are developed under the umbrella of GQM, or as a function of strategic planning. Business goals must exist; they must be identified and be the focus for establishing the measurement goals. Without them, the measurement program has no focus. Without this alignment, it is unlikely that implementing the rest of GQM will have a significant impact. When business goals exist, then multiple projects or subgroups within an organization have a basis for identifying the measurement goals relating to their role or scope of influence within the organization.

The goals at the top of the GQM tree (see Figure 5.12) are the measurement goals that are the outcome of step 1 of the GQM process. They are conceptual, not quantitative. They are quantified by their linkage to questions and metrics, as noted in the mapping.

Basili and his followers express GQM goals (measurement goals) using five facets of information to define what the measurement should accomplish in precise terms. Each GQM goal statement explicitly contains these facets:

Object: The product or process under study, e.g., testing phase or a subsystem of the end product.

Purpose: Motivation behind the goal (why), e.g., better understanding, better guidance, control, prediction, improvement.

Focus: The quality attribute of the object under study (what), e.g., reliability, effort, error slippage.

Viewpoint: Perspective of the goal (who's viewpoint), e.g., project manager, developer, customer, project team.

Environment: Context or scope of the measurement program, e.g., project X or division B.

Step 2: Generating Questions

The purpose of Basili's step 2 is to clarify and refine the measurement goals, moving from a conceptual level to an operational level by posing questions. By answering the questions, one should be able to conclude whether a goal is reached. Questions help identify interpretations of the goal that may exist among the stakeholders, as well as constraints imposed by the environment. Typically, at the project level (or perhaps for a group of related projects), conceptual measurement goals are identified relating to product quality, process, resources, or the environment. The project team then identifies questions that the team (individually or collectively) feels should be asked to capture various perspectives of the goal, and addresses whether the goal is being met. These questions would typically get at all of the nuances and perceptions relating to the goal, addressing both perceptions of quality and the context or environment in which the object will evolve. This is essentially a process of stakeholders converging on a common understanding and interpretation of the goal at the appropriate level of abstraction. In other words, the individual project managers and software engineers provide their perspective of what the goal means in the given environment. They do this by posing questions and responding to them with their metrics.

On the surface this step may appear to be trivial, and for some goals that may be the case, but GQM experts (Basili 2005; van Solingen 1999; PERFECT 1997) and implementers have found that getting the right level of abstraction for GQM questions can be difficult. If questions are too abstract, the relationship between the metrics and the question may be muddied. If they are too detailed, it becomes more difficult to get a clear interpretation of the goal. In many instances, particularly where the purpose of the goal is to understand or characterize the process or product, questions may need to be broken into many subquestions to drive appropriate identification of metrics. The implementing organization may tailor this step of the process as needed to ensure that the level of questioning is sufficient to drive the identification of the right metrics. Some excellent examples of ensuring the appropriate level of questioning are provided in the case studies section of van Solingen's book (van Solingen 1999).

In some implementations (van Solingen 1999), a GQM team interviews the stakeholders (members of the project team) individually to capture their perspectives of the goal (their questions) and to have them formulate expected answers as hypotheses. These hypotheses make explicit the current knowledge that is in the minds of the team members, thus forming a baseline for later analysis of metrics. Comparing actual results with these hypotheses during the interpretation phase of GQM increases the learning effect from measurement.

Step 3: Specifying the Measures

Step 3 is about examining how the questions could be answered, moving from the qualitative (or operational level) to a quantitative level. Once goals are refined into a list of questions (GQM process step 2), metrics need to be defined that provide all the quantitative information needed to answer the questions in a satisfactory way. Stakeholders, those directly involved with the object of the goal, must be directly involved in the metric identification step as well as the question step. Direct involvement of these stakeholders minimizes ambiguities and false assumptions and contributes to the overall consistency and completeness of the metrics identification.

In this context, the term *metric* is loosely defined; it can mean a base measure, a derived measure, a composite or aggregate of measures, or what some would call an indicator. The level of definition depends on the scope of the goal and the environment of the GQM implementation. Further details are provided later in the section describing GQM implementation.

The diagram is intentionally oversimplified in order to convey the notion of how one gets from a conceptual level goal to the right quantitative data that renders the goal measurable. It also conveys the multiple mapping of metrics to questions and questions to goals (Figure 5.13).

Note a distinction between the metrics that are defined and the data elements that support them. The metric is at a more abstract level than the actual data items and measurements that need to be collected to provide the correct data for preparing the metric.

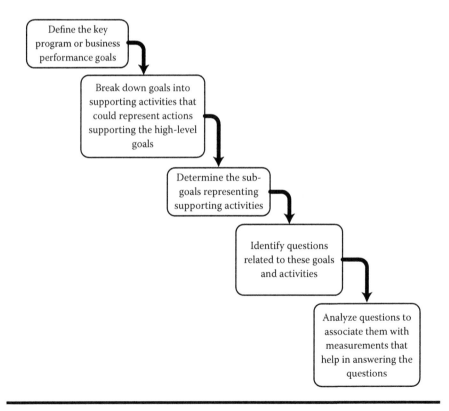

Figure 5.13   Sample of GQM definition phase.

Step 4: Preparing for Data Collection

Once the metrics are identified, one can determine what data items are needed to support those metrics, and how those items will be collected. The metric provides insight regarding how the data need to be organized in order to be meaningful to the viewer/recipient of the information. A significant amount of planning is necessary to provide the detailed procedures for data collection that support the identified metrics. Most projects accomplish this detailed planning by preparing a measurement plan that includes at least the following (van Solingen 1999):

- Formal definitions of direct measurements
- Textual descriptions of direct measurements
- All possible outcomes (values) of the direct measurements
- The person (role) that collects each direct measurement
- The moment in time (or frequency) when the direct measurement should be collected
- The medium (tool or form) that should be used for collecting the measurement

The plan also defines and describes all types of data collection forms and automated data collection tools that should be used. It addresses the question of how the data can be collected most efficiently and effectively and to whom it should be delivered.

Referring to the example in Figure 5.14 of change request processing time, one cannot assume that all stakeholders have the same understanding of what constitutes CR processing time. Does it begin when the CR is first documented, or after it is diagnosed and categorized for action? When is processing considered done? Which CRs are included for averaging—only closed out CRs, or also those on hold? The measurement plan anticipates and addresses such questions.

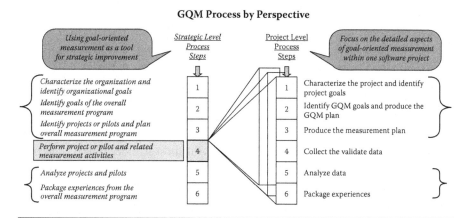

Figure 5.14   GQM process—strategic vs. project level.

Once a plan is developed, the measurement procedures need to be tested and validated before implementing the program. Exercising the forms and procedures during a trial period will reveal flaws that can subsequently be corrected before full-scale implementation of the measurement program begins, or before adding the new procedures and data to an existing program (van Solingen 1999).

In addition, it is important to train individuals involved in data collection to ensure that they understand why the data are needed, how they are going to be used, and how their action contributes to the overall validity of the data collection process.

Step 5: Collecting, Validating, and Analyzing the Data for Decision Making

This step presumes that data collection follows the procedures predefined in the measurement plan. It is often a continuous (or periodic) process rather than a one-time activity. However, it is only a means to an end. Data collection is a worthless process if one does not do anything with the data. The focus needs to be on preparing the data for optimal usage. Regardless of the collection medium, data need to be validated before they are used for analysis.

Recently a project manager told the DACS a story about a group of developers responsible for maintaining an application that was particularly volatile. Each time they fixed a problem they entered a 1 in the problem report (PR) form field that asked for actual time spent on the fix. From their perspective, this was an irrelevant field because nothing was ever done with the data. They were very busy with a backlog of PRs, and it took time to accurately estimate the time to fix each problem. Their manager, who knew that many PRs required extensive time to fix, showed them a request for additional staff that had been denied based on a report of staff utilization that showed a graph of average time per PR, clearly demonstrating that the current staff was underutilized. Once the staff understood the significance of that data item, what decisions it affected, and that it was not measuring their personal performance, they started entering their estimates of time appropriately and the manager began to get valid data for his management purposes.

Automation can assist, but it cannot replace all forms of data collection and validation. The key is to minimize the overhead imposed on the people who are required to provide data while ensuring that they understand the significance of their data collection effort. Validation consists of checking the data collected for correctness, completeness, and consistency. Completeness is the most significant data collection problem. What does one do with a form that is only half completed? How does one ensure that all instances of data are actually captured? These, and similar questions, need to be addressed in planning the measurement program so that there is a proper course of action available to those people tasked with validating.

As the story about the maintenance staff showed, leaders need to reinforce the purpose and value of data collection to promote better data collection quality. A significant part of the validation process is checking validity as close to the data source as possible and taking immediate corrective action for invalid data.

Once validated, it is important to store the measurement data in such a way that it can be accessed for varying analysis and reporting purposes. Because of the sheer volume of measurement data needed for all but the smallest projects, it is useful to develop and use a measurement support system that contains a database for the storage of the metric data and tools for analysis (spreadsheets) and presentation. Flexibility and accessibility are the most important features of such a system.

Analysis is about organizing the data and preparing the metrics for presentation to the stakeholders to address the questions pertaining to the measurement goal. Typically, a GQM team, together with the project team, develops an analysis plan as soon as they know what metrics are needed. The plan details how the data should be organized, what presentation formats are needed, who will review the data, and when. Developing the analysis plan often helps with decisions about data collection. Basili (2005) uses the term *analysis* to mean both analysis and interpretation, but some implementers of GQM make a distinction between the two terms, primarily to assert that the analysis can be done by a GQM team (measurement expert), but the interpretation must be done by the project team, who are the owners of the measurement goals.

Some form of feedback is required to communicate measurement results to the appropriate stakeholders. These sessions are focused on the measurement goal and reviewing the measurement results to answer the questions posed in step 2 of the GQM process. The project team can then decide on corrective action when progress toward goals is not deemed adequate.

Analysis and interpretation is an iterative step typically integrated with the progress reporting cycle of a project.

Step 6: Analyzing the Data for Goal Attainment and Learning

The last step in Basili's GQM process is about looking at the measurement results in a postmortem fashion to assess goal attainment, and also to determine lessons learned and what might be valuable to pass on to future projects.

When GQM is implemented to support an organization-wide improvement process, the experiences and lessons learned from each implementation are packaged in the form of policies, procedures, and best practices, to support future projects and improvement initiatives and to help the organization achieve greater leverage from its measurement program.

Applying GQM at Varying Levels within an Organization

The GQM methodology is quite generic, and thus its scope of implementation can range from somewhat narrow (an individual using GQM to achieve desired goals) to very broad, such as when it is used in strategic planning. The open literature delineates the GQM approach in terms of a six-step process, but the descriptions and boundaries (entry and exit points) of each step vary, depending on the context of implementation and the publication period within the body of literature.

The major distinction between strategic level GQM and project level GQM relates to the data collection phase. The strategic level implementation identifies pilots and projects as the source of data for strategic-level metrics. Therefore, strategic-level data collection is dependent on the designated projects actually implementing GQM at their project level and packaging results to feed back to the strategic level implementation.

When applied at a strategic level, GQM is still a six-step process, with the first three steps focusing on goal and metric identification and planning the measurement implementation, step 4 addressing data collection, and steps 5 and 6 addressing analysis and interpretation. The objects of focus differ slightly at the strategic level from those at the project level. Data collection (strategic level, step 4) is about gathering the information, experiences, and lessons learned from the multiple targeted projects, as the basis for the strategic-level analysis phase.

In summary, the result of the application of GQM is the specification and implementation of a measurement plan for a particular set of goals and a set of rules for the interpretation of the measurement data within the context of these goals. The GQM model has three levels:

Conceptual level (goal): A goal is defined for an object (product, process, project, or resource), for a variety of reasons, with respect to various models of quality, from various points of view, relative to a particular environment.

Operational level (question): A set of questions is used to characterize the way the assessment/achievement of a specific goal will be performed based on some characterizing model. Questions try to characterize the object of measurement (product, process, etc.) with respect to a selected quality issue, and to determine either this quality issue from a selected viewpoint or the factors that may affect this quality issue.

Quantitative level (metric): A set of data is associated with every question in order to answer it in a quantitative way. The data can be objective (e.g., person-hours spent on a task) or subjective (level of user satisfaction).

A GQM model has a hierarchical structure starting with a goal that specifies the purpose of measurement, the object to be measured, and the viewpoint from which the measure is taken. The goal is refined in several questions, which usually break down the issue into its major components. Each question is then refined into metrics. The same metric can be used in order to answer different questions under the same goal. Several GQM goals can also have questions and metrics in common, provided that when the measure is actually collected, the different viewpoints are taken into account correctly (i.e., the metric might have different values if taken from different viewpoints).

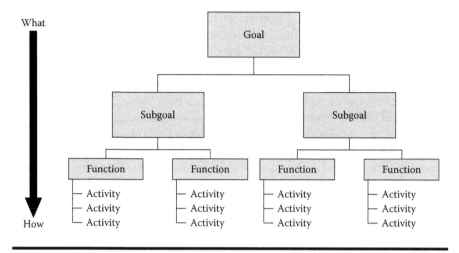

Figure 5.15 Connecting goals and activities.

With the GQM method, the number of metrics that need to be collected is focused on those that correspond to the most important goals. Thus, data collection and analysis costs are limited to the metrics that give the best return. On the other hand, the emphasis on goals and business objectives establishes a clear link to strategic business decisions and helps in the acceptance of measurements by managers, team leaders, and engineers.

Mohammad Modarres, professor of mechanical engineering, director of the Center for Reliability Engineering, and codirector of the Center for Technology Risk Studies, University of Maryland, has published an extensive body of research on the goal tree–success tree methodology.* A method and system are provided for managing goals of an organization. A goal tree is generated having a high-level organization goal and one or more hierarchically organized subordinate goals aligned with the high-level organization goal. Each goal is owned by one or more individuals associated with the organization. The goal tree is accessible to one or more of the individuals through a graphical user interface for their use in monitoring progress toward the goals.

Nuclear engineers have used a modeling concept called the goal tree methodology for many years. A goal tree is simply a hierarchy of goals and functions that are broken down into the technical means available to accomplish the goal (see Figure 5.15). It is a pragmatic approach that is goal and success oriented and can be used to understand how the successful outcome of a complex project can be achieved by looking at the means needed to achieve the goal.

---

* Department of Mechanical Engineering, http://www.enre.umd.edu/faculty/modarres/index.html#menu7.

A success path refers to a bottom-up chain through the tree by which the goal can be accomplished. Thus, the tree can be used to determine how success is achieved and to assess the impact of a specific process on the global results. The objective of the goal tree is to lay out a logical path to accomplish the goal through subgoals, which are in turn accomplished through functional activities made up of technical means. In short, the goal tree starts with "what needs to be accomplished" and defines "how it is accomplished."

The goal tree concept can be adapted to different levels of user-oriented services. For example, one goal can be increased customer satisfaction for an interaction between a customer and the business, or customer satisfaction for a specific business process, which is part of the overall interaction. The concept can also be adjusted for internal and external customers (Figure 5.15).

The goal tree analysis brings another level of management metrics. The process outcome metrics coming from IT operations indicate the root causes and are used by IT management to identify, for example, that the application management processes need to improve. Also, collected at the process level, they show where the process needs to be improved. By using the process models, all levels of IT management—from the CIO down to the line manager—can benefit from metrics that accurately represent their performance.

However, while each specific process model can easily determine a set of internal metrics, a main problem still exists—the inability to define a set of global metrics for the higher levels of IT management to identify process deficiencies.

The goal tree analysis procedure is:

Identify the system goal.
Proceed to the next lower level of the system and identify the subsytem success that could lead to the top event.
Determine the logical relationships between the goal, subgoals, and functions that are required to produce the top event.
Proceed to the next lower system level.
Quatify the goal tree.

In summary, the purpose of GTA is to identify success pathways, or success trees, that can lead to the fulfillment of a specific goal. The goal tree is a graphical illustration of various combinations of goals, subgoals, equipment, or system successes that can result in the success of the top event.

References

Victor R. Basili. 2005. Using measurement to build core competencies in software. Seminar sponsored by Data and Analysis Center for Software.

Lewis Carroll. 1865. Alice's adventures in wonderland. London, UK: Macmillan & Co., Chapter 6.

John Case. 1995. The open book revolution. *Inc.* June 1. www.inc.com/magazine/19950601/2296.html

Matt Evans. www.exinf.com/workshop.com

Antony Jay. 1967. *Management and Machiavelli.* New York: Holt, Rinehart and Winston.

John Pearce II and Richard Robinson Jr. 2000. *Strategic management: Formulation, implementation, and control* (7th ed.). Burr Ridge, IL: Irwin.

PERFECT. 1997. Goal-oriented measurement using GQM: A booklet from the perfect ESPRIT project 9090 handbook. PERFECT Consortium. www.iese.fraunhofer.de/PERFECT/Handbook/handbook.html

Rini van Solingen and Egon Berghout. 1999. *The goal/question/metric method: A practical guide for quality improvement of software development.* London, UK: McGraw Hill. www.mcgraw-hill.co.uk/html/0077095537.html

Gene Weingarten. 2007. Pearls before breakfast: Can one of the nation's great musicians cut through the fog of a D.C. rush hour? Let's find out. *Washington Post.* April 8. www.washingtonpost.com/wp-dyn/content/article/2007/04/04/AR2007040401721.html

Chapter 6

Value Management Domain

He had bought a large map representing the sea,
Without the least vestige of land:
And the crew were much pleased when they found it to be
A map they could all understand.
"What's the good of Mercator's North Poles and Equators,
Tropics, Zones, and Meridian Lines?"
So the Bellman would cry: and the crew would reply
"They are merely conventional signs!
"Other maps are such shapes, with their islands and capes!
But we've got our brave Captain to thank:
(So the crew would protest) "that he's bought us the best—
A perfect and absolute blank!"

—Lewis Carroll (1876)

Strategic Planning

Strategic planning is a process of defining the mission and long-range objectives for conducting the business and developing the strategies for achieving them (Speweek and Hill, 1993) (Figures 6.1 and 6.2). It is a dynamic process of continuously looking at your current situation and plotting your next move. This requires a solid understanding of the organization as well as an understanding about the

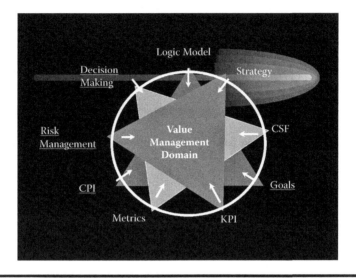

Figure 6.1   Value management domain.

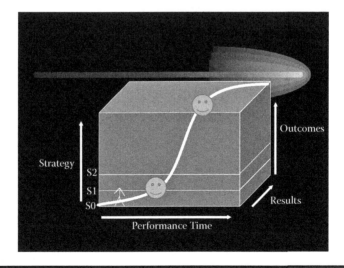

Figure 6.2   Connecting strategy and outcomes.

environment in which the organization operates. The best organizations are always engaged in some form of strategic planning, for example:

Corporations often experience cyclical periods of growth and downturns instead of sustainable growth. Why?

Emerging ventures with innovative products and technologies (hardware) sometimes may not have the business skills and resources to commercialize the market and sell (software).

Should organizations build capabilities to do in-house (i.e., become more vertically integrated), or partner to outsource or buy capabilities to accelerate market implementation?

Companies are often challenged with investing in innovation versus delivering revenues and profits today, and vice versa.

Strategic planning helps management understand the current situation. This in turn allows management to plan for the future. In a world of rapid change, it is becoming imperative for management to think strategically (plan for the future). And since the rate of change seems to be escalating, the importance of strategic planning continues to grow. In fact, the best managed companies tend to engage in continuous strategic planning. Some organizations have intuitive thinkers who almost seem to see into the future. Therefore, strategic planning is a way of preparing for the future by attempting to simulate the future.

Strategic planning has a tendency to force people to think about the future. This is extremely important since many organizations are inward thinking, focusing too much on the short term. Strategic planning looks at the long term, which is how organizations survive and thrive. It has been proven that organizations that focus on the long term through strategic planning outperform organizations that lack long-term planning. Consequently, one of the benefits of strategic planning is long-term performance and growth. Another benefit of strategic planning is communication. Strategic plans communicate the intentions of management to employees, shareholders, and others.

The Balanced Scorecard

These original findings that helped Kaplan and Norton to define and formulate the balanced scorecard in the mid-1990s is still true today. These can be summarized as follows:

A clear, strategic vision is not enough. It requires communicating to the entire company and being understood.

When a strategic vision is in place, it typically has little or no impact on the operating goals of departments and individuals. It must be tied to the goals and objectives of the individuals and departments concerned.

Day-to-day decisions ignore the strategic plan. The plan must be broken down into objectives and initiatives that have direct relevance to the day-to-day activities of personnel.

Companies fail to collect the right information to monitor progress toward their strategic goals. It requires the right data gathered and input to provide an effective measurement of objectives.

Companies do not identify or learn from their mistakes. If an objective is not attained, it must be clearly understood why, with initiatives created to modify the objective or change the approach.

What is a good strategy? What is a bad strategy? Good strategy answers the questions:

What existing and new customers? (and not)
What existing and new products/services? (and not)
What criteria for new product or market opportunity?
What current product and market focus?
What future product and market focus?
What is important to our customers?
What is our competitive advantage?
What goals, measures, and time frame?
What values guide us?
What are our key assumptions?
What are our key operational links (organization systems, processes, and jobs)?

The indicators of good strategy are:

Stakeholders are linked by strategy and goals commensurate with their assigned role and mission.

Performance indicators are standardized within stakeholder levels to allow traceability, roll-ups, and more credible acquisition decisions.

Cascade and align strategy down to the outlet level (and beyond—personal scorecards) where execution takes place.

Capture cause-effect linkages as you cascade and align down. This will ensure that all of the company is moving in the same strategic direction.

Identify and commit to projects and initiatives that will drive strategic execution.

Establish performance outcomes in the form of measurements and targets.

Review results on a regular basis.

Development of Strategies for Each Goal

The next step in strategy development is the definition of strategy for each goal. Strategies are statements of a major approach or method for attaining goals and resolving specific issues. Ideas for strategy emerge from the earlier internal, external, and market assessments, especially the strengths and weaknesses identified in the internal assessment as well as the implication statements developed as part of the market and external assessments. A strategy is judged potentially effective if it does one or more of the following:

Takes advantage of environmental opportunities
Defends against environmental threats
Leverages organizational competencies
Corrects organizational shortcomings
Offers some basis for future competitive advantage
Counteracts forces eroding current competitive position

Here are examples of strategies for our sample goal: expand and diversify our revenue base in order to support anticipated growth.

First strategy: Generate revenue from special events.
Second strategy: Increase funding from public sources.
Third strategy: Expand individual giving from major donors.

How to Formulate Strategy? Strategy Map Development

According to the Harvard Business School, a strategy map provides a better way to communicate and align strategy to all levels of the organization. Research by the Harvard Business School suggests three major benefits to using a strategy map:

Helps build consensus on what the organization must do strategically
Effectively communicates strategy across the stakeholders
Helps ensure that all components in the organizaton are aligned around strategy

Now we can connect the strategy map and measurements (Figure 6.3). To establish a framework for the suite of tools to operate within, embedded strategic planning capability should be developed (Figure 6.4) that cascades and links strategic strategy with operational metrics that can be aggregated into an enterprise representation of successful process change (Figure 6.5).

Connection Strategy and Goals

Cascade from the top of the strategic plan—mission, vision, guiding principles.
Look at your strategic analysis—strengths, weaknesses, opportunities, and threats (SWOT), environmental scan, past performance, gaps, etc.
Limit to a critical few, such as five to eight goals.

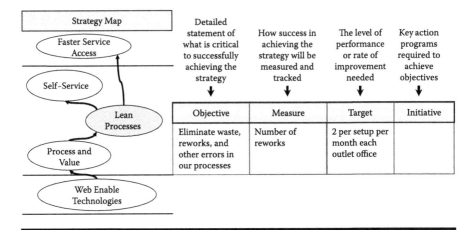

Figure 6.3 Connecting strategy map and measurements.

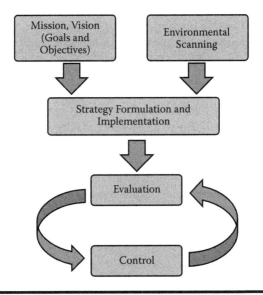

Figure 6.4 Strategy development.

Broad participation in the development of goals—consensus from above and buy-in at the execution level (Figure 6.4).

Should drive higher levels of performance and close a critical performance gap.

Strategy can be described as a series of cause-and-effect relationships. It povides a "line of sight" from strategic to operational activities, working on the "right" things.

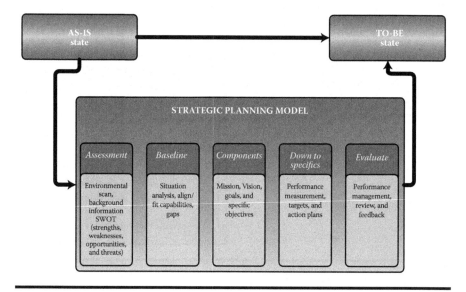

Figure 6.5   Strategic planning model.

Key Performance Indicators

Can we make decisions based on indicators? Two days after Bill Clinton won the 1992 U.S. presidential election, the *Wall Street Journal* ran a front-page humor story by reporter Ron Suskind entitled "Incredible: Vikings Win Football Game, GOP Loses Election." Suskind's story outlined how many once reliable election predictors had missed the mark in this latest presidential contest. The Minnesota Vikings football team had won a Monday night game the evening before the polls opened, and the Vikings victory on the election eve had always correlated with a Republican victory the following day. Likewise, grammar school children favored the Republican candidate in the annual poll conducted by the *Weekly Reader*— another surefire indicator of electoral success suddenly off target. Suskind's story went on to mention a handful of other once reliable election indicators that had failed on this latest contest, among them the baseball World Series winner (an American League victory coincides with a Republican victory, and the tall-short man indicator [taller candidates usually win]). The story quoted Allen Lichtman, a professor at American University and a builder of forecasting models, saying, "For some of these predictors it's just a matter of time before the statistical probabilities catch up with them—and then they disappear."

What Is a Key Performance Indicator?

A key performance indicator is a financial or nonfinancial measure used to help an organization measure progress toward a stated organizational goal or objective (Figure 6.6).

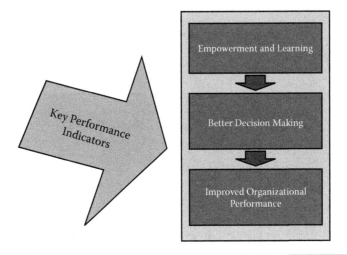

Figure 6.6   Benefits of key performance indicators.

Definition

> "Key Performance Indicator is a performance measure or a combination of performance measures that helps in measuring progress towards long term organizational goals. KPIs are means to track the planned versus actual process performance over a period of time".

KPI is the rate of change or deviation from original goals, sub-goals, strategies and priorities of the organization. They provide a high level snapshot of performance of business, process or program based on certain predefined measures. KPIs provide insight into a process, project or product of the organization. Once the drift between the planned versus actual process performance is understood with the help of KPIs, organization can optimize areas by efficiently allocating resources, changing processes or eliminating unnecessary tasks within the processes.

Purpose of the Key Performance Indicators

KPI helps in understanding the trend of effectiveness of the process performance. KPI monitors the effect of any change made to a process, or implementation of a new strategy. KPI can show different perspectives on an event. It can detect potential problems and it can drive improvement. KPIs help in answering questions as:

What are we ahead or behind on? What was the set metric?
How far ahead or behind are we? How much have we drifted from Planned?
What is the minimum we have achieved to date? How far have we reached?

Benefits of Key Performance Indicators

KPIs are important for tracking progress made to achieve a set goal

KPIs reveal the vital aspects of the business and are usually customer focused.

KPIs enable process improvement by highlighting areas requiring attention.

KPIs are easy to understand and focus on the areas needing immediate improvement

KPIs help prepare for Audit process as it determines the drift between Planned versus Actual

Category of Key Performance Indicators

Classification of KPIs: There are three major types of KPIs that help us in measuring business performance.

Success KPIs: These KPIs determine if the defined goals are met

Progress KPIs: These KPIs track the progress and execution of the tasks defined

Analysis KPIs: These KPIs assist in analyzing the output of each task

Types of KPIs: Which One Should I Use?

Depending upon the requirements of the organization, the KPIs can be distinguished as:

Process KPIs: These measure the efficiency or productivity of a business process. These indicators emphasize on how to track performance for an end to end activity. Few examples include ìDays to deliver and orderî, ìNumber of certified employeesî etc.

Input KPIs: These measure assets and resources invested in business ventures. These indicators directly or indirectly relate to resources used to accomplish a goal. They specify how organization is performing in terms of the utilization of resources.

Output KPIs: These measure the results pertaining to financial and nonfinancial aspects of business activities. These indicators reveal loss or success after an investment is made.

Few common KPIs in Business relate to Quality, Cost, Delivery and People. Key Performance can be differentiated into various sub-categories as mentioned below:

Features Key Performance Indicators Should Encompass

Like Goals and Objectives, Key Performance Indicators should be SMAART.

Specific: KPIs help in answering questions that helps set specific objectives for well defined and concrete goals that are set at the beginning.

Measurable: It is best to associate the goals with measurements to track the progress. In case of deviations corrective actions can be taken up. These measurements are also used as standard for comparison and help us in understanding if we have accomplished the objectives.

Achievable: Goals should be achievable, if the objective is too far in the future, it would be difficult to be motivated and to strive to attain it.

Action Oriented: Goals should be action oriented. Tasks and activities need to be defined to accomplish a goal.

Realistic: Achievable goals may not be realistic; Realistic does not mean easy to achieve rather, means that you have the resources (skills, money, and equipment) to get to it.

Time: Goals should be time-bound which means having a deadline for the achievement of the goal. Deadlines need to be both achievable and realistic. Time frames create the necessary urgency and prompts action.

Few questions which need to be answered to support specific goals are:

WHAT is to be done? – These are written using strong, action verbs such as conduct, develop, build, plan, execute, etc.

WHY is this important to do?

WHO is going to do what? Who needs to be involved?

WHEN do we need it to be completed?

HOW are we going to do this?

Benefit: Answering this question helps the goal to be action-oriented and focused on the most critical aspects.

How to Establish Effective KPIs for Your Organization

KPIs help us in establishing a Metric to validate the success criteria. They can be graphically represented. The Key Performance Indicators are established on the basis of Goals and Objectives set in the beginning (Figure 6.7).

In order to establish KPIs on the basis of set goals, objectives and critical success factors, steps below can be followed:

Key Facts:

CSFs are elements that help in identifying the success criteria set for a particular activity whereas; KPIs measure the strategic performance in moving towards the goal and showing if the criteria has been met.

Start with the high level goals and objectives that need to be achieved.
Check the Critical Success Factors for the goals and objectives.

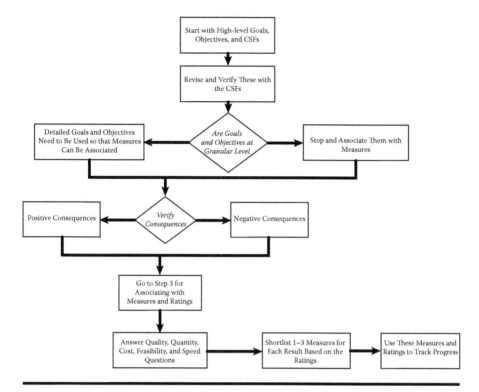

Figure 6.7 Exhibit illustrates the steps to form sound key performance indicators which are based on the goals and objectives. Based on the requirements of the indicators that needs to be formed, Measurement Analyst, Requirements Manager, Configuration Management Manager establishes means to collect data. The data is collected at least monthly, more frequently during activity periods. All requirement data needs to be collected at this stage.

Each of them needs to be detailed. Granular level helps in understanding how to associate measures to track the progress.

Verify the consequences, some of which might be unintended. Check both for positive and negative consequences in achieving the result.

At this point, Step 3 needs to be validated, go back to that step and list the potential things that can be counted or measured and gives the evidence regarding each description actually occurring. For each potential measure identify a high, medium or low rating for how relevant it is to the desired result and how feasible it would be to measure it.

Answer questions related to Quantity, Quality, Cost, Return, Feasibility and Speed.

Examples:

> What measures the unit cost of the product or service, including that of the activities and resources involved?
>
> What measures tell us the number of occasions of service, quantity of output?

Shortlist 1 to 3 measures for each result based on the high, medium and low ratings.

These high, medium and low ratings are used to track the progress and deviation from the desired results.

Key Performance Indicator Measures Overview

As mentioned before, Key Performance Indicators help in monitoring and controlling the process performance. It is important to track the deviation of these from the desired results. The deviation is tracked and accordingly, corrective actions are taken. Usually this deviation is seen as Planned versus Actual. Few examples of such measurements are given as:

Total effort in hours by task, activity or event (Planned)
Total effort in hours by task, activity or event (Actual)
Software Engineering Effort in hours by task, activity or event (Planned)
Software Engineering Effort in hours by task, activity or event (Actual)
Number of staff by task, activity or event (Planned)
Number of staff by task, activity or event (Actual)

Few measurements can also be derived and depicted (Figure 6.8) as Planned versus Actual

% of Software Engineering effort (SE effort/ total effort) (Planned)
% of Software Engineering effort (SE effort/ total effort) (Actual)
% of Software Engineering staffing (SE staffing/ total staffing) (Planned)
% of Software Engineering staffing (SE staffing/ total staffing) (Actual)
Variance of effort (per task and total)

Additional Key Facts: Lead and Lag Indicators

Definitions

Lead Indicators

> "Lead Indicators are performance drivers. They are measures of performance which is envisioned between factors and ultimate accomplishment of desired results."

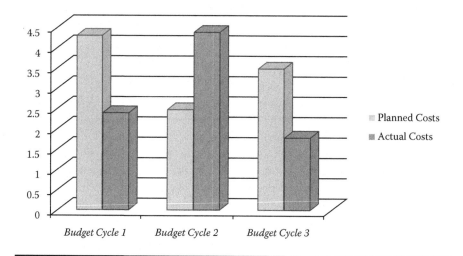

Figure 6.8   Description of the exhibit: KPI cost example in terms of Planned and Actual for 3 budget cycles.

These measures indicate progress against a process or behavior. They are helpful in predicting the future outcome of an objective. Lead indicators tend often appear in the Internal and Learning & Growth perspectives of the Balance Scorecards.

Lag Indicators

"Lag Indicators are outcome measures. They are used to measure the success of achieving results usually on the basis of financial metrics as revenue, profit, growth and loss ratio."

These measures determine the outcome of an objective indicating company performance at the end of a period. They are results-oriented and do not reflect a process. Lag indicators often appear in Balance Scorecardsí outcome-oriented Financial and Customer perspectives.

Lead and Lag Indicators are used to depict the four perspectives in the Balance Scorecard which would be discussed in the latter chapters.

KPI versus CSF

Key performance indicators should not be confused with a critical success factors (CSFs). CSFs are elements that are vital for a given strategy to be successful. KPIs are measures that quantify objectives and enable the measurement of strategic performance. A critical success factor (CSF) needs to be in place to achieve that objective, for example, the launch of a new product or service. For example, KPI = number of new customers and CSF = installation of a call center for managing the customers.

By using graphical representations of KPIs, you can easily visualize answers to the following types of questions:

What are we ahead or behind on?
How far ahead or behind are we?
What is the minimum we have achieved to date?

In his article, Art Schneiderman suggests:

> If the process view of an organization is taken, it is as the sum of a number of interconnected processes. Each of these processes has customers and suppliers. The customers have requirements, and organizations strive to match the process output to these requirements. Results metrics measure how well the organization performs this. Internal to the process are a few key variables that drive its output. In general, they are invisible to the processes' customers. Measurement of these variables produces a set of process metrics. In mathematical terms, results metrics are the dependent variables and process metrics are the independent variables associated with a process.
>
> Process knowledge is the set of tangible and intangible operating procedures used to convert the inputs to outputs. If knowledge is constant (i.e. operating procedures unchanging), and the process variables are stable, then the output of the process will also be stable, subject only to statistically predictable variability. This phenomenon is the purview of statistical process control (SPC). Process improvement requires new knowledge that manifests itself in changed operating procedures.
>
> This change in knowledge is called learning. Note also that process knowledge can be lost. For example, undocumented procedures that rest in volatile human memory can be lost when the process executors move on to other assignments. This loss of knowledge is called forgetting.
>
> As process knowledge increases, the gap between the processes' inherent capabilities and actual outputs will decrease. Inherent capabilities represent the ultimate limit the process can achieve without significant capital investment. Consequently, any results metric should also decrease, defined as a measure of that gap. Therefore, the rate of change of a results metric is a function of net process learning. Conversely, the rate of change of a results metric is itself a measure of net process learning.[*]

---

[*] Art Schneiderman, "Measurement: The Bridge between the Hard and Soft Sides," *Journal of Strategic Performance Management*, April/May 1998.

Leading Indicators

What are leading indicators? A leading indicator is a measure for evaluating the effectiveness of a how a specific activity is applied in a program in a manner that provides information about impacts that are likely to affect the system performance objectives. A leading indicator may be an individual measure or collection of measures that are predictive of future system performance before the performance is realized. Leading indicators aid leadership in delivering value to customers and end users, while assisting in taking interventions and actions to avoid rework and wasted effort.

Leading indicators provide insight into potential future states to allow management to take action before problems are realized. While there are some leading indicators that cover the management aspects of program execution (e.g., earned value), we lack good leading indicators specifically for systems engineering activities.

The primary users are the program-specific systems engineering leadership, program management, and IPT leadership who use the indicators to assess and make adjustments for ensuring systems engineering effectiveness of the program. Selected indicators may also be used by the program customers, program partners, and program suppliers depending on the phase of the program and the nature of the contractual relationship. Secondary users include executive and business area management, as well as process owners, for the purpose of predicting the overall effectiveness of systems engineering within and across a program, and for early detection of problems that require management attention.

Conventional measures provide status and historical information, while leading indicators use an approach that draws on trend information to allow for predictive analysis (forward looking). By analyzing the trends, predictions can be forecast on the outcomes of certain activities. Trends are analyzed for insight into both the entity being measured and potential impacts to other entities. This provides leaders with the data they need to make informed decisions and, where necessary, take preventative or corrective action during the program in a proactive manner. While the leading indicators appear similar to existing measures and often use the same base information, the difference lies in how the information is gathered, evaluated, interpreted, and used to provide a forward-looking perspective.

Most organizations have an organizational measurement plan and a set of measures. Unfortunately, they measure what is easy to measure and not what's really important. Yes, it leads to the low-cost reporting system, but it does not deliver any value to the company and management process.

These leading indicators are meant to augment the existing set of measures. For optimal efficiency, these should be implemented via the organization's measurement infrastructure (typically based on CMMI® practices), thereby enabling mechanized data gathering, analysis, and evaluation. It should also be noted that leading

Indicators	Description
Quantitative indicators:	These are indicators that can be quanitified and represented as a number.
Practical indicators:	These are indicators that are in line processes existing in the organization.
Directional indicators:	These are indicators that help us to know if organization has improved or not.
Actionable indicators:	These are indicators that control to effect change in the organization.
Financial indicators:	These are indicators that are used in performance measurement of how the organization has performed.

Figure 6.9 Types of indicators.

indicators involve use of empirical data to set planned targets and thresholds. Where organizations lack these data, expert opinion may be used as a proxy to establish initial targets and thresholds until a good historical base of information can be collected, but should not be relied on as a long-term solution for measurement projections. Rather, organizations must build the collection of the historical measurement data into its collection practices. For example, see Figure 6.9. This indicator is used to evaluate the trends in the growth, change, completeness, and correctness of the definition of the system requirements. This indicator provides insight into the rate of maturity of the system definition against the plan. Additionally, it characterizes the stability and completeness of the system requirements, which could potentially impact design and production. The interface trends can also indicate risks of change to and quality of architecture, design, implementation, verification, and validation, as well as potential impact to cost and schedule.

An example of how such an indicator might be reported is shown in Figure 6.10. Refer to the measurement information specification in Section 4.1 of the *Systems Engineering Leading Indicators Guide* V2. Lean Airspace Initiative. for the details regarding this indicator; the specification includes the general information, which would be tailored by each organization to suit its needs and organizational practices.

The graph in Figure 6.11 illustrates growth trends in the number of requirements with respect to the planned number of requirements (which is typically based on expected value based on historical information of similar projects as well as the nature of the program). Based on actual data, a projected number of requirements will also be shown on a graph. In this case, we can see that there is a significant variance in actual versus planned requirements, indicating a growing problem. An organization would then take corrective action, where we would expect to see the

> **Executive Information: Mission Results**
>
> • Cyclical (e.g., annual or quarterly) information that focuses on Mission results used for policy decisions and strategies

> **Management Information: Unit Results**
>
> • Periodic (e.g., quarterly or monthly) information that focuses on unit results associated with management and operational improvements

> **Activity Information: Workplace Results**
>
> • Immediate (e.g., daily or weekly) information that focuses on activity and task level data used to make tactical decisions and execute management decisions

Figure 6.10   Types of KPIs reporting.

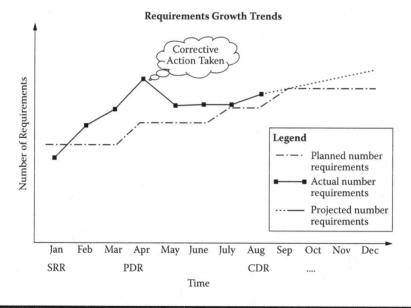

Figure 6.11   Requirements growth trend.

actual growth move back toward the planned growth subsequent to this point. The requirements growth is an indicator of potential impacts to cost, schedule, and complexity of the technical solution. It also indicates risks of change to and quality of architecture, design, implementation, verification, and validation.

The graph in Figure 6.11 illustrates the rate of change of requirements over time. It also provides a profile of the types of change (new, deleted, or revised), which allows root cause analysis of the change drivers. By monitoring the requirements volatility trend, the program team is able to predict the readiness for the system requirements review (SRR) milestone. In this example, the program team initially selected a calendar date to conduct the SRR, but in subsequent planning made the decision to have the SRR be event driven, resulting in a new date for the review wherein there could be a successful review outcome.

Performance Measures[*]

Section 1: Understand Objectives

What Is Involved in This Step?

Objectives are expressions of some future desired end state you want to achieve. Objectives represent a response for meeting a challenge, such as new customer requirements, changes in technology, or declining resources. Objectives can exist at any organization level, from an organizational unit down to an employee level. Objectives at the organizational level tend to be strategic—cutting across numerous departments and functions. Strategic-related objectives usually address major performance issues, such as improving customer service, reducing processing times, or developing new products.

Objectives tend to compel some form of action—setting forth a challenge and future direction for the organization. Objectives also have certain characteristics:

Specific and quantifiable in measurable terms
Realistic and achievable at some future date
Convey responsibility and ownership
Acceptable to those who must execute

The best approach for coming up with an objective is to work your way down from the highest strategic level (mission/vision/goals). Once you get down to a lower strategic level where execution takes place, then you can define your critical success factor (CSF) for the overall unit—department, division, organization, agency, etc. This grounds the objective, validates its importance, and puts focus on what matters. This is important since everyone ultimately contributes to overall strategic success, from the mailroom up to the boardroom. Therefore, objectives at lower levels should drive success at upper levels of the organization. Also, when you derive or define an objective by looking up (connecting/linking) to a higher goal, this helps galvanize or mobilize the entire organization around what's important—less effort and high focus on strategic execution and performance. This overall alignment is a major watershed event in creating an enterprise-wide performance management system. And the best way to get there is to start at the top (highest strategic level) and work your way down.

---

[*] Matt Evans. www.ecinf.com/workshop.com.

Why Is It Important?

You cannot get somewhere unless you define the destination point. Failing to establish an objective almost guarantees no improvement or movement with the current performance conditions. It also contributes to the inability to execute a higher-level goal.

Given the complexity of today's global world and the escalating rate of change, no organization can sit still and accept the status quo. Therefore, it is imperative to adjust, change, and continuously seek out objectives that ensure organizational success for the future. This is a very dynamic process, requiring some form of assessment between the current conditions and the desired conditions. The gap between the current and desired end state is the basis for establishing an objective. This gap analysis is often expressed in the form of strategic goals, leading to the objectives. Regardless, you are trying to drive higher levels of performance in relation to where you are currently. Objectives give you the direction and guidance for how the organization must improve going forward.

How Do You Do It?

Objectives are typically derived by going through some form of assessment—comparing your current level of performance against some desired level of performance. This performance gap is typically identified by going through an assessment of strengths, weaknesses, opportunities, and threats (SWOT). The SWOT approach is easy to understand and can be used to establish objectives at any level—agency, program, department, section, or individual (Figure 6.12).

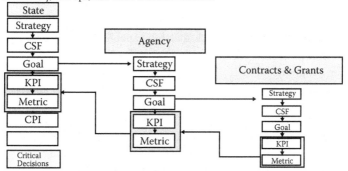

Figure 6.12   Cascading strategies.

Example of strengths
- Stable customer base
- Good delivery channels for services
- Solid reputation
- Funding is adequate to meet basic demands
- Management is committed and confident

Examples of weaknesses
- Lack of innovation in transforming services
- Limited budget
- Delivery staff need training
- Processes and systems are very fragmented
- Management cover is insufficient

Example of opportunities
- Could develop new services
- End users want newer types of services
- New specialist applications
- Support core business economies
- Could seek better supplier deals

Examples of threats
- Legislation could impact our funding
- Existing core business distribution risk
- Service demand is somewhat seasonal
- Retention of key staff critical
- Vulnerable to nonprofits that offer same services

As you work your way down from the highest strategic level, objectives become more task oriented, or tactical. Unlike strategic-level objectives, which cut across a large part of the agency, tactical-level objectives will be specific to a department- or section- or working team. These might be expressed in the form of a project plan since projects often drive execution of higher-level objectives. Here is an example of how it works:

Strategic objective ⇒ Grow the leadership capabilities of the organization
Initiative or project to drive execution strategic objective ⇒ Leadership development program
Tactical objective or task—leadership development program ⇒ Design an assessment survey template to measure leadership effectiveness

In the above example, objectives associated with the project are specific tasks to be performed that should translate into meeting the higher-level strategic objective. The output of producing an assessment survey should help achieve the outcome of growing leadership capabilities. This can also get translated into individual goals for employee development, such as participation in the leadership development program. Employee participation (outputs) in the leadership development program should lead to the desired outcome of employee's assuming more active leadership roles.

Where possible, you should follow a top-down methodology—start at the highest strategic level and work your way down, aligning and connecting objectives from the abstract level (mission/vision) down to the execution level (action plans/tasks). This top-down process binds all parts of the organization together, ensuring successful execution of what's important (strategy). Here is a basic example:

Mission ⇒ To corporately manage public facilities
Goal ⇒ Sound management of public resources
Objective ⇒ Distribute funding for services in an equitable manner across the entire agency
Task ⇒ Define those services that will be subject to a consistent allocation process

It is sometimes useful to follow a set of criteria for creating your objectives. The SMART criteria can help set the stage for good performance measures:

Specific: Provide clear direction on what actions must be taken, easy to understand.
Measurable: Quantifiable and verifiable through measurement.
Attainable: Realistic given organizational capabilities.
Results oriented: Focused on an outcome, not the method by which you get there.
Time bound: Set around some reasonable time frame.

If for some reason you are unable to follow a top-down methodology in developing your objective, then you might consider referring to a common set of critical success factors. Many critical success factors are generic, applying to most organizations regardless of size or type. For example, we can derive some critical success factors by looking at layers (perspectives) in the balanced scorecard.

The internal process perspective can be broken down into three objective categories:

Predelivery objective ⇒ Innovative processes that meet customer needs, provide solutions, and address emerging trends. Example of measurement ⇒ Number of new products introduced.
Delivery objective ⇒ Operations that produce and deliver products and services to customers. Example of measurement ⇒ Delivery response time to customer.
Postdelivery objective ⇒ Value-added services provided to customers once products or services have been delivered. Example of measurement ⇒ Cycle time for resolving customer complaint.

The learning and growth perspective might look at employees, systems, and the organization.

Objective for employees ⇒ Employee satisfaction, productivity, and retention. Example of measurement ⇒ Percentage of key personnel turnover.

System objective ⇒ Engaging to the end user, accessibility, and quality of information. Example of measurement ⇒ Percentage of employees who have online access.*

Objective for the organization ⇒ Climate for change, strong leadership, empowering the workforce, and other motivating factors. Example of measurement ⇒ Number of employee suggestions.

Design Measures

What Is Involved in This Step?

Measurements tell you whether you are meeting an objective. The easiest way to go from an objective to a measurement is to express your objective in quantifiable terms. This gives you a one-to-one relationship between the objective and the measurement. Performance measurement experts often use the so-called blindfold test: Can I tell what your objective is by simply looking at your measurement?

Objective	Measurement
1. Reduce employee turnover by 20%	Percent turnover in workforce
2. Reduce delivery times to customers by 10%	Percent error rate in order form processing

Example 1 in the table passes the blindfold test, but example 2 does not. Therefore, measurements must be meaningful and relevant to the objective. There are several other criteria to consider in the design of measures. They include:

Valuable: Measuring what is important.
Balanced: Inclusive of different types of measures.
Practical: Affordable price to retrieve or capture the measurement data.
Comparable: Useful in making comparisons with other data over time.
Credible: Based on accurate and reliable data.
Timely: Designed to use and report data in a usable time frame.
Simple: Easy to calculate and understand.

If the objective is vague and not very specific, then you should define your critical success factors associated with the objective. The example below goes from an objective to a set of critical success factors to the appropriate measurements:

---

* Adapted from Matt Evans, Methodology for Developing Performance Measures. www.exinf.com

Objective	Critical Success Factors	Measures
Happy customer	Accurate order	Error rate
	Fast order fulfillment	Wait time
	Friendly service	Customer complaints

Not only will you need to define each specific measurement according to a set of criteria (such as the criteria listed above), but you must also understand how measurements are used within an overall framework or hierarchy. As you move through the hierarchy or organizational levels, measurements may change. If the measurements remain the same, then you may have to index and roll up the measurements for reporting purposes.

Why Is It Important?

A good fit between the measurement and objective is critical; otherwise, you could drive the wrong behavior. What you measure sends a signal to everyone—this is what we hold you accountable for. Measurements provide the feedback on how well you are doing. You must define the right kind of feedback to drive the right kind of results—the old adage "What gets measured gets done in an organization."

How Do You Do It?

Once you have clearly articulated what must be measured (quantifiable objective or critical success factor), then you can follow a set of criteria for design of the appropriate measurement. It is sometimes useful to assign scores to each criteria for evaluating the measurement before moving to the design stage. Listed below is a simple example using three criteria: Is the measurement relevant, measurable, and actionable?

Measurement	Relevant	Measurable	Actionable
Percent of training facilities that are operational	3	1	2
Percent of agency facilities using ABC models	3	2	2
Percent of division offices with security points	2	3	3

Scoring scale: 0 = does not apply, 1 = poor, 2 = acceptable, 3 = good.

Each performance measure should be designed in the context of a larger overall framework. Most organizations will start the process by developing a strategic plan.

This sets into motion how we get to the "right" set of objectives, and once we have the right objectives, we can design the right measurements. For larger organizations, a hierarchy consisting of layers may be required, aligning different measurements as you work your way down to lower levels:

Measurement Layer	Objective	Measurement
Strategic (organization wide)	Customer loyalty	Customer retention ratio
Operational (division, section, department)	Customer satisfaction	Customer survey rating
Tactical (team tasks)	Fast service to customers	Average processing time
Individual	Cross-functional skills	Number of proficient skills

Measurements at the highest levels are often outcome-based-type measurements, whereas at lower levels, you may be measuring activities and processes. Each is linked or aligned for driving performance.

Activity	Process	Outcome
Shape the bricks	Build the wall	Newly constructed facility

One of the more popular frameworks for aligning measurements is to use the balanced scorecard. Since the balanced scorecard is rooted in the strategic plan, it lends itself well to the alignment of both objectives and measurements (Table 6.2). This tight end-to-end model (balanced scorecard) helps ensure successful execution of the strategic plan.

Table 6.2   The Basic Structure of the Logic Mode

Goal	Objective	Measurement	Target	Initiative
Achieve leading levels of operational efficiencies and effectiveness, competitive with the best in the private sector	Reduce by five times operational service costs	Cost per person served, cost of program delivery	Reduce service costs 50%	Use activity-based costing
	Reduce defect/ rework by two times	Defect rate	Reduce waste/cycle time by 75%	Use Lean/ Sigma

Table 6.3   Connecting Strategy and Measurements

	Quantity	*Quality*
Input	How much service did we provide? (4%—least important—to 10% weight)	How well did we deliver the service? (2–25% weight)
Output	How much service did we produce? (3–15% weight)	How good were the services? (1%—most important—to 50% weight)

Table 6.4   Categorizing and reporting measurements

Audience	*Format*	*Timing*	*Venue*
Nonmanagerial employees	Charts/graphs	Quarterly	Newsletter
Executives	Scorecard	Quarterly	Briefing
Stakeholders (investors)	Text with tables	Annually	Annual report

Depending upon the performance constraints associated with an objective, you most likely will have to consider a mix of different types of measurements. For example, you may have to start by putting resources in place for a project, then generating outputs that lead to outcomes. A good framework for understanding different measurements is to follow the logic model. The basic structure of the logic model is shown in Table 6.3.

Larger organizations may also require rolling up and indexing common measurements for different reporting units. In some cases, you might want to weigh different types of measurements to place emphasis on outcomes as the most important type of measurement. For example, you could use the so-called four-quadrant approach for categorizing and reporting measurements (Table 6.4).

As a final point, the alignment of all measurements into a common single framework helps us go from performance measurement (what is occurring) to performance management (what actions we should take). And if we can use one common framework to pull all parts of the organization together, then it becomes much easier to drive performance than having to work with desperate silos of measurements scattered across the organization.

Define Measures

What Is Involved?

After designing and choosing its measures, the next step for an organization is to add the requisite detail behind those measures in order to calculate and collect accurate and valid measurements. In other words, step 4 is how an organization operationalizes its measures. It is this operational detail underlying the measures that makes them usable. Without the detail, the measures are simply good ideas on a page.

There are six main categories of detail behind any measure:

1. The definition of a measure gives a detailed description or formula.
2. The unit of measure conveys the mathematical format in which the quantified measurement should be presented.
3. Data requirements specify the precise data elements that comprise the measure.
4. The sources of data indicate where the data requirements can be found.
5. Frequency displays the period of reporting for the measure.
6. The owner of the measure identifies a specific individual or group responsible for the periodic reporting of the measurement.

Why It Is Important?

Capturing the operational detail behind a measure is critical for several reasons. First, as mentioned above, performance measures bring no value to an organization unless they are implemented and used. Second, the detail promotes reliability and validity of the performance data by preventing the measurer from misinterpreting the measure, using the wrong sources, or reporting the result at an incorrect frequency.* Designating an owner of a measure promotes accountability for the reporting of the measurement. If there is more than one individual reporting against a measure, the detail provides for consistency between measurers. Also, in the case where the owner of a measure changes or is absent, the captured detail assists the new owner in quickly understanding the measure and adopting the correct way to report against it.

How Do You Carry It Out?

Define the measure: Expand on the title of the measure to more fully describe what should be captured by the measure.

Determine the unit of measure: How should the result of the measurement be expressed—as a straight count, a percentage, a ratio, in dollars, minutes, or months?

Specify data requirements: What specific data points are needed to calculate the measurement—inputs, outputs, products, cases, or resources?

Identify sources of data: Where are these data points stored, or where can they be found—in a system, in a file, from a Web site, or an individual?

Set the reporting frequency: How often should this measurement be reported— weekly, monthly, biannually, or daily? Since both errors and customer waits

---

* Reliability refers to the extent to which a measuring procedure yields the same results on repeated trials. Validity refers to data that are well grounded, justifiable, or logically correct.

happen several times a day, and both are such key indicators, our sample organization decided to report them on a weekly basis. In both cases, reporting
weekly is feasible for the organization, produces a manageable measurement,
and allows the organization to spot and react to trends. Had the data been
reported daily, the organization would not have had time to act on it, and if
the frequency was monthly, the data would be too old to act on by the time it
was reported, and short-term trends would be missed.

Nominate an owner for each measure: Who will be held accountable for reporting this measure—an individual or group, the process manager, the database manager, or the supervisor of an organizational unit? Nominating an
individual position (and an alternate) is preferred because it precisely locates
accountability for the measurement data.

Operational detail can include as much information as is wanted or deemed
necessary by the measurement team. For instance, owner information can include
e-mail addresses and phone numbers. Data sources might list precise file and document names. Measurement efforts often begin with the six categories above, and
the detail expands and becomes more comprehensive over time as the organization
matures in its measurement capability.

Setting Performance Targets

Some organizations include "performance target" in their definitions. However,
keep in mind that targets move over time while definitions are static for as long as
a particular measure is used. A performance target is the level or measurement an
agency is aiming to achieve over a certain period of time. Under "frequency," we
can see that this measurement could be reported weekly, so the organization can
track its weekly (and monthly) progress toward this goal.

In the federal government, Office of Management and Budget (OMB) guidance documents include "target" in their definition of "performance goal." "A
performance goal sets a target level of performance over time expressed as a tangible, measurable objective, against which actual achievement can be compared."[*]
A performance goal is frequently described as "measure plus target plus time
frame," since none of these three elements should exist in the absence of the
other two.

Target performance figures can be incremental or radical or anything in between.
Of course, the optimal target levels are challenging but realistic. Performance targets decisions can be based on customer desires or stakeholder demands, an analysis
of past performance trends, a performance level from another organizational unit
(a.k.a. internal benchmark) or external organization (a.k.a. external benchmark), or
any combination of these three.

---

[*] OMB Circular A-11, Part 6, 2005.

Implement and Evolve Measures

What Is Involved?

Once measures have been operationalized, measurement results can be collected, reported, and used to make management decisions. Based upon the applicability of measurement results to management decisions, the measurement team can reassess and redesign measures for greater efficacy.

> Reporting: Ensuring that the right people see the right information at the right time and in the right place.
>
> Making decisions: Based on results, managers may reassign resources from one activity/function to another, reprioritize activities, or reset workload targets.
>
> Evolving measures: Assessing the value of the measures to decision makers and rewriting measures to produce more useful data.

Why It Is Important?

Step 5 is critical because it is here that the whole effort produces value for an organization in two ways: (1) providing data that managers can use to make decisions about the organization, and (2) publicizing performance results to customers, stakeholders, business partners, and the general public to show progress and return on investment. Using performance data to manage an organization is the fundamental purpose of any performance measurement effort, so this is where "the rubber meets the road." Without this step, a performance measurement effort has no value. This is also where the measurement team can assess the value delivered by the measurement effort and make changes to the measures to increase that value.

How Do You Carry It Out?

Reporting Measurement Results

> Identify all audiences: How many different (internal and external) audiences are there and who sits in each one? At a minimum, an organization has an executive audience, a managerial audience, an employee audience, a customer audience, and a stakeholder/investor audience. Other audience segments might be human resources and information technology divisions, and vendors or contractors.
>
> Determine report content for each audience: Not all audiences want or need to see the same performance information. For instance, an executive steering committee might be interested in higher-level measures like return on investment (ROI) and other financial measures, while a site manager would be interested in lower-level, more detailed measures, like workload efficiency and effectiveness measures. Lastly, there may be some measures that are common to all audiences. The easiest and most accurate way to determine the data each audience needs to see is simply to ask.

Select data format: What is the preferred way to present results to each audience—scorecard, dashboard, table, or text? Some audiences prefer the red-green-yellow "stoplight" format of a scorecard, while other audiences may prefer the dials and graphs of a dashboard construct. Some helpful hints to keep in mind are:

Use consistent data collection and analysis techniques to report performance results.

Graphs are a very effective format for presenting performance results since they convey findings with few words.

Including comparative data, in the form of past performance results or external benchmarks, adds more value to the report because it conveys trends in performance or progress toward a performance target.

Determine report timing: How often does each audience expect to be updated—quarterly, annually, or monthly? The answer to this often depends on the frequency of reporting of the measures themselves.

Select the venue/delivery vehicle for report: What is the preferred delivery medium of each audience—e-mail, Internet, newsletter, voicemail broadcast, town hall meeting, or one-on-one briefing? An audience is more likely to review performance results if they are delivered via a commonly used vehicle (Table 6.4).

Managing by Measures

Performance results should assist all levels of an organization in making decisions. At the front lines, supervisors can use performance data to determine how they can improve performance and to what degree. For instance, upon seeing the performance results, a supervisor may elect to change a process to increase efficiency or make staffing changes to increase productivity. Managers can use performance results to determine whether there are more effective ways of implementing the leadership's strategy, such as finding and importing best practices, investing in technology, or reassigning resources from a high-performing function to a struggling function to eliminate a gap in performance. Executives can use data to determine changes to their business strategy, including what products and services to offer customers, how best to structure the organization to deliver those products and services, and how to compensate and motivate employees.

Likewise, executives might have an objective to "maintain customer loyalty." Should performance results indicate a drop in repeat customers, they may decide to invest in a new advertising campaign to a certain market segment, or research and development of a new product offering. Along with the investment decisions, executives may reset the objective to "build customer loyalty" and hold the COO accountable for an increase in percentage of repeat customers.

Evolving Measures

In addition to reconsidering objectives when results are reported, the measurement team should reconsider the measures themselves. The key question here is: "Do our performance measures provide the right information to decision makers?" In the example above, the supervisor and executive were able to make decisions based on the performance information reported; however, the regional manager with the objective of "happy customer" was not able to determine whether the objective was met because she did not have any data on customer satisfaction for her region. Working with the measurement team, the manager may request a new performance measure of "average customer satisfaction score for the northwest region."

To report a result of this measure, the measurement team might have to install a customer survey process, or simply collate customer satisfaction data from all the sites in the region. Similarly, site managers may want to segment "average wait time" into two measures: one for daytime customers and one for nighttime customers, since the 10% of customers who come in at night do not require the same level of service as the 90% of customers who come in during the day.

In summary, this:

■ Facilitates and creates a framework for the strategy implementation
■ Visualizes and helps understand the strategy
■ Enables and systematizes feedback and collaboration
■ Supports decisive actions
■ Provides tools for analysis and enables drill down for real causes
■ Provides one easily accessible interface to all strategy- and performance-related information

Risk Management and Logic Model

Risk is always identified as the uncertainty associated with future events and outcomes. Risk impacts the potential outcome of the planned strategy and organizational results. Risks are usually determined through the list assumptions analyzing the extent that each objective can or cannot be achieve. At the same time, risk is a tool to manage potential results.

In the previous chapter we already discussed the logic model as a series of cause-and-effect relationships between the investment of resources to the outcomes achievement and the expected impact. Those relationships, mostly expressed in if-then structures, represent the internal logic organization applied during the strategic planning phase. For example, if the resources are available, then activities will be possible to implement, and then the outputs will be produced, and then short-term output can be achieved. Those short-term outcomes will lead to long-term outcomes and impacts. This basic model provides a frame for the stakeholder input, which is based in their past experience and knowledge of the company situation and objectives. The key question should be answered to put risk management issues into the right perspective (Table 6.5). Each answer should be put in terms of

Table 6.5   Perspectives of Risk Management

Uniqueness	Who and what make us unique?
Perspective	Why do we want to do it?
Means	How? Do we have resources?
Behavior	What should be done?
Environment	Where and when?

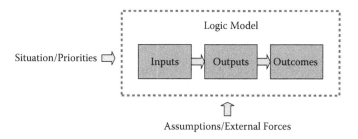

Figure 6.13   Logic model connects situation and assumptions.

expected outcomes. The next step, then, is to identify assumptions and areas of risk (Figure 6.13).

The logic model provides a good foundation to build risk management strategy. The assumptions describe the conditions that must exist if we want the planned cause-and-effect relationship from resources to the outcomes to be successful. For example, if the funding is available, then the activities can be undertaken. If the activities are delivered, and provided that the assumptions about the factors affecting the activity-output relationship hold true, then the outputs should be achievable. If the outputs are produced, and provided that the assumptions about the external factors affecting the output-outcomes relationship hold true, then the short-term outcomes should be achievable.

The INCOSE recommends the use of risk indicators to monitor the status of the assumptions.[*]

Risk Exposure Trends

This indicator is used to evaluate the risk exposure over time in terms of cost and schedule, and in context of the level of risk. It indicates whether the program is

---

[*] INCOSE Technical Product INCOSE-TP-2005-001-02.

Risk Exposure Trends

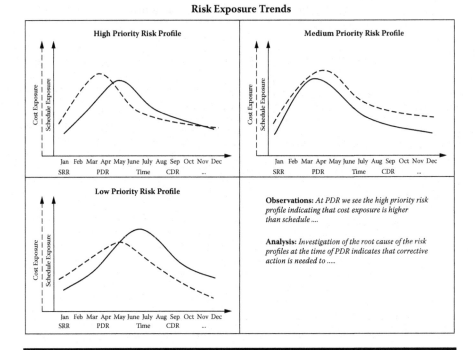

Figure 6.14   Priorities and assumptions relationship (Systems Engineering Leading Indicators Guide V2. Lean Airspace Initiative).

effectively managing the program risks, as shown by predicted exposure ratings over time. If the risk exposure continues to grow or not be reduced, the customer satisfaction will be negatively impacted due to resulting cost, schedule, or technical impacts. It is recommended that the risk exposure trend indicators be used in conjunction with the risk handling trend indicators.

The graph in Figure 6.14 illustrates risk profiles of the program in regard to cost and schedule exposure over the life cycle. In this case, profiles for high-, medium-, and low-priority risks are shown separately. For illustrative purposes, cost and schedule exposures are included in this graph. While not included, technical exposure would be another element of this indicator.

The graph in Figure 6.14 illustrates the planning and tracking of the risk exposure in terms of cost (millions of dollars). The plot of the actual risk exposure burndown shows a slow start. The program team projected the burndown for the remainder of the program to identify whether the risk exposure could be reduced to an acceptable level as the program proceeds, and where there were realistic opportunities that could significantly reduce the exposure. To build confidence in the projection, the program team needed to determine the reason for any significant movement (positive or negative). The first movement was due to late program ramp-up and requirements changes. The second movement was where the program team would be able to insert technology to eliminate a set of risks.

Risk Handling Trends

This indicator is used to evaluate effectiveness of handling risks. It indicates whether the program is proactively handling/treating potential problems or risks at the appropriate times in order to minimize or eliminate their occurrence and impacts to the program. If the actions are not closing per plan, then there is a higher probability that risks will be realized. This insight can identify where additional action may be needed to avoid preventable problems or reduce impacts. This indicator may also identify that the program does not have an iterative or continuous process implementation for risk management. Thus, new risks may not be identified and handled, and may affect the program and technical effectiveness/success. Refer to the measurement information specification in Section 4.10 for details regarding the indicator.

As an example of appropriate analysis, consider four related risk handling trends as a group (Figure 6.15):

Indicator 3.10.1—risk actions: Broadly shows that the project is not closing the actions items, and also the number of overdue actions are increasing.

Indicator 3.10.2—open actions by age: Shows risk actions beyond set acceptable thresholds.

Indicator 3.10.3—open risk actions by severity: Might temper any anxiety given the fact that the majority of the actions are of a low and medium severity.

Indicator 3.10.4—open risk actions by state: Gives an understanding that the risk management process is being followed in that the majority of actions are being implemented.

Risk Management

Risk management is an essential component of strategic management for organizations. Risks associated with the activities of the organization are addressed (Figure 6.16). The main objective of risk management is to maximize the sustainable value of the activities and understand the effects of all those factors. Risk Management can increase the probability of success. It also helps in reducing the probability of failure and the uncertainty of achieving the objectives of the organization. Its objective is to add maximum sustainable value to all the activities of the organization. It marshals the understanding of the potential upside and downside of all those factors which can affect the organization. It increases the probability of

Risk Handling Trends

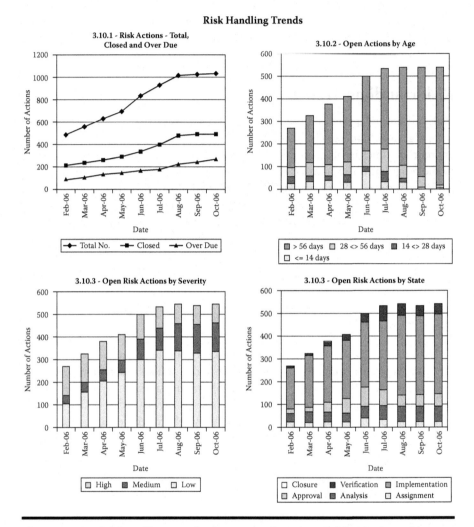

Figure 6.15   Risk handling trends. System Engineering Guide V2. Lean Airspace Inititative.

success, and reduces both the probability of failure and the uncertainty of achieving the organization's overall objectives.

Risk management is a continuous process running throughout the implementation of the Risk Management strategy. The Risk management strategy should encompass the effective measures of the risk associated with the past, present and future activities of the organization. This way the strategy can be transformed into operational and tactical objectives.

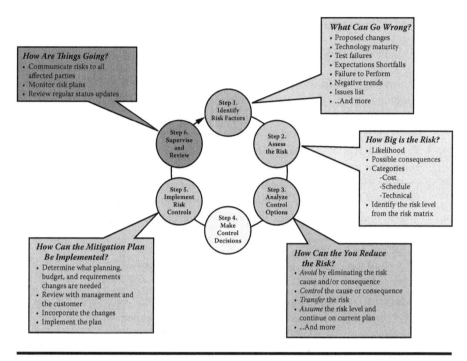

Figure 6.16   Risk management process.

Purpose and Benefits of Risk Management

The purpose of Risk Management is a continuous process improvement technique which:

- Risks can be identified at an early stage and accordingly measures can be taken to mitigate them.
- Planning risk management activities to mitigate the adverse impacts
- Forward looking continuous process improvement is enforced.
- Risk Management addresses issues pertaining to uncertainties in achievement of vital objectives.

Risk Management highlights:

- Level of organization at which the risks occur.
- Available time and resources for mitigating risks.
- Techniques to prioritize risks.
- Tools and trainings required for managing risks.

Types of Risks and Management: Which One Should I Use?

Depending upon the needs of the organization, the risks can be categorized as:

1. **Technology Risk:** It occurs when a new technology is adopted and its components might be developed or purchased from outside vendors.
2. **Business Risk:** It occurs due to external or internal business conditions as a new competitor or entrant in the market or reorganizations.
3. **Process Risk:** It occurs when the proper end to end activities are either skipped or not followed in a department, team or an organization.
4. **Project Risk:** It occurs when requirements, analysis, design or development techniques incorporated in a project are not robust. Challenges as insufficient project budget, work outside the project scope or scope creep, etc are potential risks.

To handle these risks two main techniques of risk management are identified:

■ **Tactical Risk Management:** It views a threat as a probable event that might/might not occur. It focuses on the direct consequences of that threat. The risk emphasizes on the likelihood of the potential event that would lead to loss.
■ **Systemic Risk Management:** It provides a holistic view of risk which could block fulfillment of the objectives. This is done by assessing the collective effects of various conditions and likely actions on the objectives.

Risk Factors and Drivers

The potential risks to an organization can be a resultant of both external and internal factors. Few risks that could be critical and need to be mitigated could be resulting both from external and internal drivers. The main drivers of risk are depicted by the following diagram (Figure 6.17).

A Risk Driver is any initiative which if not carefully and successfully implemented could cause unwanted situations to occur. The driver is studied to understand the risk triggered by these drivers and the potential loss that could be caused to the organization. In the above diagram it is shown that these drivers could be either due to internal or external or a combination of both the factors. Certain examples are shown in the picture which is categorized as internal or external drivers. Even within these categories, the risk drivers can be further categorized as:

Objectives: The objectives mainly target that product, cost and schedule should be realistic and achievable for avoiding any risk.
Preparation: This mainly includes the processes and plans that need to be implemented to achieve the objectives.

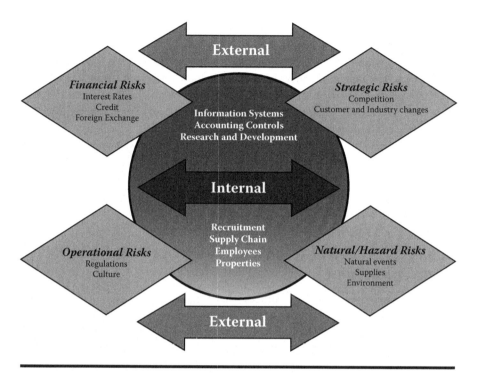

Figure 6.17 Risk factors and drivers.

Execution: This focuses on how the tasks and activities are managed and it includes techniques for assembling, organizing and managing the resources.

Environment: This helps to assess how effectively and efficiently the activities are performed. Organization structure, culture, politics and communication methods are taken into consideration.

Resilience: This mainly emphasizes on the flexibility of the organization to adapt to any changing events. It means the necessary planning and actions could be taken to avoid any unexpected results.

Result: This takes into consideration the correctness and completeness of a product or process. This is judged by the operation, usage and maintenance of the product.

The drivers for the Healthcare Industry are identified and mentioned in the Appendix.

Associating with Process Improvement

The previous chapter focuses on the fact that to provide efficiency, effectiveness and efficacy, risk management is considered an integral part of process improvement.

It is critical to have a risk management strategy to mitigate or avoid the potential threats. If the desired results are not achieved the BSC or Performance summary depicts what percentage is achieved. It is important to investigate the causes for underperformance so that risks are eliminated. Certain techniques could be applied when the desired results are not achieved. Few methods to get to the root cause include Affinity diagram, Ishikawa diagram, surveys & interviews, requirements' analysis and work breakdown structure analysis.

In the previous chapter, Performance Index P (I) depicts the safe and unsafe zones in which the performance of the organization falls. In case the unsafe zone is revealed, it is critical to investigate further and the causes why the performance is lying in this zone. There could be several factors lying in the financial, strategic, and operational or hazard risk driver categories contributing to this phenomenon.

Strategies, Tools and Techniques to Manage Risk in an Organization

Risk Management is an iterative process that runs throughout the lifecycle of any project. The stages of Risk Management process are described below:

Risks Planning: It focuses on the approaches and planning for the risk management activities. Risks need to be identified, described and quantified so that mitigation plans or contingency plans for these risks could be developed.

Risks Assessment: It includes the process of Risk Analysis and Risk Evaluation.

1. **Risk Analysis**
   - **Risk Identification:** It helps to identify the exposure to any type of uncertainty (Figure 6.18). This involves having an in depth knowledge of the organization, its markets, products, cultural and political environment etc. The knowledge of the critical success factors and objectives of the organization help in identifying the possibilities that could lead to any uncertainty or threats. The assumptions and constraints related to the process/product/project are reviewed. The drivers are identified which could be:
     - **Strategic:** These include the objectives of the organization that could be affected by capital availability, political risks, legal or regulatory changes, environmental conditions.
     - **Operational:** These include concerns to achieve the strategic objectives.
     - **Financial:** These include the effective management and control of the finances that are the effects of external factors as credit availability, foreign exchange rates, etc.

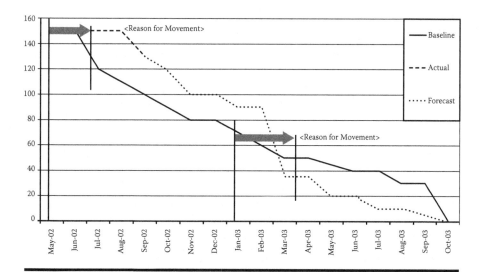

Figure 6.18   Risk burndown.

- **External factors (Hazards):** These include the unauthorized use or abuse of intellectual property etc.
- **Compliance:** These include safety, environmental, data protection, and regulatory issues etc.

■ **Risk Description:** It displays the risks that are identified in a structures format which facilitates the description and evaluation of risks. Describing the risks enables prioritizing the risks and studying them in detail. The description includes the name of risk, its scope, stakeholders involved, quantification of risk, tolerance, treatment and control techniques, improvement mechanisms etc.

■ **Risk Estimation:** This could be the probability or possibility of event along with its consequence measured quantitatively, semi quantitatively or qualitatively. Probability could be high, medium or low. It becomes possible to prioritize the risks that need to be analyzed and studied.

2. **Risk Evaluation:** This follows the Risk Analysis process. It is critical to have knowledge of associated costs and benefits, requirements, socioeconomic and environmental factors etc. It is used to take appropriate decisions regarding the risks and if they need to be accepted, treated, controlled or transferred.

Risks Reporting: Information regarding risk needs to be distributed to the various levels of management. Focus should be to protect the interests of the stakeholders, ensure that duties are performed according to formulated strategy both by the Board of Directors and individual staff, create value and monitor performance etc. Formal reporting practices including control methods for management responsibilities for risk management, processes for identifying risks and how they are addressed by the risk management systems and monitoring and reviewing control system are implemented. Any deficiencies revealed by the system should be reported for proper actions to be taken. External Reporting to stakeholders include proof of efficient management of the organization's non-financial performance as human rights, employment practices, community affairs, health and safety and the environment.

Decision: After proper reporting, decision whether to avoid the risks, mitigate, control or transfer are taken.

Risk Treatment: It is the process of implementing measures and techniques to modify the risk. Risk could be avoided, transferred or controlled. The treatment should provide effective and efficient operations, controls and should comply with the regulations. Cost effectiveness of such techniques is compared to the benefits that are expected out of implementation of these techniques. Audits occur regularly and opportunities for improvement are identified.

- **Acceptance:** The risks are accepted after careful analysis and it is assumed that it can be overcome as the project proceeds further.
- **Avoidance:** The risk can be eliminated by doing something that is less risky. Non critical requirements can be eliminated from the initial release of the project.
- **Reduction:** Likelihood of the risk is minimized. Even the impact is minimized.
- **Transference:** The risk can be shifted elsewhere including the accountability to respond to the risk event.

Risk Monitoring and Control: The process ensures that proper control measures are followed. Changes are identified and accordingly the internal working or process within the system is changed. Cost of implementation of these techniques is calculated. Proper reporting and review structure are formed. Knowledge of the potential threats and mitigation techniques helps in better decision making for managing risks (Figure 6.19).

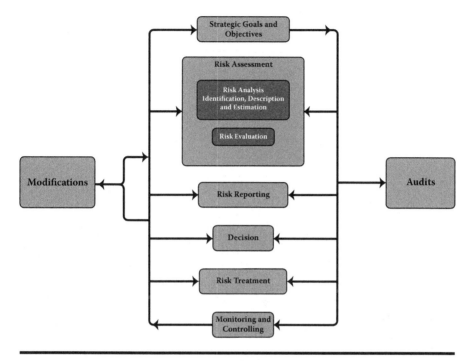

Figure 6.19   Risk monitoring and control.

References

Lewis Carroll. 1876. *The hunting of the snark—an agony in eight fits*, London. UK: Macmillan and Co.

Ron Suskind. 1992. Incredible: Vikings win football game, GOP loses election, *Wall Street Journal*, Nov. 5.

Steven Spewak and Steven Hill, *Enterprise Architecture Planning* (Wiley, 1993).

Systems Engineering Leading Indicators Guide V2. Lean Airspace Initiative.

Chapter 7

Value Sustainment Domain

Nullius in verba—"Take nobody's word for it; see for yourself"

Value Transformation Domain

In order to stay balanced on an S-curve, we have to measure and manage both strategy and operational performance (Figure 7.1). The scorecards and dashboard are the tools for meaningful decision making about effectiveness and efficiency of performing processes. Developing meaningful tools such as dashboards and scorecards for decision making is a very challenging task. It is challenging because it deals with the issues of information availablility, information perception, and information uncertainty.

In many cases we are uncertain regarding our own capabilities, and this creates the problem of undecidability. This undecidability presents a number of challenges, including relying on somebody else's experience—reducing one's own strategy and tactics to a set of best practices and past experiences—that guaranteed success to different a company, identify and collect to many measures. Another problem is that all effort associated with process improvement implies making a process repeatable. Organizations should not standardize responses to the multiple outside changes. It is easy to predict process behavior because process is repeatable. It pushes companies to create repeatable inflexible strategies.

> Decision making is a cognitive process leading to the selection of a course of action among variations. Every decision making process produces a final choice. It begins when we need to do something but do not know what. (Wikipedia)

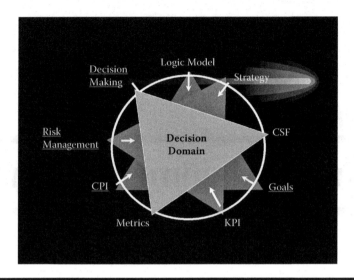

Figure 7.1   Decision domain.

Three components of information go into the decision process. For any manager, these components are goals, constraints, and alternatives. Goals are what every project manager wants out of the process: a high-quality product developed on time and within budget. How will project managers know when the goals can be achieved?

Goals should be specific, realistic, and measurable. How do you know if you are making progress toward your goal? Marvin Minsky, cofounder of the Artificial Intelligence Laboratory at MIT, formulated the process progress principle as a way to improve the blind trial-and-error search: "Any process of exhaustive search can be greatly reduced if we possess some ways to detect when 'progress' has been made. Then we can trace a path toward a solution, just as a person can climb an unfamiliar hill in the dark—by feeling around, at every step, to find the direction of steepest ascent." This principle represents a way in which an easy problem can be solved.

What do we do if the problem is really hard to solve? That is when the second statement comes into play: "Goals and Subgoals. The most powerful way we know for discovering how to solve a hard problem is to find a method that splits it into several simpler ones, each of which can be solved separately." The significance of this statement is that Minsky formulates the problems in terms of goals.

The goal should be maintained. If we do not maintain the goal, all of our efforts to solve the problem are wasted. Records of the process followed to solve the problem should be kept to provide information about how to solve a similar problem in the future (historical data collection).

Defining the goal's performance measure (what you will track to measure success) and targets (how much or how fast success is required) will provide you with criteria against which you can assess the results. For example, my son is in the ninth grade in high school and he is learning mathematics. A target for measuring his math achievement is his test performance, and a measure of success is that at least 86% of the problems on a test are answered correctly. In software project management, if your goal is to improve the accuracy of software bug descriptions in the software problem reports, the target for measuring is the number of bugs reported, and the measure for this target will be 5% of incomplete software problem reports. The measure of success is 95% of problem reports closed. So, the structure is very simple: goal-target-measure (GTM).

Constraints are limiting factors, such as amount of money allocated for a project by the contract and the availability of trained developers. Typically, there are three types of constraints: time, resources, and deliverables. Constraints are conditions we must live with. Resource constraints involve three different areas: budgets, people, and equipment. Alternatives are the choices available that we can use to minimize the risk associated with not achieving the goal. The management decision process is a mental one. During this process, the project manager is trying to connect goals and constraints with possible alternatives to determine the most valuable alternative and come to a decision. The decision arrives during the process of aggregation and quantification of collected information, in which goals and constraints are analyzed and reduced to a number. The project manager has to break the decision scenario into small pieces. This is not a big problem. The difficulty is to identify the potential problem.

You may recall a story about Rumpelstiltskin. Rumpelstiltskin was a dwarf who helped the miller's daughter weave flax into gold in return for a promise that she would give him her firstborn son. Once her son was born, she refused to keep the bargain. Rumpelstiltskin told her that if she could learn his name by midnight of the third day, she could keep the child. At midnight on the third day she told him his name and Rumpelstiltskin disappeared. Identifying your problem is the first step toward solving it!

First, name and analyze the problem in order to state project goals and constraints. It is impossible to eliminate all problems, but we can focus on the current problems and allow the process to grow and mature in order to deal with the problems of the next stage.

Managers never have any problems naming constraints; unfortunately, they seem to weigh them against goals and alternatives in isolation. Software project management requires close consideration of the goal-constraints-alternatives (GCA) relationships.

The success of the process improvement effort depends heavily on the strategy of the implementation and the type of goal-subgoals structure (Figure 4.1). This process usually begins with an understanding of the following:

- Where are all the organizational functions performed?
- How are these functions performed together?
- What is the real situation?

These three questions are typically answered by the initial process baseline, and they are the input needed to understand the present situation.

The inputs to the goals are usually the description of the ideal situation, or what you want to achieve over a certain period of time. It can be improvement of the quality of the product, to be certified by the International Organization for Standardization (ISO), or the ability to control the process of software development. At this point, the actual assessment framework or implementation of the model is not important. What is important is the ability of the organization to take the model and adapt it. The next step is to understand and resolve the differences between the current situation and goal achievement.

How is the process implementation going to affect job function?
What problems surrounding the implementation of process will we be able to solve?
Which goals are considered worthy of pursuit?
What are the methods to reach the goal?

After resolving the differences, you can start to develop the strategy for a successful implementation by developing and prioritizing the subgoals that will represent the resolution of the potential conflict. Do not rush. You have a lot to learn about your own organization. Do not skip the learning stage.

The available information, as it exists at any given moment, is the basis for the current decision that controls management action. The action or activity changes the level or condition of the software development organization as a system. This is the needed information that is the basis for the decision process. The decision depends on what data are available, what we can get, and what we know how to use.

The majority of companies are overloaded with a lot of different data. This can be very useful for analysis of project performance, but only if we have structured procedures describing how and what data should be considered, analyzed, and interpreted. Of course, there are cases when the data collection process does not exist, or collected data are distorted during the course of a project or simply truncated by the end of the development life cycle.

A typical example of how the lack of collected and analyzed information results in a big decision-making challenge for management is that of deciding whether to release software for integration, beta testing, or customer acceptance testing.

Critical success factors (CSFs) are the critical factors or activities required for ensuring the success of your business. The term was initially used in the world of data analysis and business analysis. Critical success factors have been used significantly to present or identify a few key factors that organizations should focus on to be successful. As a definition, critical success factors refer to the limited number of areas in which satisfactory results will ensure successful competitive performance for the individual, department, or organization.

A critical success factor is an element of organizational activity that is central to its future success. Critical success factors may change over time, and may include items such as product quality, employee attitudes, manufacturing flexibility, and brand awareness.

Critical success factors are also any of the aspects of a business that are identified as vital for successful targets to be reached and maintained. Critical success factors are normally identified in such areas as production processes, employee and organization skills, functions, techniques, and technologies.

How Are They Important to Your Business?

Identifying CSFs is important, as this allows firms to focus their efforts on building their capabilities to meet the CSFs, or even allows firms to decide whether they have the capability to build the requirements necessary to meet CSFs.

How Do You Write a Good Critical Success Factor?

In an attempt to write good CSFs, a number of principles could help to guide you:

Ensure a good understanding of the environment, the industry, and the company. It has been shown that CSFs have five primary sources, and it is important to have a good understanding of the environment, the industry, and the company in order to be able to write them well. These factors are customized for companies and individuals, and the customization results from the uniqueness of the organization.

Build knowledge of competitors in the industry. While this principle can be encompassed in the previous one, it is worth highlighting separately, as it is critical to have a good understanding of competitors in identifying an organization's CSFs. Knowing where competitors are positioned, what their resources and capabilities are, and what strategies they will pursue can have an impact on an organization's strategy and also resulting CSFs.

Develop CSFs that result in observable differences. A key impetus for the development of CSFs was the notion that factors that get measured are more likely to be achieved versus factors that are not measured. Thus, it is important to write CSFs that are observable or possibly measurable in certain respects such that it would be easier to focus on these factors. These don't have to be factors that are measured quantitatively, as this would mimic key performance indicators; however, writing CSFs in observable terms would be helpful.

Develop CSFs that have a large impact on an organization's performance. By definition, CSFs are the most critical factors for organizations or individuals. However, care should be exercised in identifying them due to the largely qualitative approach to identification, leaving many possible options for the factors and potentially results in discussions and debate. In order to truly have the impact as envisioned when the CSFs were developed, it is important to thus identify the actual CSFs, i.e., the ones that would have the largest impact on an organization.

CSF as an Activity Statement

A good CSF begins with an action verb and clearly and concisely conveys what is important and should be attended to. Verbs that characterize actions are *attract, perform, expand, monitor, manage, deploy,* etc. Poor CSFs start with verbs such as *enhance, correct,* and *upgrade.* For example, a good CSF would be "monitor customer needs and future trends."

CSF as a Requirement

After having developed a hierarchy of goals and their success factors, further analysis will lead to concrete requirements at the lowest level of detail.

A critical success factor method:

- Starts with a vision: mission statement
- Develops five or six high-level goals
- Develops a hierarchy of goals and their success factors
- Lists requirements, problems, and assumptions
- Leads to concrete requirements at the lowest level of decomposition (a single, implementable idea)
- Identifies the problems being solved and the assumptions being made
- Cross-reference usage scenarios and problems with requirements

Project Success: As Commonly Measured

What constitutes project success? As the previously listed definitions of project management show, many individuals define project management as meeting the budget, meeting the time schedule, and conforming to the requirements. This prevalence is so ingrained that the Standish Group has gathered statistics since 1994 on projects in IT that succeeded, failed, or were "challenged."

The Standish Group categorizes projects into three resolutions types:

Successful: The project is completed on time and on budget, with all features and functions originally specified.

Challenged: The project is completed and operational, but over budget, over the time estimate, and with fewer features and functions than initially specified.

Failed: The project is cancelled before completion or never implemented.

According to the 2001 extreme CHAOS report, the following graph shows that only 16 to 28% of projects are considered a success. With an average success rate of fewer than 30%, why are so many projects started? Or a better question: Why are projects that are challenged, the largest percentage, allowed to be fully implemented? There are obviously benefits to the originations that are implementing these projects for such a large percentage of challenged projects to continue until completion.

Project Success: A Different View

Project success tends to measured by the big three (cost, time, requirements met) as they are easy and timely to measure. With standard project management techniques, you can identify at any given point if you are currently a successful project or a challenged one.

This also leaves out one important fact: that the original specifications may not have been correct, the budget allocated to the project may have been inaccurate, and the time estimate may have been flawed. This is often perpetuated by a manager or stakeholder who, in his or her zeal to get a project started, will try to make the return on investment (ROI) look the absolute best. One of the easiest ways to increase ROI is to have the implementation costs as low as possible. This sometimes is done with best-case scenarios or wild guesses on the time and cost of the project. Also, the ramifications and true requirements may not be fully understood and may cause significant cost and time overruns.

Management has traditionally turned a blind eye to this, as once a project is implemented, everyone starts working on other projects or are in support of the new process/system/product. Very rarely is a postimplementation audit done, and when it is done, rarely does it measure the actual ROI, leaving the individuals creating the project request specifications to be free from repercussions in the event of overruns in the project.

This approach leaves the project manager without any feedback mechanisms except for the ones he or she can monitor, which puts us back to the quality, cost, and speed metrics. However this does not provide any indication as to the success of the project to the organization. Is it possible that a percentage of the challenged projects are actually successes to the organization, and vice versa—a percentage of the "successful" projects are really failures?

Project Success: New Metrics and Measurements

While not suggesting that project managers "throw the baby out with the bathwater" and eliminate the traditional PM metrics, it is obvious that additional metrics and measurements need to be added to the project managers' toolbox.

Project justification should be expanded and refined. Simply looking at the ROI for project justification is shortsighted, and usually incorrect. Metrics should be identified as to how an implementation will benefit the core business directives or mission statement. Also, how success of the project will actually be measured once implemented needs to be identified. Most important is when the measurements will be done. Organizations, vendors, and project managers should spend adequate time defining metrics, monitoring techniques, and timetables at the very beginning of a project that relate to the following categories and possible metrics.

The decisions areas for performance management support several interrelated balancing acts: between leading and lagging indicators, between top-down and bottom-up management processes, between revenue and expense trade-offs, between short-term and long-term resource allocation. Each of these decision areas has two levels: the top dashboard level and more detail operational level.

The decision should be framed:

The four performance management decision areas have to provide a clear path to drill down from goals in their underlying operational drivers. The customer-focused perspective includes information and metrics from decision areas that drive revenue. The internal process perspective focuses on operational expense drivers. The learning and growth reflects investment and leverage from long-term assets such as IT and human resources. The financial management perspective helps to analyze and monitor quantifiable financial indicators.

Over the past decade, organizations have adopted the balanced scorecard (BSC) as a key framework for managing their businesses. This concept has spread through businesses and consulting communities at the speed of light. This concept instantly appealed to CEOs. It was easy to comprehend because on one sheet of paper it was possible to capture not only financial goals, but also the nonfinancial drivers for their achievement. No longer will the operational side of the business be disconnected from the financial measures that stockholders used to judge the performance. Most CEOs would fail to be committed to the creation and management of this balanced scorecard? Given that lack of management commitment has repeatedly been identified as the single most important factor in explaining the failure of organizational change initiatives.

In addition to being a strong tool for communication of key strategies, the assumption was that BSC provides clear linkages between strategies, the business processes by which the strategies are executed, and the key measures needed to gauge business performance.

From a performance management perspective, the BSC provides the baseline for performance measurement, and according to industry research, many companies who adopt the BSC are satisfied with the method and plan to continue its use. Whether you call it enterprise performance management, business performance management, or corporate performance management, there is no denying that the ability to measure performance from financial, customer, operational, and learning perspectives is valuable.

The balanced scorecard was introduced in 1992 as a business performance system designed to implement organizational strategy. The scorecard uses the process of setting specific/challenging goals (and not only financial) that translate an organization's mission and strategy into a comprehensive set of performance measures. It is called balanced because:

1. Organizations should focus on more than financial objectives and indicators. It is supposed to balance financial and nonfinancial indicators and measures. It balances internal and external processes. It should balance lagging (past performance) and leading (future drivers of performance) measures.
2. It is a scorecard showing how you are doing against targets you choose. And, of course, targets are based on selected strategy.

The balance is a part of the strategic plan. It supports the items shown in Table 7.1.

There are five principles to focus and align every process and system within an organization to match its overall strategy:

1. Translate the strategy into operational terms. Everybody must understand the strategy of the organization so it is presented in a cause-and-effect linkage that reveals how the strategy will be implemented.
2. Align the organization to strategy—to create synergy within the organization. The activities of the individual functional divisions must be aligned and integrated.
3. Strategy is a part of everyone's job. Everybody should be aware of how he or she contributes to the overall strategy.
4. Strategy is a continual process. Organizations must be able to adapt their strategies as external changes happen or the existing strategy matures.

Table 7.1 Balancing Mission and Objectives

Mission	Why do we exist?
Core values	What do we believe in?
Vision	What do we want to be?
Strategy	What will our game plan be?
Strategic initiatives	What do we need to do?
Personal objectives	What do I have to do as an individual?

Everyone must be linked to the strategy environment to create a collaborative environment and open communications.

5. Educate and mobilize leadership for change. Every member of the executive team must realize that the change is a good idea and keep the strategy transparent—in front of the people.

Another view of performance measurement is as a recurring management process (Figure 7.2). After the initial strategy maps have been created and cascaded, the objectives have been decided, and the targets have been defined, there is a regular performance measurement and reporting cycle, which is often monthly. As you might imagine, for a company of any size and complexity, the number of measures to be reported every month as the measures are "cascaded" into the organization can become unwieldy. Further, the scope of business information required to report the measures can be quite broad and may require data integration from several sources. Many companies use largely manual methods for reporting, expending large sums of money to produce monthly reports.

More broadly, performance measurement is only one part of the performance management cycle.

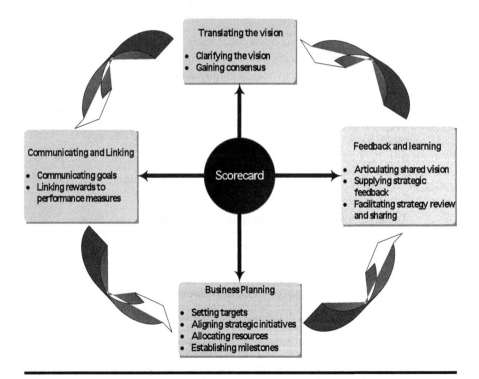

Figure 7.2   The benefit of the scorecard.

Unfortunately, these measures—and the BSC in general—do not provide the business information, analytical tools, and structured decision support that are needed to actually improve business performance in relation to specified targets. For that, we need a unified framework.

Alignment Process Improvement with Business Goals

Process improvement is not a goal by itself. ISO defines process improvement as an "action taken to change an organization's processes so they meet the organization's business needs and achieve its business goal more effectively." Therefore, continuous process improvement is the means to achieve better business results by continuously improving the performance of the organizational processes.

Internal processes should reflect the strategy selected. Going back to BSC, Kaplan and Norton address two critical issues: the alignment of the processes with the strategic business goals and the identification and application of measures to manage the performance of business unit. When the strategic and the operational level are not aligned, the organization suffers negative consequences, such as:

■ A corporate strategy that is unknown or not used in the development project goals
■ Financial indicators are the driver of the corporate decision making
■ Measurements are implemented without a clear purpose
■ Measurements are not connected to each other

There is a correspondence between the Goal Question Metric (GQM) methodology and a BSC (Table 7.2).

Table 7.2

GQM	BSC	Comments
Goal	Goal	GQM goals refer to a project, while BSC goals refer to a certain particular perspective and a certain particular tier in the organizational hierarchy
Question	Driver	The BSC drivers can be compared to GQM questions since they represent how a goal can be achieved
Metric	Indicator	The BSC indicators can be compared to the GQM metrics since they reflect the control mechanisms and values used to verify the achievement of goals (through the selection and use of a particular driver)

"We run the company by questions, not by answers," said Eric Schmidt, the CEO of Google.

> So in the strategy process we've so far formulated 30 questions that we have to answer. I'll give you an example: we have a lot of cash. What should we do with the cash? Another example of a question that we are debating right now is: we have this amazing product called AdSense for content, where we're monetizing the Web. If you're a publisher we run our ads against your content. It's phenomenal. How do we make that product produce better content, not just lots of content? An interesting question. How do we make sure that in the area of video, that high-quality video is also monetized? What are the next big breakthroughs in search? And the competitive questions: What do we do about the various products Microsoft is allegedly offering? You ask it as a question, rather than a pithy answer, and that stimulates conversation. Out of the conversation comes innovation. Innovation is not something that I just wake up one day and say "I want to innovate." I think you get a better innovative culture if you ask it as a question.[*]

A Range of Strategic and Operational Measures

The measures used to manage the performance of a business comprise a range of strategic measures:

Strategic measures: Market attractiveness (industry structure, growth, concentration, innovation, customer power, logistical complexity) and competitive strength (relative market share, relative quality, intellectual property, customer coverage).

Organizational measures: Culture, leanness, incentives, training and development, structure, purpose, process.

Operational measures: Customer satisfaction, product or service excellence, capacity utilization, capital intensity, productivity, outsourcing.

Depending on the emphasis placed on different measures in an organization, its information and performance measures can vary between operational fixed (for example, the 99% replenishment rate on the shelves of a Sainsbury's store) and strategic flexible (for example, Microsoft's goal of standards ownership on the information superhighway).[†]

---

[*] www.1000ventures.com.

[†] http://www.1000advices.com/micro/ten3_micro_sets_biz_success.html - 6W.

A Framework for Designing a Set of Measures

Many project managers do not conduct a postimplementation audit (Table 7.3), but this is essential to reviewing the successes, failures, challenges, and lessons learned. For those who do them, it is usually within a month or two of completion of the project and usually focuses on the traditional metrics, successes/failures, and how the project team did in performing the project implementation. However, for many projects, including IT projects, this may not be enough time to get a clear picture of the success/failure of the project. To demonstrate how time plays a factor in monitoring success/failure metrics, consider the Empire State building (ESB).

The building was the brainchild of John J. Raskob, the vice president of General Motors, who wanted this new building to exceed the height of the rival car manufacturer's Chrysler Building, still under construction when the plans were released on August 29, 1929. The program given to the architects called for a tight schedule of completion, one and a half years after the start of the project.

The Empire State Building in New York City was completed "[in] one year and 45 days … (ahead of schedule)" and "cost \$40,948,900 (including land). Building alone \$24,718,000 (the onset of the Depression halved the anticipated cost of the building)." (Empire State Building official Internet site). So the ESB was completed ahead of schedule, under budget, and was to the specifications as designed. If the measurement were to be done on traditional PM metrics, the project would be a complete success! However, if the metrics also looked at rented space, they would tell a completely different story. For the very reason that it came in at half the production cost (the Great Depression), rental rates at the building's opening were a meager 20%. In fact, it was nicknamed the "Empty State Building." So if measured on rented space on completion of the project, it would be a failure. So let's expand the timeline: you have to go to 1948, or seventeen years later, for the building to have enough tenants to turn a profit. But today it is again the tallest building in New York, and it has always been a representation of New York, and as of 2002 it was 97% occupied.

This example brings up an important point: that success metrics may need to be monitored over a period of time to determine the true success/failure of the project. This may or may not be possible at, or just after, implementation time.

This time factor of measurement is very important, as many projects are either creating something new or implementing a new process or system. Metrics that look at many of the goals of a system need time to realize the true impact, "despite [that] management's introduction of an extensive set of organizational change initiatives, managerial goals of improved flexibility and responsiveness are not immediately attained" (Melville, 2004).

One last important metric is use. Whether it is in construction, like the above ESB, or a computer system, it is the use of the final product that ultimately decides the success of many projects. This should be an important metric that is identified during project approval and monitored throughout product testing and rollout.

The five critical success factors are based primarily on leadership effectiveness, clear performance measurement goals, and well-designed change management plans:

1. Strong executive leadership and alignment
2. Clear and measurable goals
3. Actionable business case and performance measures
4. Clearly defined roles and responsibilities
5. Well-designed execution and continuous improvement plan

Metrics

Customer-Oriented, Outcome-Based Metrics

The outcomes to measure are those that have value in supporting the customer's mission. Several DOD organizations are currently employing customer-oriented, outcome-based metrics. The Navy, for example, uses a ready for tasking (RFT) metric to calibrate key processes and measures in its enterprise value chain in terms of aircraft that are available to fleet commanders. Management of this kind of metric requires focusing on preventive and predictive actions.

Criteria for Evaluating Metrics

CPI metrics should have five key characteristics:

1. *Valid* metrics actually measure what they are intended to measure.
2. *Obtainable* metrics can actually (and practically) be gathered in a timely manner.
3. *Accurate* metrics can be trusted to give the right information.
4. *Repeatable* metrics give the same answer under the same conditions every time.
5. *Actionable* metrics allow us to do something with the information they provide, which requires both relevance and timeliness.

Other considerations related to metrics include the following:

1. *Face validity.* It may not be obvious that a given metric actually relates to a given goal, even though a causal analysis shows that it does.
2. *Level of aggregation.* Some metrics are only valid or reliable at certain levels of aggregation. The actual cost for any given piece of the organization is likely different from the calculated value. In other cases, aggregated metrics can be misleading or incorrect, even though the individual metrics are correct (this is generally known in the statistics community as Simpson's paradox).

3. *Data ownership.* Even if the data exist, we might not be able to get access if the data are under the control of an individual or organization that chooses not to make them available. This might require elevation to a higher level to achieve cooperation and overcome resistance to cultural change.

Purpose of the Metrics

Metrics are useful to efficient decision making. It provides organizations with the ability to develop certain baselines that can be used to measure improvements in different areas as performance, growth, client satisfaction etc. The major quadrants that the Metrics (Figure 7.3) fall into are:
Metrics help in answering questions like:

■ Are we on the correct track?
■ Are there any risks associated?
■ Are we getting to our goals?
■ Are we in line with the goals and CSFs?
■ Are we deviating from our goals?

Benefits

Metrics help in having a clear perception about what needs to be measured. Establishing Metrics for an organization are important as they can be used to develop various measures for improving a process, product or system.

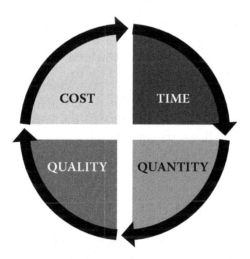

Figure 7.3 Four major quadrants of Metrics.

Types of Metrics: Which One Should I Use?

Depending upon the requirements of the organization, the metrics can be distinguished as:

1. **Software Metrics:** It is a measure of property of software, its component or its specification. It is the mathematical number showing relationship between different variables. These are used to quantify the software, software development resource or software development process.
2. **Performance Metrics:** It is a measure of the performance of the organization. These metrics are used for assessing the status of the project by measuring the six criteria which are time, cost, scope, quality and actions. These are established by developing critical processes on the basis of customer requirements, developing measures and establishing targets or baselines for measuring against. Performance metrics are usually linked with corporate strategy and are used to measure performance against the CSFs.
3. **Process Metrics:** These are used to measure the characteristic of the methods, techniques and tools employed in developing, implementing and maintaining a product.
4. **Product Metrics:** There are used to measure the characteristics of the documentation, coding etc required developing a product. An important example of metric is the number of defects found in internal testing compared to the defects found in customer tests, which indicate the effectiveness of the test process itself.

Descriptions and Features Metrics Should Encompass

Metrics can be represented in numeric form, percentages or ratios. Few important characteristics of Metrics for providing efficient process improvement encompass the following:

KEY FACTS:

GQM reveals that Metrics need to be in conformance with the business goals.

1. **Relevant:** Does the measurement fit with the performance objective?
2. **Measurable:** After collecting relevant data it is important to see and report the measurements that make sense.
3. **Actionable:** Can one take action on the measurement in a timely way to correct and improve what is happening?

The measures could be connected to the Logic Model (Figure 7.4).

How to Establish Metrics for Your Organization

As a practice, Metrics should be setup for each KPI. The following questions should be answered to create effective Metrics:

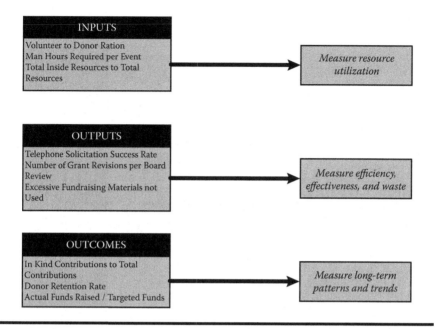

Figure 7.4 Connecting the Logic Mode to Measures.

- The type of information this metric is going to provide
- The management question is it going to answer
- Does all collected data relate to the question or information need?
- Are we collecting too much data? Are we collecting sufficient data?
- How does the metric support higher level goals or answers questions about CSF or Risk factors?

The Methodology to setup metrics is called Goal Question Metric Methodology (GQM).

Goal Question Metric is a software metrics technique used to understand whether the set goals have been successful or not (Figure 7.5). GQM was developed by Dr. Victor Basili of the University of Maryland, College Park.

GQM aligns measures and indicators with previously set goals. GQM takes into consideration three levels in terms of Goal, Question and Metric as described below:

- Conceptual level: Goals are defined at this level. It is defined for attaining desired results relative to a particular environment.
- Operational level: Questions are defined at this level. These are defined to describe the assessment or achievement of a specific goal.
- Quantitative level: At this level the metrics are defined. These are associated with the questions formed at the operational level. It is important to identify the right metrics associated with the questions in order to understand the

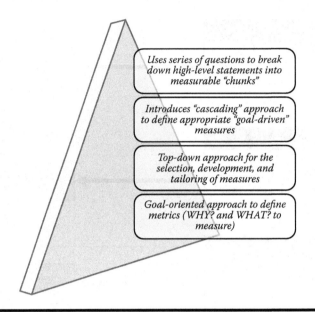

Figure 7.5 GQM and goal setting.

progress being made for achieving the goals. The uses of measurements result in effective decision making strategies.

The GQM can be found as a six step process. The first three steps relate to the business goals to drive identification of the right metrics and the rest deal with gathering the measurement data and making using the results to drive efficient decision making and process improvements.

Taking into consideration the 5 aspects of information, *Object, Purpose, Focus, Viewpoint* and *Environment* (as mentioned in Goals chapter), GQM method is described below. The method is enlisted as the steps that need to be followed.

Steps for the Goal Question Metric methodology (Figure 7.6) are:

1. Set of organization or business goals are developed and they are associated with quality and productivity goals.
2. Questions that could define goals as completely quantifiable way are developed.
3. Measures are required to answer the questions and track the conformance of the process and product to the business goals.
4. Mechanism for data collection are developed
5. The data is collected, validated and analyzed in real time to show if the project is in alignment with the business goals and if corrective actions are required.
6. The data is analyzed to assess its conformance to the business goals and to make future recommendations for process improvements.

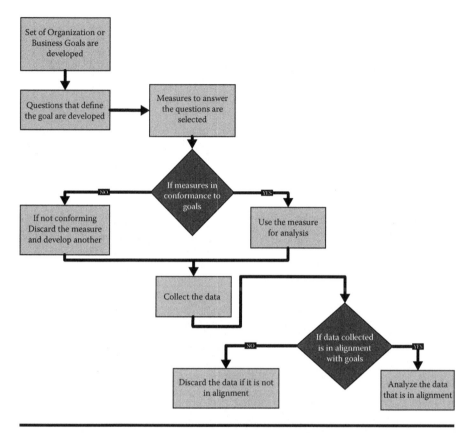

Figure 7.6 Steps of GQM.

References

ISO/IEC 15504-4:2004(E)

Nigel Melville. 2004. Review: Information technology and organizational performance: An integrative model of IT business value, *MIS Quarterly*, 28(2), June, 283–322.

Marvin Minsky. 1988. *The society of mind*. New York: Simon & Schuster.

www.esbnyc.com/index2.cfm?noflash=1

www.pmforum.org/library/papers/2006/Proj_Mgmt_Metrics.pdf

www.schneiderman.com/Activities/publications.htm#BS article

www.wikipedia.com

www1.standishgroup.com/newsroom/chaos_2009.php

Chapter 8

Business Process Management: It Is All about Strategy and Outcomes!

Companies have high hope that business process management (BPM) will enable them to monitor and control specific activities, to predict future internal and external states, to monitor state and behavior relative to its goals, to make decisions within needed time frames, and to alter the firm's overall orientation and behavior (Figure 8.1). It can serve as a real-time system that alerts managers to potential opportunities, impending problems, and threats, and then empowers them to react through models and collaboration.

There are four questions that must be looked at in order to understand the core issues and opportunities in BPM:

1. How do we know what we know?
2. Do we know what we do not know?
3. Do we know when and how to react and what we should be doing?
4. Do we know who should react?

Although we hear about many successful attempts to transform organizations, the overall track record is very poor. In recent surveys, CEOs reported again and again that their organizational change efforts did

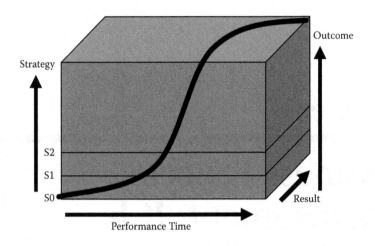

Figure 8.1 Connecting strategy and outcomes.

not yield the promised results. Instead of managing new organizations, they ended up managing the unwanted side effects of their efforts. At first glance, this situation seems paradoxical. When we observe our natural environment, we see continuous change, adaptation, and creativity; yet our business organizations seem to be incapable of dealing with change. (Fritjof Capra)

Inefficiencies in process management produce product quality issues and cause more testers to be hired. In a vast majority of the situations when requirements are not clearly defined, the customer is willing to accept mediocre quality product. Attempts to improve or change processes in large organizations are met with resistance. The survival law requires one to be a team player and not to make any waves. But in order to be a team player, you have to have an environment that supports the team.

Process, structure, and long-term policies are annoying and boring. We still prefer a creative art form. We have to look at BPM from a business perspective, not from technology perspective. There are more and more different definitions of BPM: automated workflow, SOA (services-oriented architecture) that deviates companies from the path that you need to manage the actual business.

In 2001, KPMG published a study of U.S. and European business and government executives that revealed that one of the most common disappointments reported was the lack of data integrity and the inability of their system to product meaningful information to support decision making. The study also discovered that BPM systems are not aligned with strategic business measures, dependent on lagging, not leading indicators, are poorly integrated with internal and external information, and rely too heavily on financial measures. Some factors for failed BPM systems included: measuring things that are easily measured versus what should be measured, data inaccuracy, measures that were too complicated, and users not understanding the system and its measures.[*]

So what are the requirements of the BPM? According to Vince Kellen,[†]

> the BPM system should help the firm accurately perceive relevant internal and external phenomena. These include threats and opportunities, shortcomings in its ability to perceive phenomena, as well as shortcomings in its ability to control its actions (breadth, depth, coherence, and predictability).

Measurement information needs to be delivered, processed, and acted upon within the time frame needed for market survival (latency, propagation, and response). The BPM system must aid the decision-making process. The BPM system needs to operate self-reflexively and largely below the threshold of the firm's awareness (adaptability, measurability, autonomic).

The BPM Standards Group has developed a common definition of BPM that provides an appropriate context for performance management, including the following principles:

BPM is a set of integrated, closed-loop management and analytic processes, supported by technology, that address financial as well as operational activities.
BPM is an enabler for businesses in defining strategic goals, and then measuring and managing performance against those goals.
Core BPM processes include financial and operational planning, consolidation and reporting, modeling, analysis, and monitoring of key performance indicators (KPIs) linked to organizational strategy.

Wayne Eckerson, director of research, TDWI, said, "In order to drive a successful BPM initiative, companies should identify strategic business drivers up front, select metrics and measures derived from their drivers, and assess the ability of their current systems to support BPM. These are all important parts of the process companies should follow for BPM success." There are three dimensions of BPM: the value dimension, the transformation dimension, and enabling dimension (Figure 8.2).

---

[*] KPMG, *Achieving Measurable Performance Improvement in a Changing World: The Search for New Insights* (KPMG, 2001).
[†] Vince Kellen, Business Performance Measurement at the Crossroads of Strategy, Decision-Making, Learning and Information Visualization.

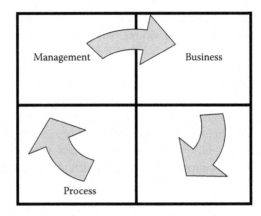

Figure 8.2 Three dimensions of BPM.

The Value Dimension: Business

The first dimension of BPM is the value dimension. This dimension is very important because it creates value for the customers and stakeholders. The correct approach to BPM is to be able to facilitate and formulate the strategy, goals, and objectives of the enterprise.

Business Process Goals

The goal(s) of any organization is driven by the strategy of the organization. Commonly accepted competitive factors include:

- Quality
- Delivery lead time
- Time to market
- Delivery reliability
- Design flexibility
- Volume flexibility
- Cost/price
- Innovation
- Trustworthiness

The operations should be aligned with goals and strategies. The value comes as the result of the focused activity and resource allocation. The BPM approach could serve as a tool to enable faster response to the presented challenges and will facilitate change and flexibility needed for staying competitive.

There are new BPM approaches recently emerged in industry. The OMG Group recently announced a new initiative called Business Ecology™. According to OMG,

"Business Ecology is more than just the mechanics of process optimization; it's a way of thinking about your business processes that eliminates the outdated concepts of business and IT silos or stovepipes and focuses on the benefits of ubiquitous IT," said Richard Mark Soley. "We look forward to working with IBM and other interested organizations on promoting Business Ecology as a way to streamline operations, remove waste, survive in difficult economic times and thrive in the recovery to come."

This initiative was immediately supported by IBM. "IBM's sponsorship of this new Business Ecology Initiative is a continuation of our long-term support for the OMG SOA Consortium," said IBM's Sandy Carter, VP, SOA, BPM, and WebSphere. "Business Ecology will help provide the next milestone in support of IBM's focus for improved Business/IT alignment as a key element in long term client success."

OMG is the leading proponent of the drive toward Business Ecology through the Actionable Architecture™, which will provide details on how to create sustainable business processes. This movement requires standards, but also relies on a stronger relationship and communication mechanism for IT and business alignment. OMG uses its proven ability to bring communities together and motivate new initiatives through offerings beyond standards work and into industry collaboration forums such as the SOA Consortium, BPM Consortium, and Green Computing Impact Organization (GCIO).

OMG recognizes that there must be a way to measure, model, and drive the effectiveness of this transition to closer IT and business alignment through standard maturity models. OMG supports this through its growing work in maturity model definitions, such as the Business Process Maturity Model (BPMM) and the forthcoming Green Computing Maturity Model (GCMM).

IBM saw value in supporting a cross-organizational non-vendor-specific group that works to help clients be successful in today's new economy. The OMG Business Ecology Initiative is focused on bringing together business and IT to create business capability around sustainable BPM and SOA. The idea that IT become a full partner with business is one that IBM has been espousing based on SOA for a number of years, including as a sponsor of the SOA Consortium.

The Actionable Architecture

As business and IT move closer to a convergence then ever before, we must approach transparency with an even broader view. Business will access technology resources not just through a common infrastructure or application platform, but also through a transparent business methodology. OMG calls this the Actionable Architecture.

This requires information technology (IT) to no longer be viewed as a utility but rather as an integral and vital asset to the company. IT must lead quality initiatives, drive efficiency and revenue, and provide measurable, clear return on investment.

To support this role, it's not enough to merely use technology as a means to an end, but rather as a driving force of the business. The business must have access to all the necessary underlying architecture it requires from IT without effect to the business services it needs to supply. OMG is taking a leading role in this charge through the Business Ecology Initiative—an initiative that brings together best practices in process management to develop and deliver on the actionable architecture.

An actionable architecture is one that provides the business with a number of important attributes, including:

Quality: To ensure that business products and services are of competitive substance, and processes are repeatable and improvable.

Efficiency: To ensure that the products and services delivered to the customer are available within a better than reasonable time frame to support the business, with minimal use of corporate resources.

Compliance: To comply with standards, whether these are through mandates or supporting best practices.

Agility: To prepare for what cannot be forecast, being in a position to adapt to the changing business climate with ease and speed.

Scale: To support business growth with little impact to the quality and efficiency of the delivery of the product or service, based on standard technologies, standard processes, and standard methodologies across the enterprise.

Reuse: To make use of corporate investments to save resources and time.

Leverage: To build on the existing investments in a way that supports new investments moving forward.

Value: To improve the business investments so that they deliver real value to the business by supporting return and cost of ownership metrics.

Effectiveness: To ensure the business services delivered yield their intended outcomes, based on agreed upon and public metrics.

Optimization: To improve the speed at which products and services are delivered with minimal impact on resources.

Sustainability: To allow the business to remain operational during hard times.

In summary, Actionable Architecture, an output of business process analysis, includes decisions that maximize value and minimize waste. Examples include:

Creation, automation, or termination of a business process

Movement of an automated process to the public cloud, private cloud, or in-house computing utility

Initiating governance of a process—computing related or not—to lean or green that process

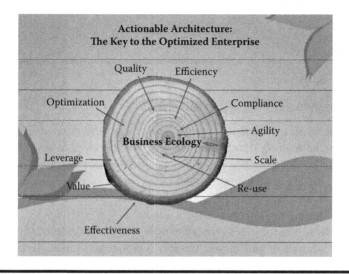

Figure 8.3   Actionable architecture (OMG).

Identification of opportunities to minimize waste (of people, computing resources, electricity, water, paper, etc.)

Reuse of existing processes in new ways to support a new business capability

The essential factors shaping business success are the value cycles: value creation, value management, and value sustainability (Figure 8.3). The measure of the business ecology is efficacy of the organization or the capability to stay on a mapped glide path represented by the S-curve with minimum volatility.

Transformation Dimension: Processes and Business Process Management

Processes are structured activities that create value. Processes transform company resources into product and services for the marketplace. They are a direct link between transformation and organizational success in value creation.

The transformation is usually represented by an input-process-output model. BPM is flexible enough to apply a number of different methodologies to make the process more effective and agile. Those methodologies are well known to industry: Six Sigma, Lean, quality cycles, etc.

This interesting study below was provided to me by Dr. Thomas L. Honeycutt from North Carolina State University.

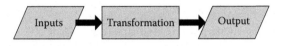

Figure 8.4   Basic processes.

A Systems Model of a Business Firm

The systems model of a business firm attempts to capture the dynamic process of information and resource flow for a firm within the context of its surrounding environment. The model described here is an extension of one proposed by Raymond McLeod Jr.* To facilitate an in-depth understanding of the model, this chapter will construct the model in steps from its components. Each step will included an explanation of the components and their function.

The model is divided into a *conceptual layer* and a *physical layer*. In the conceptual layer, management and various support components provide the direction for the processes in the physical layer. The physical layer is where resources are turned into goods and services. Performance data from the physical layer are fed back to the conceptual layer for analysis. The analysis is then incorporated into decisions, which in turn provide direction for the processes in the physical layer. So, as you can see, a continuous cycle of information flow exists between the two levels.

Basic Processes of the Physical Layer

The production of goods and services occurs within the physical layer of the model. Figure 8.4 depicts the three major components of the physical layer and the process flow between them:

Input: The raw resources required in production processes.
Transformation: The conversion of raw resources into final products.
Output: The end products of the transformation process represented by the goods and services produced by the company.

The Environment

Both the physical layer and the conceptual layer interact with the *environment*. Figure 8.5 shows the processes of the physical layer of the firm surrounded by the environment. Simply stated, the environment is the total context within which the firm exists. The environment includes entities such as vendors, customers, stakeholders in the firm, unions, governmental bodies, competitors, etc. Resources such as raw materials, information, and data flow into the firm from the environment,

---

* McLeod (1998).

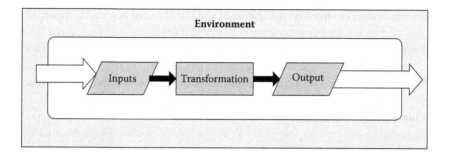

Figure 8.5 The environment.

go through a transformation process, and then flow from the firm back into the environment. This outward flow is in the form of goods, services, responses to regulatory requirements, and outputs related to business necessity (advertisement, publications, community relations, etc.).

Environmental Interaction at the Physical Layer

Several entities within the environment are of particular interest at the physical level of a business firm. These components are essential to operations at this level. Figure 8.6 depicts the model's interaction with the environment. Important environmental components include:

Upstream vendors: These are the resource suppliers. They are represented by other companies and even by internal organizations within the using firm.
Resources: Any material required by the using company in the transformation process. The standards are money, manpower, material, machines, and information.

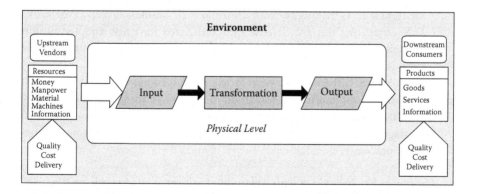

Figure 8.6 Interaction with the environment.

Downstream customers: Recipients of the transformed resources. Again, these could be independent businesses or internal organizations within the firm.

Products: The goods, services, or information produced by the firm for a customer (internal or external).

Resource and product information categories: These are the most significant attributes of resources and products coming into and leaving the firm.

Quality: The quality of a resource is vital to the firm's product. A poor-quality resource will detract from a firm's ability to achieve Six Sigma product quality, which in turn will impact product sales.

Cost: Costs for resources and products directly affect the firm's revenue flow. High costs for resources on the input side impact the cost of the products on the output side with measurable effects upon profitability.

Delivery: Delivery times have a greater influence on a firm's operations now than in the past. The modern trend toward just-in-time delivery to cut costs and increase efficiency has put immense importance on this attribute. Firms depend upon reliable resource delivery to carry out their operations and to deliver their own products on time. Additionally, cutting overall delivery times is a path to increased profits.

One particular section of the model deserves a closer look in the discussion of quality cycles. The flow of information in the upper left quadrant of the model changes depending on the type of quality improvement process involved. Two quality improvement terms borrowed from the Japanese are particularly relevant to this topic. The terms and their definitions are:

Hoshin: A breakthrough innovation or dramatic change in level of performance. The hoshin concept was developed in Japan to communicate company policy to everyone in the organization. Hoshin's primary benefit is to focus activity on the key things necessary for success. Japanese Deming Prize winners credit hoshin as being a key contributor to their business success. Progressive U.S. companies like Hewlett-Packard and Xerox have also adopted hoshin as their strategic planning process. Hoshin plans map out a framework for substantial increases in performance.

Kaizen: Kaizen is the Japanese term for continuous improvement. It refers both to a statistical/quantitative evaluation of process performance and an adaptive framework of organizational values and beliefs that focuses workers and management alike on zero defects. Kaizen plans lay out an ongoing refinement process.

Hoshin and kaizen, along with a plan-do-check-act (PDCA) cycle, will be used to describe the previously mentioned information flows and demonstrate the quality improvement cycles.

Breakthrough Innovation (Hoshin) Cycle

When Cp ≤ 4/3, an unstable process is indicated and a major innovative change, or hoshin, is suggested. A hoshin could also be considered even when a process is stable. For a business firm to maintain its competitive edge or increase revenue, it may be necessary to initiate a hoshin cycle for a process that is already at a high sigma level of quality. Figure 8.7 depicts the information flow within the model when a jump in productivity or level of performance is desired.

PDCA Quality Cycles

In this view of quality improvement cycles, the upper and lower PDCA cycles of Figure 8.7 correspond to hoshin and kaizen, respectively. For illustrative purposes, we will assume an unstable process as a starting point and follow it through the eight steps of this process improvement procedure (Eddlestone 1992).

Beginning at the plan element of the upper cycle, the steps are as follows:

- Develop process innovation/breakthrough plans.
- Implement plans.
- Check impact on capability.
- Act on results (decision point). If Cp > 4/3, process has stabilized. Go to plan element of lower PDCA (kaizen) cycle.
- Develop process improvement plans.
- Implement plans.
- Check process variation.

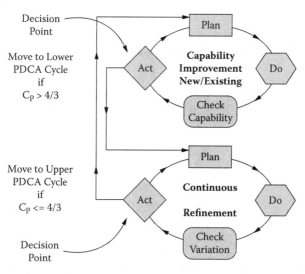

Figure 8.7   PDCA cycle.

Act on results (decision point). If Cp ≤ 4/3, the process is now unstable. Go to plan element of the upper PDCA (hoshin) cycle.

Process Representation

There are usually three views of a process:

1. What you think it is (Figure 8.8)
2. What it actually is (Figure 8.9)
3. What it should be (Figure 8.10)

The first view is what you think the process is in terms of its size, how work flows, and how well the process works. In virtually all cases, the extent and difficulty of performing the process is understated.

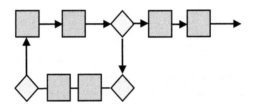

Figure 8.8   What do you think?

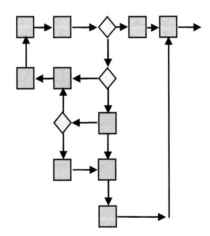

Figure 8.9   What it actually is.

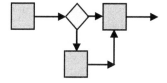

Figure 8.10   What it should be.

The questions that must be looked at in order to understand the core issues and opportunities in BPM are:

Which processes that I work in are key to the success of the organization, the customer, or are in need of improvement?

What specific problem can I solve to improve the performance of this process or my company?

What is the current baseline level of performance that quantifies this problem or process performance.

By how much and by when do I want to improve the performance? What is my objective?

How much money would I save if I improved the process performance to the level stated in the objective?

If I make an improvement, which of the company's goals and objectives does it support?

Why Measure Business Performance?

In 2002 Bititci, Carrie, and Turner identified the following reasons why companies measure business performance:

- To monitor and control
- To drive improvement
- To maximize the effectiveness of the improvement effort
- To achieve alignment with organizational goals and objectives
- To reward and discipline

Simons (2000) looks at business performance measurement as a tool to balance five major tensions within a firm:

1. Balancing profit, growth, and control
2. Balancing short-term results against long-term capabilities and growth opportunities

3. Balancing performance expectations of different constituencies
4. Balancing opportunities and attention
5. Balancing the motives of human behavior

Looking at the firm as a complex organism seeking to survive or thrive in its competitive environment, performance measurement systems serve as a key contributor to the perceptual and coordination/control capabilities of the firm.

Process Management

It is through processes that work is performed in order to deliver value to the customer. The value, of course includes product and service. The ultimate goal of any organization is definition and management of these processes.

The management of these processes so that they are effective, efficient, and adaptable is the ultimate goal. You may elect to use various tools, methodologies, management approaches, and technologies to achieve this goal. Process management is the collection and orchestration of these efforts in order to ensure our business success. Approaching all aspects of business from a process perspective will enable you and your organization to significantly improve and succeed.

Processes have a natural architecture (Figure 8.11). A major process, typically owned by an executive or senior manager, involves more than one function within the organization, and its operation has a significant impact on the organization.

Simply stated, processes transform inputs into higher-value outputs by blending the inputs together in a prescribed way. Inputs are provided to the process by suppliers. A supplier is an entity, person, or another process that provides an input to the process under consideration. Therefore, a supplier can be internal to our company or external to it.

A supplier can be as close as the output of the previous step in the process or a vendor more than a thousand miles away. The outputs of a process always go to a customer. A customer is any entity, person, or another process that receives an output from the process under consideration. Just like inputs, the customer can be as close as the next process step or a customer external to your company, many miles away.

The process is a set of activities and tasks that are accountable for the blending of the inputs to create a higher-valued output. For now you can generally categorize inputs as materials, information, people, energy, tools, and equipment. Processes are also supported or governed by such things as methods, procedures, process rules, and customer requirements.

A process is generally repeated over and over, although the frequency of replication may be low. The output of one process can become the input to another process, and a business is made up of a large number of processes to produce a product or service that a customer is ultimately willing to purchase.

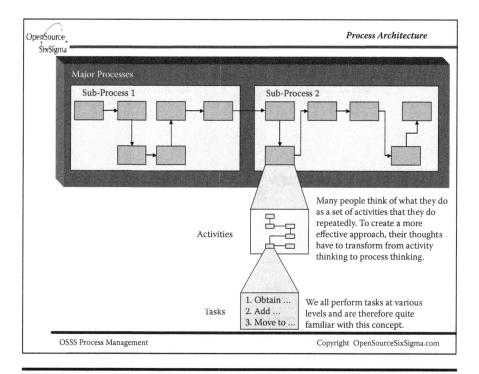

Figure 8.11   Process architecture.

A major process could be, say, accounts receivable, including such subprocesses as invoicing, posting, quality control, reconciliation, approvals, tracking, etc.

The next level of detail is the various activities that occur in a subprocess. These are logically grouped to form the steps of the process. The various activities are usually documented and performed by a single unit (a person, machine, or department). Many people think of what they do as a set of repeated activities. To be more effective in their approach, their thoughts have to be transformed from activity thinking to process thinking.

Finally, the lowest level of the process architecture is the task level—the individual elements of an activity. Normally, tasks relate to how someone or some machine performs a specific assignment. We all perform tasks at various levels and are therefore quite familiar with this concept (Figure 8.12).

Inputs are provided to the process by suppliers. A supplier is an entity, person, or another process that provides an input to the process under consideration. Therefore, a supplier can be internal to our company or external to it.

A supplier can be as close as the output of the previous step in the process or a vendor more than a thousand miles away. The outputs of a process always go to a customer. A customer is any entity, person, or another process that receives an output

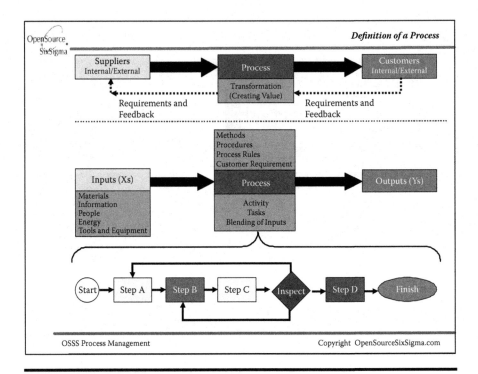

Figure 8.12 Definition of a process (OSSS).

from the process under consideration. Just like inputs, the customer can be as close as the next process step or a customer external to your company, many miles away.

Processes are classified as either core or enabling. A core process is directly related to generating revenue, providing products or services to a revenue-generating customer, or creating a strategic advantage for the company. Typically, there are only four to six core processes in a company, and they are made up of various major processes and subprocesses. Typical core processes are sales and marketing, manufacturing/fulfillment, design engineering, order entry and processing, etc. As you can readily begin to comprehend, these are large processes that many departments contribute to.

Enabling processes exist to enable and support the execution of the core processes. A core process could not sustain itself without the support and services provided by the enabling processes. Typical enabling processes are information technology, human resources, finance, legal, documentation, etc. Enabling processes do not touch or directly impact the external customer.

A part of process management is to identify those processes and process steps that are critical to the success of these higher-level processes. Metrics are generated to either monitor or control the performance of these processes. Because the processes are critical to success, the associated metrics are tracked on a periodic basis in what is called a process management summary report. The process management summary is most often owned by middle management and is a simple aggregation of the key inputs and outputs of each critical process.

A process owner is a person who manages the process end to end to ensure optimal overall performance, coordinates functional/cross-functional activities at all levels of a work process, has the responsibility to approve changes in the process, and sponsors improvement efforts (teams).

It is important for us to understand that the core processes are made up of major processes, which are then made up of subprocesses. Some, but not all, of these subprocesses are critical to the success of the business. In an ideal world, we would immediately know all the critical processes. In reality, we discover them either systematically or because it is obvious they are causing problems.

Many people who have learned to think of processes tend to see process in terms of departments or functions. This is referred to as the silo or vertical view of process flow. Value actually flows horizontally across the many silos of a company; in other words, core processes expand horizontally across the company. This is where process management can make a significant difference. Process management is all about creating a framework and an actionable effort aimed at configuring, coordinating, and aligning both core and enabling business processes to achieve the goals of the organization.

Process management creates the insight to see how value flows across the various stovepipes or functional organizations of the company. Key inputs and outputs of these value-creating and -supporting processes are identified, and their performance or capability is characterized. The organization can see how outputs of one process become inputs to another process until, finally, an output to an external customer is made.

Process management is all about your ability to better manage the behavior and performance of your processes. Process management provides a systematic approach and knowledge about the true workflow, allowing you to achieve improvement efforts. The benefits of process management include:

- Creates indicators to help manage objectively
- Focuses on the needs of the customer, the process, and the business
- Provides a structure for the continuous monitoring of an organization's capability to meet customer requirements
- Establishes work improvement priorities
- Provides a common language within and across departments
- Links together all process activities so the team can better understand and perform the necessary work
- Maintains the gains achieved by problem-solving teams and process redesign teams levels (and you most likely will use them in order, from the macro map to the micro map)

The macro map contains the least level of detail, with increasing detail as you get to the micro map. You should think of and use the level of process maps in a

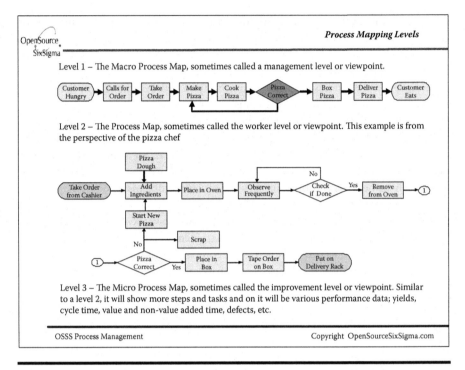

Figure 8.13 Process mapping levels (OSSS).

way similar to that in which you would use road maps. For example, if you want to find a country, you look at the world map. If you want to find a city in that country, you look at the country map. If you want to find a street address in the city, you use a city map. This is the general rule or approach for using process maps (Figure 8.13).

The macro process map, what is called the level 1 map, shows the big picture; you will use this to orient yourself to the way a product or service is created. It will also help you to better see which major step of the process is most likely related to the problem you have, and it will put the various processes that you are associated with in the context of the larger whole. Management level process has the following characteristics:

■ Combines related activities into one major processing step
■ Illustrates where/how the process fits into the big picture
■ Has minimal detail
■ Illustrates only major process steps
■ Can be completed with an understanding of general process steps and the purpose/objective of the process

The next level is generically called the process map, referred to as a level 2 map, and it identifies the major process steps from the workers' point of view. But can you fully understand why the process performs the way it does in terms of efficiency and effectiveness, and can you improve the process with the level of knowledge from this map? Probably not; you are going to need a level 3 map, called the micro process map. It is also known as the improvement view of a process. There is, however, a lot of value in the level 2 map, because it helps you to see and understand how work gets done, who does it, etc. It is a necessary stepping stone to arriving at improved performance.

There are four types of process maps that you will use. They are the linear flow map, the deployment or swim lane map, the SIPOC map, and the value stream map.

While they all show how work gets done, they emphasize different aspects of process flow and provide you with alternative ways to understand the behavior of the process so you can do something about it. The linear flow map is the most traditional and is usually where most start the mapping effort.

The swim lane map adds another dimension of knowledge to the picture of the process: now you can see which department area or person is responsible. You can use the various types of maps in the form of any of the three levels of a process map (Figure 8.14).

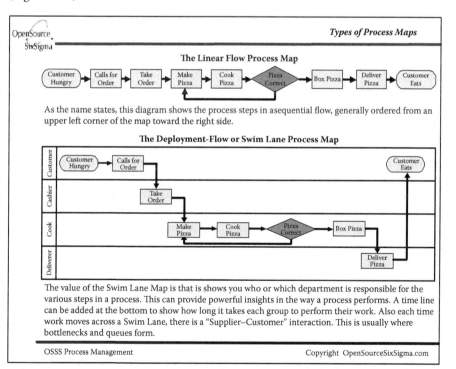

Figure 8.14   Types of process maps (OSSS).

Process knowledge is the set of tangible and intangible operating procedures used to convert the inputs to outputs. If knowledge is constant (i.e., operating procedures unchanging) and the process variables are stable, then the output of the process will also be stable, subject only to statistically predictable variability. This phenomenon is the purview of statistical process control (SPC). Process improvement requires new knowledge that manifests itself in changed operating procedures.

This change in knowledge is called learning. Note also that process knowledge can be lost. For example, undocumented procedures that rest in volatile human memory can be lost when the process executors move on to other assignments. This loss of knowledge is called forgetting.

As process knowledge increases, the gap between the processes' inherent capabilities and actual outputs will decrease. Inherent capabilities represent the ultimate limit the process can achieve without significant capital investment. Consequently, any results metric should also decrease, defined as a measure of that gap. Therefore, the rate of change of a result metric is a function of net process learning. Conversely, the rate of change of a result metric is itself a measure of net process learning.[*]

Enabling Dimension: Management

Performance management is a dynamic system. Dynamics system management is what makes an organization agile.

A manager needs information about projects to be able to make decisions, plan and schedule, and allocate resources for the different activities. Sources of information are documents produced during the development and direct contact with the developers. However, these sources are not sufficient, and the manager must rely on experience and estimations. It would be better to know instead of estimating, but when this is not possible, the approach has to be to make as good estimations as possible. To be able to make good estimations, the manager needs to have in-depth information about the organization and the staff. Also, there is a need for validation of the estimations. The underlying problem for a manager is that it is very difficult to control something that one has little knowledge about.

Inability to make a decision or discriminate between different states of events affects a company's bottom line and, as a result, drives the cost of doing business high and profitability low. This leads to the problem of the decision-making process and makes the questions below difficult to answer.

From the customer prospective: "How do our customers see us?"
From the financial prospective: "How do we get the best results for the funds?"

---

[*] "Measurement, The Bridge between the Hard and Soft Sides," *Journal of Strategic Performance Management*, April/May 1998.

From the internal processes prospective: "What must we excel at?"

From the improvement perspective: "How do we continue to improve and create value?"

Therefore, if the management of the organization wants to minimize the number of problems it is constantly facing, it has to change its focus and learn how to "manage for results and by the process." The effect of change will give the organization a sense of control. If the process manages the organization, the organization can achieve continuous improvement, which, in addition, will be measurable.

The process-focused approach means that attention is concentrated on the process, rather than the product. For example, you would be able to identify (using planned schedule metrics versus actual schedule) that your project is behind schedule and that the number of defects discovered is not acceptable. You then adjust the process, making sure that the design specifications contain enough detail, which helps developers translate designs into accurate code more easily. If instead you decide to increase the test cycle to improve the quality after the fact, you are using a product-focused approach.

Managing the process refers to managing the rate of change presented by different volatility metrics. There are two major patterns involving change, depending on whether the change is rapid or slow—whether it occurs in a day or months. You have to define what a good change is, what makes good process, and how the process reacts to such a positive change. There are some important questions that should be asked continuously:

- Do we have the ability to respond to change?
- Who is managing the process?
- How is the process tracked?
- What actions should be taken to improve the process?

In his article, Art Schneiderman suggests:

> If the process view of an organization is taken, it is as the sum of a number of interconnected processes. Each of these processes has customers and suppliers. The customers have requirements, and organizations strive to match the process output to these requirements. Results metrics measure how well the organization performs this. Internal to the process are a few key variables that drive its output. In general, they are invisible to the processes' customers. Measurement of these variables produces a set of process metrics. In mathematical terms, results metrics are the dependent variables and process metrics are the independent variables associated with a process.

The measurements should not be limited by just four categories, as the balanced scorecard (BSC) suggests. They should provide quantitative information showing trends that may influence change in the S-curve trajectory.

Process Performance Monitoring and Metrics

Performance monitoring is simply to find out whether we are meeting our objectives. It shows the trends and inconsistencies. It does not provide you any information on cause or outcome. It just tells you what is going on and whether you are on a right track. The data points that you are collecting are the measures. In order to find out why the results are what they are, you must develop metrics that support your indicators. The performance evaluation comes after collected information is analyzed, correlated, and cross-referenced.

After you understand and define how the process delivers value to the customer, the measurements and metrics should flow naturally. Expressing metrics in terms of value-added activities helps to define customer perception of value. Those measures across organizations should lead to a higher level of process performance through continuous process improvement. They should be aligned with the business strategy and present decision making and actionable information for management.

The balanced scorecard concept is often considered a means to provide needed information to the identified stakeholders.

Balanced Scorecard

Strategic dashboards are frequently based on the balanced scorecard methodology of David Norton and Robert Kaplan, a widely adopted method for determining and achieving organizational goals. Organizations using this approach are significantly more successful in achieving their goals.

The balanced scorecard process gets its name from a balance of financial and nonfinancial measures, a balance of short-term and long-term indicators, and a balance of leading and lagging indicators.

The balanced scorecard translates the vision and strategy of a business unit into objectives and performance measures in four different areas: the financial, customer, internal business process, and learning and growth perspectives. The financial perspective identifies how the company wishes to be viewed by its shareholders. The customer perspective determines how the company wishes to be viewed by its customers. The internal business process perspective describes the business processes at which the company has to be particularly adept in order to satisfy its shareholders and customers. This description leads to the identification of the main process indicators that the company wants to control and which will be part of the balanced scorecard itself. Similarly, the organizational learning and growth perspective analyzes the changes and improvements that the company needs to realize if it is to make its vision come true (Kaplan and Norton 1996, pp. 30–31).

The identification of these key factors leads to the identification of key indicators. Kaplan and Norton (1996, p. 31) assume the following causal relationships: measures of organizational learning and growth → measures of internal business processes → measures of the customer perspective → financial measures. The measures of organizational learning and growth are therefore the drivers of the measures of the internal business processes. The measures of these processes are in turn the drivers of the measures of the customer perspective, while these measures are the drivers of the financial measures. Each strategic area should have both lead and lag indicators, yielding two directional cause-and-effect chains: lead and lag indicators apply horizontally within the areas and vertically between areas. This procedure implies that strategy is translated into a set of hypotheses about cause and effect (Kaplan and Norton 1996, p. 30).

The balanced scorecard is not just a strategic measurement system but also a strategic control system that may be used to (1) clarify and gain consensus about strategy, (2) align departmental and personal goals to strategy, (3) link strategic objectives to long-term targets and annual budgets, (4) identify and align strategic initiatives, and (5) obtain feedback to learn about and improve strategy (Kaplan and Norton 1996, p. 19).

In order to obtain these results with the balanced scorecard, the company must start by clarifying and translating the vision and strategy into specific strategic objectives and measures. The next step includes (1) the communication of the vision and the strategy to teams and employees, (2) the translation of strategic objectives and measures into objectives and measures for teams and employees, and (3) the creation of a link between rewards and performance measures.

Process Improvement

For the purposes of the IMPACT framework a combination of the above techniques are used to develop the process improvement strategy.

The Process Improvement involves focusing and improving the most critical processes of the organization critical for meeting the goals and objectives. It helps the organization to focus on "doing things the right way". Most of the techniques had been devised for manufacturing companies and soon after its successful implementation they were adapted in the service based industries.

The IMPACT framework focuses on the Performance Improvement aspect of this component: According to the framework, in order to have processes aligned to the goals and objectives of the organization, it is important to ensure that performance of the individuals is in compliance with the conditions of the organization. The inability to adapt to the complexity and changing dynamics of the real world can lead to failure.

Organizations view Performance Improvement techniques as means to deliver better products and services while increasing the organizational effectiveness. Performance Improvement ensures effectiveness, efficiency and efficacy of the organizations. Organizational goals and objectives are set on the basis of the organizational efficacy. Continuous Performance Improvement is imperative and should be integrated with Continuous Process Improvement techniques.

Purpose of Process Improvement Techniques

The main purpose of the Process Improvement techniques is to follow an approach of continuous improvement. Process Improvement techniques focus on reducing the waste or non value added activities in processes.

1. They emphasize on defining the strategic goals of the organization.
2. They focus on the stakeholders of the organization.
3. The main task is to align the business process with the corporate goals.

The above mentioned three factors help in long term sustainability and growth of the company. The organization is left with the most important processes for its efficient functioning.

Benefits of Continuous Process Improvement

- The Process Improvement techniques are developed in alignment with the organizational goals.
- The Improvement techniques should be devised in a way that customer focus is increased.
- Process Owners can be identified for devising effective improvement strategies.
- Benchmarking helps in assessing the progress and understanding if appropriate improvement techniques are being adopted.
- Performance Improvement techniques need to be integrated into Continuous Process Management and alignment with organizational goals.

Types of Process Improvements: Which One Should I Use?

Depending upon the needs of the organization, the process improvement techniques can be categorized as:

1. **Continuous Process Improvement:** It is an ongoing constant improvement effort for products, services and internal operations of an organization. It is

targeted that the impact of such improvement techniques are for long term sustenance. It focuses on the quality of services, products, processes.

2. **Business Process Improvement:** It is a systematic approach to optimize the underlying processes of an organization and reduce inefficient, irrelevant activities. It focuses on improving quality, productivity, timeliness, business, strategic or functional processes of the organization.

3. **Software Process Improvement:** It relates to quality of processes used for developing or maintaining a software system. It focuses on the solution to process related challenges. It is based on the fact that product quality is predominantly dependent on the quality of process used to develop it.

Continuous Process and Performance Improvement Technique

The Continuous Process Improvement diagram (Figure 8.15) depicts the correlation between the Metrics, Indicators, and Scorecards. For industry specific processes, the goals and objects are defined. These goals need to be accomplished in a defined timeframe and in an allocated budget. Effort in terms of money, manpower is invested accordingly to meet the targets. Once the initiative is undertaken it needs to be compared to the baselines which have been developed. The performance results are compared to earlier results to check any deviation from the desired results, targets or the benchmarks. Performance summary is reviewed

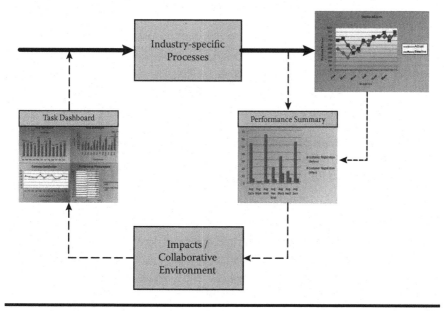

8.15 Continuous Process Improvment.

consistently, Impacts are studied. The Dashboard or the Scorecard illustrates and summarizes how successful the initiative has been. The complete cycle acts as a "Feedback Loop". The performance is assessed and changes are made on a continuous basis. The indicators also help to devise a mechanism to measure the performance. Consistent measures are used to analyze the performance and in case when the environmental conditions change, changes can be made to the measures. The details are given in the next section of this component.

Techniques and Components of Process Improvement

There are various techniques to identify the critical processes of the organization. The techniques can be used in combination or individually depending upon the requirements of the organization. The IMPACT framework suggests using a combination of these techniques to better understand the important processes of the organization:

Performance Improvement

Performance Improvement is a critical aspect of improving processes of an organization. Performance can be in terms of individuals, teams or organization. Performance Improvement techniques need a collaborative approach for prioritization of the desired results. Just like any other area, Performance Improvement faces a number of challenges. Few facts that need to be emphasized for improving performance with maximum efficiency are:

1. It is important to associate the initiative with proper leadership role. The feeling of ownership helps drive performance improvement.
2. Performance goals need to be set and prioritized.
3. Performance framework can be developed to facilitate the implementation organization wide.
4. Performance statistics can help enhance the knowledge of the processes and the gaps of the organization.
5. Success Factors for performance improvement need to be identified.

Measuring Performance

Performance of an organization can be measured and depicted graphically. This can be depicted in the Scorecards or as separate Performance Charts. Both techniques are helpful in understanding the gaps and improving performance. The details of devising appropriate means of measurement are mentioned in the next section of this chapter.

Process Measurement Tools:

1. **Key Prioritization Matrix:** The Key Prioritization Matrix is a tool that helps to understand the processes needing immediate attention.
   - The Impact on customer focus (internal or external) are recorded as "Voice of Customer"
   - Improvement required is recorded as the "Voice of the Process"
   - Importance in terms of meeting the goals and objectives are recorded as the "Voice of the Business."
2. **SIPOC:** It stands for Suppliers, inputs, process, outputs, and customers. It is started from right from the suppliers and ends at the customers.
3. **Identification of Value Added and Non Value Added processes:** *Identifying the waste*
   The motive is to have an end-product or service having cost that exceeds the cost of producing the product or providing the service.

Measuring Performance for an Organization:

Performance Improvement can be possible if we have certain benchmarks. Performance targets usually reflect the throughput and quality of the process. These targets are based mainly on the scorecards. Measuring Performance becomes easier if we have defined the appropriate Key Performance Indicators and Metrics used for them. The classifications of Process metrics are mainly in four major quadrants as mentioned in the last chapter. These are Cost, Time, Quality and Quantity.

The Example of Measures

Measures			
Cost	Time	Productivity	Quality
Cost per appointment	Call wait time per customer	Increase in calls per day	Number of patients returning
Cost per treatment	Time taken to schedule an appointment	Increase in number of patients	Available treatments
Payment per customer	Time taken to admit a patient	Number of patients treated	
	Time taken to process the bill	Number of bills processed	

Summary

There are five principles to focus and align every process and system within an organization to match its overall strategy:

1. Translate the strategy into operational terms. Everybody must understand the strategy of the organization so it is presented in a cause-and-effect linkage that reveals how the strategy will be implemented.
2. Align the organization to strategy—to create synergy within the organization. The activities of the individual functional divisions must be aligned and integrated.
3. Strategy is a part of everyone's job. Everybody should be aware of how he or she contributes to the overall strategy.
4. Strategy is a continual process. Organizations must be able to adapt their strategies as external changes happen or the existing strategy matures. Everyone must be linked to the strategy environment to create a collaborative environment and open communications.
5. Educate and mobilize leadership for change. Every member of the executive team must realize that the change is a good idea and keep the strategy transparent—in front of the people.

Another view of the performance measurement is as a recurring management process. After the initial strategy maps have been created and cascaded, the objectives have been decided, and the targets have been defined, there is a regular performance measurement and reporting cycle, which is often monthly. As you might imagine, for a company of any size and complexity, the number of measures to be reported every month as the measures are "cascaded" into the organization can become unwieldy. Further, the scope of business information required to report the measures can be quite broad and may require data integration from several sources. Many companies use large manual methods for reporting, expending large sums of money to produce monthly reports.

More broadly, performance measurement is only one part of the performance management cycle.

Unfortunately, these measures—and the BSC in general—do not provide the business information, analytical tools, and structured decision support that is needed to actually improve business performance in relation to specified targets. For that we need a unified framework (Figure 8.15 and Figure 8.16).

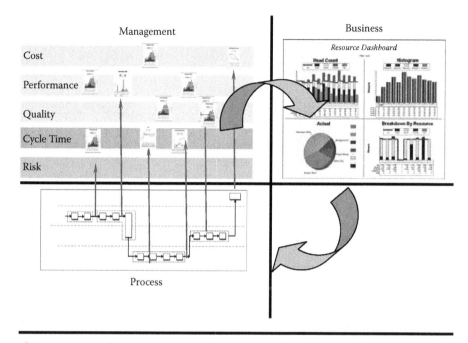

Figure 8.16   Business process management.

References

Umit Bititci, Allan Carrie, and Trevor Turner. 2002. *Integrated performance measurement systems: Structure and dynamics, in business performance measurement: Theory and practice.* Andrew Neely, editor. Cambridge, U.K.: Cambridge University Press.

Fritjof Capra. *Life and leadership: A systems approach.* www.fritjofcapra.net/seminars.html

Robert S. Kaplan and David P. Norton. 1996. *The balanced scorecard.* Boston: Harvard Business School Press.

Raymond McLeod Jr. 1998. *Management information systems (seventh edition).* Englewood Cliffs, NJ: Prentice Hall, Inc.

Robert Simons. 2000. *Performance measurement and control systems for implementing strategy.* Upper Saddle River, NJ: Prentice Hall.

www.kellen.net/bpm.htm

www.omg.org

www.schneiderman.com/AMS_publications/.../Bridge.doc

Chapter 9

Tools of Probletunity

Determine where the probletunity lies, and then build a proactive approach to solving the problem or taking advantage of the opportunity:

Tools of Probletunity
Fishbone
SWOT, etc.
SIPOC
Pareto
Lean

Value Analysis

A value stream is all of the actions (both value added and non-value added) currently required to deliver a product or a service. It is the work activity and information flow occurring as raw material or information becomes a product/service that is delivered to a customer. It is the flow of paper and information from its origin or initial request, to the desired service or action, to its final delivery to the user or customer. It is the entire flow, from door to door. It can be comprised of several key process areas that together achieve the deliverable.

Using a value stream perspective means working on the big picture, not just individual process steps, to find individual opportunities to optimize the whole. For any given product or service, a value stream spans all of the processes, from the delivery of supplied parts, material, and information, to the delivery and receipt by the user or customer.

It is an analysis that helps you to see and understand the flow of materials, documents, and information as a product or service flows through all of the processes, from the customer back to the supplier.

The analysis is performed by drawing a visual representation with specific information about every major process of the material and information flow, from the customer to the supplier. The end goal is to achieve an efficient future state of process flow that integrates individual optimizations achieved from Six Sigma projects and other appropriate methods.

A value stream map will provide you with these six essential benefits, and if you add Six Sigma metrics to the value stream map, you will have a door-to-door characterization for a product or service you deliver to a customer. It helps you visualize more than the just the single process level, i.e., order entry, invoicing, shipping, assembly, test, welding, etc. You can see the complete flow. Value stream analysis is a qualitative process that allows you to understand in detail how your business should operate to achieve breakthrough performance levels. It helps you see sources of inefficiency and problems in the complete generation and delivery of your service or product. It forms the basis of an improvement vision and plan by helping you understand how door-to-door flow should be performed to optimize costs, cycle times, and quality. It conceptualizes Six Sigma projects as well as other improvement efforts.

Value stream analysis is good for describing what you will do to change business performance levels.

Performing a Value Stream Analysis

Each process, i.e., a key process from your workplace project, is linked together to form the total value stream of a given product or service. Value stream mapping can be thought of as being done at the key process level. By thinking about linking the key processes together, you will be interested in the performance from the key process level.

Always start at the shipping end in your facility and work upstream. This way, you will first see the processes linked most closely with the customer and will better understand the impact of the upstream process. Begin with a quick walk along the entire door-to-door work stream to get a feel for what activities, resources, inventories, and other noticeably important things are occurring. Remember, you are acting like you are the product or service that is being produced for a customer (Figure 9.1).

A fishbone diagram is an analysis tool that provides a systematic way of looking at effects and the causes that create or contribute to those effects (Figure 9.2).

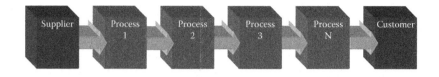

Figure 9.1 Producing product or service.

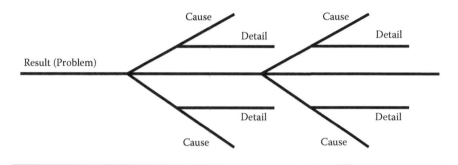

Figure 9.2 Cause and effect diagram.

Root Cause Analysis

Root cause analysis is used to clearly understand what's driving or causing a problem. The key is to identify the factors influencing the effect you are starting with. One way to jump-start the analysis is to look at:

4 Ms: Methods, manpower, materials, machinery
4 Ps: Policies, procedures, people, plant

Root cause analysis is often expressed in the form of a fishbone diagram. The steps for doing the diagram are:

Specify the effect to be analyzed. The effect can be positive (objectives) or negative (problems). Place it in a box on the right side of the diagram (Figure 9.3).
List the major categories of the factors that influence the effect being studied. Use the 4 Ms or the 4 Ps as a starting point (Figure 9.4).
Identify factors and subfactors. Use an idea-generating technique to identify the factors and subfactors within each major category. An easy way to begin is to use the major categories as a catalyst, for example, "What policies are causing …?" (Figure 9.5).

Figure 9.3   First define the goal or problem.

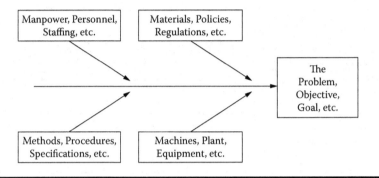

Figure 9.4   List the major categories.

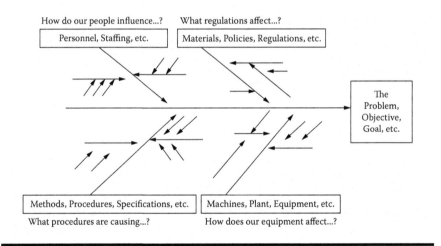

Figure 9.5   Factors and subfactors.

Identify significant factors. Look for factors that appear repeatedly and list them. Also, list those factors that have a significant effect, based on the data available. Prioritize your list of causes. Keep in mind that the location of a cause in your diagram is not an indicator of its importance. A subfactor may be the root cause to all of your problems. You may also decide to collect more data on a factor that had not been previously identified.

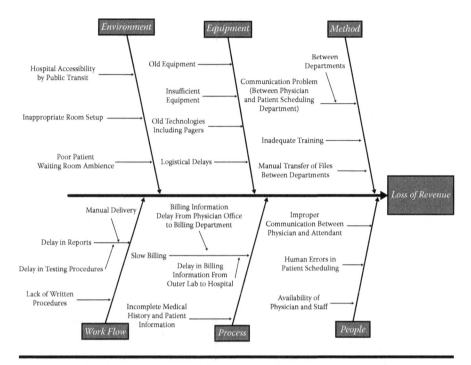

Figure 9.6 The 6 domains, People, Process, Workflow, Environment, Equipment, and Method, are used to do the root cause analysis. The causes and subcauses are depicted in the exhibit through smaller arrows.

A less formal approach to root cause analysis is to simply use the five whys technique. With each reiteration of *why* (say five times), you pull out additional information that possibly helps you identify the root cause of a problem.

The value of the fishbone diagram is that it provides a method for categorizing the many potential causes of problems or issues in an orderly way and in identifying root causes (Figure 9.6).

Root Cause Analysis Technique: The Five Whys

Sometimes the thing we think is the problem is not the real problem, so to get at the real problem, probing is necessary. Root cause analysis is an effective method of probing; it helps identify what, how, and why something happened.

The definition of root cause is as follows:

Specific underlying cause
Those that can reasonably be identified
Those that management has control to fix

Figure 9.7   5 whys.

Table 9.1   Basic Questions to Ask In Defining the Problem

Who?	What?	Where?	When?	Why?	How?
Who is causing the problem? Who says this is a problem? Who is impacted by this problem? Etc.	What will happen if this problem is not solved? What are the symptoms? What are the impacts? Etc.	Where does this problem occur? Where does this problem have an impact? Etc.	When does this problem occur? When did this problem first start occurring? Etc.	Why is this problem occurring? Etc.	How should the process or system work? How are people currently handling the problem? Etc.

The five whys refers to the practice of asking, five times, why the problem exists in order to get to the root cause of the problem (Figure 9.7, Table 9.1, and Figure 9.8).

Issue Analysis

It is often useful to break a problem down into components. Issue analysis is used to define the elements of a problem and show these elements in some logical way. This is often accomplished by using an issue tree.

An issue diagram is an effective method for breaking down problems and for-mulating hypotheses. The key to identifying issues follows:

Develop a comprehensive list of all possible issues related to the problem.
Reduce the comprehensive list by eliminating duplicates and combining over-lapping issues.
Using consensus building, get down to a major issues list (usually two to five issues).
Issue diagrams provide a framework for brainstorming and documenting the issues driving the problem and identifying the facts (i.e., data) required to support conclusions and recommended solutions.

Hypotheses and the key questions will help shape data collection requirements and ensure that only relevant data are collected.

Formulation of hypotheses and key questions is an evolving process—they will need to be revised as new insights and discoveries are made.

Use the issue diagram to identify data and information needs.

SWOT

Where processes are impacted by both internal and external factors, it can be useful to apply (strengths, weaknesses, opportunities, and threats [SWOT] analysis. SWOT analysis is a standard tool used by all types of analysts for identifying major strategic issues. SWOT can be used at any organizational level—function, department, group, etc. SWOT is defined as:

Strength: Any existing or potential resource or capability within the organization that provides a competitive advantage in the market.

Weakness: Any existing or potential internal force that could serve as a barrier to maintaining or achieving a competitive advantage in the market.

Opportunity: Any existing or potential force in the external environment that, if properly exploited, could provide a competitive advantage.

Threat: Any existing or potential force in the external environment that could inhibit the maintenance or attainment of a competitive advantage.

SWOT analysis:

Provides an objective means to identify areas of need for problem-solving efforts.

Identifies strengths, weaknesses, opportunities, and threats by asking: What things are we good at? What things are we not good at? What things might we do? What things should we not do?

Is probably the most common analytical tool for strategic planning

Is somewhat subjective

Is easy to understand and follow

Is very useful for identifying the core competencies of any organization

The aim of any SWOT analysis is to identify the key internal and external factors that are important to achieving the objective. SWOT analysis groups key pieces of information into two main categories:

Internal factors: The *strengths* and *weaknesses* internal to the organization.

External factors: The *opportunities* and *threats* presented by the external environment.

The internal factors may be viewed as strengths or weaknesses, depending upon their impact on the organization's objectives. What may represent strengths with respect to one objective may be weaknesses for another objective. The factors may include all of the above, as well as personnel, finance, manufacturing capabilities, and so on. The external factors may include macroeconomic matters, technological change, legislation, and sociocultural changes, as well as changes in the marketplace or competitive position. The results are often presented in the form of a matrix.

SWOT analysis is a strategic planning tried and tested technique that is normally adopted for obtaining a balanced perspective. SWOT analysis is just one method of categorization and has its own weaknesses. For example, it may tend to persuade companies to compile lists rather than think about what is actually important in achieving objectives. It also presents the resulting lists uncritically and without clear prioritization so that, for example, weak opportunities may appear to balance strong threats. It is prudent not to eliminate too quickly any candidate SWOT entry. The importance of individual SWOTs will be revealed by the value of the strategies they generate. A SWOT item that produces valuable strategies is important. A SWOT item that generates no strategies is not important.

Strengths:
Strengths are those things that you do well—the high value or performance points.
Strengths can be tangible: loyal customers, efficient distribution channels, very high quality products, excellent financial condition.
Strengths can be intangible: good leadership, strategic insights, customer intelligence, solid reputation, highly skilled workforce.
Often considered core competencies, strengths are your best leverage points for growth without draining your resources.

Weaknesses:
Weaknesses are those things that prevent you from doing what you really need to do.
Since weaknesses are internal, they are within your control.
Weaknesses include bad leadership, unskilled workforce, insufficient resources, poor product quality, slow distribution and delivery channels, outdated technologies, and lack of planning.

Opportunities:
Opportunities are potential areas for growth and higher performance.
External opportunities include marketplace, unhappy customers with competitors, better economic conditions, and more open trading policies.
Internal opportunities should be classified as strengths.
Timing may be important for capitalizing on opportunities.

Threats:

Threats are challenges confronting the organization are external in nature.

Threats can take a wide range, from bad press coverage to shifts in consumer behavior to substitute products to new regulations.

Threats may be useful to classify or assign probabilities to threats.

The more accurate you are in identifying threats, the better position you will be in for dealing with the "sudden ripples" of change.

SWOT Example for Clinical Trials

Strengths:

New drugs are high demand on the market

Strong and well-developed manufacturing base

Proficiency in path-breaking research

Opportunities:

High-demand market

Globalization

Future growth

Weaknesses:

Small number of discoveries

Fragmented capacities

No data management system

Manual process

Threats:

Competitive market

Lost market share

Compliance issue

Change protocol

Unsustainable partners

SIPOC

Value chain analysis is the study of all links to an organization—from original suppliers through delivery processes to the customer—that add value to goods or services provided. This is typically a higher-level, big-picture mapping analysis of an enterprise that subsequently leads to lower-level SIPOC (suppliers-inputs-process-outputs-customers) and value stream mapping analyses.

The SIPOC diagram is especially useful because it facilitates your gathering of other pertinent data that are affecting the process in a systematic way. It will help you to better see and understand all of the influences affecting the behavior and performance of the process (Figure 9.8).

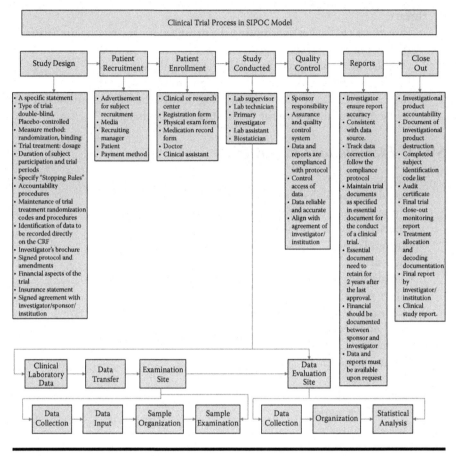

Figure 9.8 Examples of SIPOC Model for clinical trial process.

You may also add a requirements section to both the supplier side and the customer side to capture the expectations for the inputs and the outputs of the process. Doing a SIPOC is a great building block to creating the level 3 micro process map. The two really complement each other and give you the power to make improvements to the process.

The SIPOC tool is particularly useful in identifying:

■ Who supplies inputs to the process?
■ What are all of the inputs to the process we are aware of?
■ What specifications are placed on the inputs?
■ What are all of the outputs of the process?
■ Who are the true customers of the process?
■ What are the requirements of the customers?

The preferred order of the steps is:

1. Identify the outputs of this overall process.
2. Identify the customers who will receive the outputs of the process.
3. Identify customers' preliminary requirements.
4. Identify the inputs required for the process.
5. Identify suppliers of the required inputs that are necessary for the process to function.
6. Identify the preliminary requirements of the inputs for the process to function properly.

Pareto

In order to focus on significant problems, you can rank the importance in descending order of occurrence. This is typically done using the Pareto chart (Figure 9.9). In order to chart problems, you must:

Identify the problems that need to be ranked.
Use a standard measurement for ranking, such as frequency, costs, etc.
Determine the time frame for evaluating the problems.
Collect the data from existing reports or use new data.
Label the units of measure on the left vertical axis and label the problem areas on the horizontal axis.
Plot the data, showing the descending order from left to right.

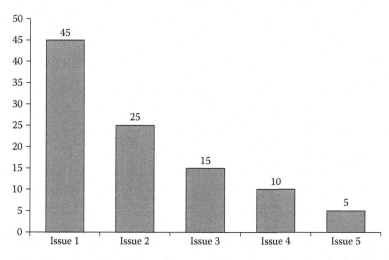

Figure 9.9   Pareto chart.

Lean

Developed in Japan, this method assumes no effective and quality job can be done without a clean and safe environment and without behavioral rules. The roots of both Lean and Six Sigma reach back to the time when the greatest pressure for quality and speed was on manufacturing. Lean rose as a method for optimizing automotive manufacturing; Six Sigma evolved as a quality initiative to eliminate defects by reducing variation in processes in the semiconductor industry. It is not surprising that the earliest adopters of Lean Six Sigma arose in the service support functions of manufacturing organizations like GE Capital, Caterpillar Finance, and Lockheed Martin.

Lean Six Sigma for services is a business improvement methodology that maximizes shareholder value by achieving the fastest rate of improvement in customer satisfaction, cost, quality, process speed, and invested capital. The fusion of Lean and Six Sigma improvement methods is required because:

> Lean cannot bring a process under statistical control.
> Six Sigma alone cannot dramatically improve process speed or reduce invested capital.
> Both enable the reduction of the cost of complexity.

Ironically, Six Sigma and Lean have often been regarded as rival initiatives. Lean enthusiasts note that Six Sigma pays little attention to anything related to speed and flow, while Six Sigma supporters point out that Lean fails to address key concepts like customer needs and variation. Both sides are right. Yet these arguments are more often used to advocate choosing one over the other, rather than to support the more logical conclusion that we blend Lean and Six Sigma.

How is it that Six Sigma and Lean are complementary? Here's a quick overview.

Six Sigma:
> Emphasizes the need to recognize opportunities and eliminate defects as defined by customers
> Recognizes that variation hinders our ability to reliably deliver high-quality services
> Requires data-driven decisions and incorporates a comprehensive set of quality tools under a powerful framework for effective problem solving
> Provides a highly prescriptive cultural infrastructure effective in obtaining sustainable results
> When implemented correctly, promises and delivers $500,000+ of improved operating profit per Black Belt per year (a hard dollar figure many companies consistently achieve)

Lean:

Focuses on maximizing process velocity

Provides tools for analyzing process flow and delay times at each activity in a process

Centers on the separation of value-added from non-value-added work with tools to eliminate the root causes of non-valued activities and their cost; the eight types of waste/non-value-added work are:

Wasted human talent: Damage to people

Defects: Stuff that's not right and needs fixed

Inventory: Stuff waiting to be worked

Overproduction: Stuff too much/too early

Waiting time: People waiting for stuff to arrive

Motion: Unnecessary human movement

Transportation: Moving people and stuff

Processing waste: Stuff we have to do that doesn't add value to the product or service we are supposed to be producing

Provides a means for quantifying and eliminating the cost of complexity

The two methodologies interact and reinforce one another, such that percentage gains in return on investment capital (ROIC%) are much faster if Lean and Six Sigma are implemented together.

In short, what sets Lean Six Sigma apart from its individual components is the recognition that you cannot do just quality or just speed; you need a balanced process that can help an organization focus on improving service quality, as defined by the customer, within a set time limit.

The essence of Lean is to concentrate effort on removing waste while improving process flow to achieve speed and agility at lower cost. The focus of Lean is to increase the percentage of value-added work performed by a company. Lean recognizes that most businesses spend a relatively small portion of their energies on the true delivery of value to a customer. While all companies are busy, it is estimated for some companies that as little as 10% of their time is spent on value-added work, meaning as much as 90% of time is allocated to non-value-added activities, or waste.

Forms of waste include wasted capital (inventory), wasted material (scrap), wasted time (cycle time), wasted human effort (inefficiency, rework), and wasted energy (energy inefficiency). Lean is a prescriptive methodology for relatively fast improvements across a variety of processes, from administrative to manufacturing applications. Lean enables your company to identify waste where it exists. It also provides the tools to make improvements on the spot.

Lean focuses on what it calls the value stream, the sequence of activities and work required to produce a product or to provide a service. It is similar to a linear process flow map, but it contains its own unique symbols and data. The Lean method is based on understanding how the value stream is organized, how work is performed, which work is value added vs. non-value added, and what happens to products and services and information as they flow through the value stream. Lean identifies and eliminates the barriers to efficient flow through simple, effective tools.

Lean removes many forms of waste so that Six Sigma can focus on eliminating variability. Variation leads to defects, which is a major source of waste. Six Sigma is a method to make processes more capable through the reduction of variation—thus the symbiotic relationship between the two methodologies.

Chapter 10

Dashboards and Scorecards

Everybody wants to have a dashboard. It became very popular and fashionable, and the reason is that management dashboards can provide a number of benefits to the organization. Some of the key benefits include:

Goal and progress alignment: The selection of which indicators to include in the dashboard helps communicate to the business organization what tasks and activities are most critical to the company's success. This ensures that everyone in the organization has a consistent view of the status of these activities.

Performance monitoring and measurement: Dashboards help users easily monitor and measure business performance without having to manually wade through a variety of nonintegrated reports and files.

Business analysis: Dashboards provide the capability for the user to dig deeper into an indicator to determine the root cause of the issues, opportunities, or changes that have been identified by that indicator.

Improved decision making: Dashboards help users make quicker, better-informed decisions by highlighting business issues and opportunities in a real-time, understandable format.

Before looking at any underlying technology or specific solutions, a basic understanding of the types of dashboard and what sorts of things they measure will provide a foundation for any dashboard project.

We see them everywhere; dashboards are another product of the astonishing capabilities of contemporary hardware and software—correct? The dashboard is a powerful metaphor for monitoring business process trends, but like many applications apparently enabled by Web technology, it has a long history, almost as long as the automobile dashboard. In France, the *tableau de bord* is standard on every Citroën and is also the name of a management reporting tool in general use since the mid-1950s.

Tableau de bord

The description of the *tableau de bord* is not an easy task. On the one hand, the *tableau de bord* is much older than the scorecard and has, for this reason, experienced many changes over time; on the other hand, there are almost as many versions of *tableaux de bord* as management control authors. We shall briefly review the historical evolution of the concept, before concentrating on the current consensus about *tableau de bord*. Indeed, whereas many definitions may be given for *tableau de bord*, most authors agree on its main characteristics.

Malo (1995) dates the use of *tableau de bord* in the management field to 1932. In French, *tableau de bord* is the name of the dashboard, and the manager is thus metaphorically compared to a pilot. According to this tradition, the *tableau de bord* is "a tool for the top management of the firm, allowing it a global and quick view of its operations and of the state of its environment" (Malo 1995). Malo suggests that its development could be a consequence of the inappropriateness of local accounting data for decision making: in France, the relatively limited size of firms, their frequent management by their owners, and the creation of income tax (1917) would have diverted financial accounting from producing data usable for the management. Besides, cost accounting was focusing on the production of true full costs. *Tableaux de bord* would then have met the need for management tools, given the lack of accounting-based data. At that time, the *tableau de bord* was a set of physical performance measures, which belong more to the engineer's language than accounting's, which is consistent with the important part played by engineers in France in the development and management of French industry (Malo 1995).

In the late 1950s, the diffusion of American management methods brought about the introduction of responsibility centers in firms, and the diversification of *tableaux de bord*. There is henceforth one *tableau de bord* for each responsibility center, and budgetary data are added (Malo 1995). According to this prevailing viewpoint (until the late 1980s), the *tableau de bord* is basically presented as a "reporting device, making it possible to control the realization of previously fixed objectives, as well as a tool for diagnosis, reaction and hierarchical dialogue" (Ardoin, Michel, and Schmidt 1986, p. 143).

Dashboards have three well-defined categories with different goals and audiences. Before describing these categories, I will introduce the concept of analysis mind share, which both helps to explain the appeal of dashboards and puts the various types of dashboards in context. We will also look at guidelines for selecting key performance indicators to populate dashboards.

Analysis Mind Share

In a large organization, there is a continuum of responsibility, from the line worker responsible for putting widgets in boxes to the CEO. At both ends of this organizational hierarchy, the primary functions do not leave a significant amount of time—mind share—for data analysis (Figure 10.1). At the bottom of the organization, the focus is on specific production tasks; at the top, the focus is on strategy. Neither of these individuals can afford the time to sift through the enormous amounts of data produced by today's enterprises.

Dashboards fall into three well-established categories:

■ Strategic dashboards for organizational alignment
■ Tactical dashboards for measuring progress in projects or initiatives
■ Operational dashboards for monitoring specific business activities

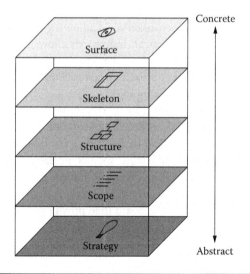

Figure 10.1   The elements of dashboard construction (Garrett 2003).

Strategic

According to Gartner's report on business intelligence (BI), scorecard takes the metrics displayed in a dashboard a step further by applying them to a strategy map that aligns key performance indicators with a strategic objective. Scorecard metrics should be linked to related reports and information in order to do further analysis. A scorecard implies the use of performance management methodology such as Six Sigma or balanced scorecard frameworks.

Strategic dashboards measure progress toward strategic objectives; they help align the organization with strategy in ways that static mission statements cannot. An executive-level dashboard might reflect enterprise-wide strategic goals and corresponding key performance indicators (KPIs). A good security model will support enterprise-wide strategic dashboards that cascade down to the department level with gradually more restrictive views of data, while retaining alignment to corporate objectives. Working down from global to departmental helps avoid creating dashboards that pit department against department. Strategic dashboards are typically highly summarized, highly graphical, less frequently updated, and include global, external, trend, and growth measures.

Tactical

Tactical dashboards measure trends and progress toward strategic initiatives or special projects, frequently against established goals. They may involve just one of the four balanced scorecard perspectives. Starting to move away from the stoplight model, tactical dashboards frequently include summary data as well as visual indicators, and make full use of hyperlinked tools, allowing drill down and root cause analysis. The focused nature of tactical dashboards allows more detailed information to be displayed—the context is clear from the outset. Incidentally, many dashboards created without a formal approach are actually tactical dashboards with the aim of maximizing profit or increasing sales.

Tactical dashboards, which are updated daily or weekly, trigger alerts to exception conditions and then guide users on the appropriate actions to take. For example, a grocery manager uses a tactical dashboard to track his daily progress toward achieving corporate objectives for the store, such as increasing the percentage of staff who greet customers in the aisles. If the manager notices a yellow or red light next to this KPI, he can drill down to view staff members who failed to greet the secret shoppers who compiled the data. The dashboard then provides a list of steps the manager should take to remedy the problem, including talking to the staff person or asking him or her to watch a training video or attend a Web-based training course.

Operational

Operational dashboards are used to monitor business or manufacturing processes in near real time with the aim of intervening quickly to resolve issues or take advantage of opportunities. Operational dashboards are usually departmental in scope, and absolute values and thresholds based on averages and norms are frequently as important as trends. Like tactical dashboards, the focused nature of operational dashboards allows more detailed information to be displayed. It would be unusual for a top-level manager to use an operational dashboard; a traffic light summarizing operational capacity trends would be more appropriate.

Operational dashboards, on the other hand, monitor events as they happen. They do this by capturing events in real time, from an organization's messaging backbone (an enterprise service bus), via data replication, or by continuous polling (querying). The dashboard engine then aggregates and correlates the events in a dimensional schema, compares them to historical data in a data warehouse, a local cache, or some other repository, and calculates the relevance of events based on predefined metrics of acceptable performance. When performance exceeds thresholds, the dashboard automatically triggers alerts, launches workflow ("send an e-mail message and report to the head of eastern region sales and request an update in three days"), or executes tasks ("submit a purchase order to supplier X for 50 widgets").

These automated actions are governed by a rules engine that business users define within the dashboard or an external business process management (BPM) system. Some industry experts refer to this type of event-driven analytical system that monitors key business processes as business activity monitoring (BAM). This type of reverse embedding is critical for helping companies streamline business processes and optimize performance. Thus, it's a critical piece of most business process management strategies.

Building the Dashboard: From the Concept to Useful Tool

In my opinion, the best definition for dashboards, found by searching the Internet, appears in a paper written by Dan Dubriwny and Kurt Rivards of Advizor Solutions: "Are You Drowning in BI Reports? Using Analytical Dashboards to Cut through the Clutter."

> They provide visibility into key performance indicators (KPIs) through simple visual graphics such as gauges, charts and tables within a web browser. Dashboards are appealing because they:
>
> Present a wide number of different metrics in a single consolidated view
> Roll up details into high-level summaries
> Provide intuitive indicators, such as gauges and stoplights, that are instantly understandable—for example, red bar means problem, green bar means everything is on plan

Steven Few, in his article for the www.intelligententerprise.com, writes:

A Working Definition

Ready to pin it down? My bias is simple: I want a definition that captures the essence of this thing we call a dashboard, expressing it in a way that is meaningful and useful. I want to promote a definition we can all share, so we can move on to fruitful discussions about how we can use dashboards most effectively as a medium of insightful business information. I don't want to define the term to uniquely specify any particular BI vendor's solution.

I believe that the real meaning of a dashboard is not based on any particular type of information (such as KPIs), but in the way it displays information to serve a particular purpose. This can be expressed in a single sentence:

A dashboard is a visual display of the most important information needed to achieve one or more objectives; consolidated and arranged on a single screen so the information can be monitored at a glance.

Just as the automobile's dashboard provides all the critical information needed to operate the vehicle at a glance, a BI dashboard serves a similar purpose whether you're using it to make strategic decisions for a huge corporation, run the daily operations of a team, or perform tasks that involve no one but yourself. The means is a single-screen display; the purpose is to efficiently keep in touch with the information needed to do something.

Additional Characteristics

This is the fundamental nature of dashboards. Now let's add some supporting attributes required for dashboards to do their job effectively:

High-level summaries. The information displayed in a dashboard should consist primarily of high-level summaries, including exceptions, to communicate at a glance. It quickly tells you what's happening, but not why it's happening, just like the gauges, meters, and indicator lights on a car. Diagnosis requires further investigation and detail. A dashboard can serve as the starting point for this investigation, letting you drill down into further detail to perform an analysis, but this feature isn't required for something to be called a dashboard.

Concise, clear, and intuitive display mechanisms. Display mechanisms that clearly state their message without taking up much space are required so the entire collection of information will fit into the limited real estate of a single screen. If a graphical representation that looks like a fuel gauge, traffic signal, or thermometer is relevant and appropriate for a particular piece of information, that's what you should use. However, insisting on sexy widgets or displays similar to those found in a car when other mechanisms would work better is counterproductive.

Customized. The information on a dashboard must be tailored specifically to the requirements of a given person, group, or function; otherwise, it won't serve its purpose to help achieve specific objectives.

The need to have effective and useful dashboards has become more and more important. This importance comes from the information it has to deliver for situation analysis and decision making. The factors that determine the decision-making process are understanding and correlation of information presented.

I adapted this methodology from a very good and useful book written by Jesse James Garrett (2003).

The effectiveness of dashboard utilization heavily depends on the user's personality. The Myers-Briggs Type Indicator (MBTI), which is one of the most common psychological assessment tools, can help in the process of information design and representation. It is based on psychologist Carl Jung's theory of personality types and addresses how people set priorities, acquire information, relate to others, and make decisions. Jung claimed that people are guided by their information-gathering and decision-making preferences for problem solving. The preference for types of data is referred to as the perceiving function. Individuals have a preference to intuitive input. They are most comfortable with facts or ideas, and the problem-solving capabilities depend on their preferred viewpoints. The MBTI distinguishes between this preference for sensing (S) or intuitive (N) information gathering. Deciding what to do with the information is referred to as judging function. According to Jung, people make choices based on analysis and logic and personal subjective value. The MBTI distinguishes between those preferences as thinking (T) and feeling (F). It extends Jung's theory and goes beyond Jung to help to identify which function—perceiving (P) or judging (J)—is dominant. Taken as a whole, the MBTI identifies sixteen different personality types. There is a significant volume of research available on MBTI, and it is practical in every facet of life.[*]

How are you energized (extrovert/introvert)?
What do you pay attention to (sensing/intuition)?
How do you make decisions (thinking/feeling)?
How do you live and work (judgment/perception)?
How do you pay attention?
　Sensing (S)
　Focus on real

---

[*] Andrzej Niesler, Gracja Wydmuch, Proceedings of the International Multiconference of Engineers and Computer Scientists, IMECS 2009, Hong Kong, March 18–20, 2009, Vol. 1 (IMECS, 2009).

Five senses
Concrete/factual
Present focused
Practical
Trust experience
Detailed
Sequential
Intuition (N)
Sixth sense
Big picture
Future oriented
Imagination/insight
See patterns
Trust inspiration
Leap of faith
Novelty
How you make decisions?
Thinking (T)
Analytical
Logical
Cause and effect
Objective
Critique
Reason
Firm/fair
Tough minded
Feeling (F)
Heart
Value based
Harmony
Empathy
Compassionate
Mercy
Accepting

Table 10.1 summarizes the MBTI characteristics. Those characteristics can be divided by two dimensions: perceiving information processing and problem solving and decision making (Table 10.2).[*]

---

[*] Ibid.

Table 10.1   Characteristics of the MBTI Types

MBTI Characteristics	*Type Description*
Extraversion (E)	Dealing with situations and facts from outer world
Introversion (I)	Dealing with ideas, information, explanations
Sensing (S)	Dealing with facts, known things, information fitting with the direct here and now experience, clear and tangible data
Intuition (N)	Dealing with ideas, conceptual information
Thinking (T)	Deciding on the basis of objective logic, using analytical and detailed approach; emphasizing tasks and results to be accomplished
Feeling (F)	Respecting values and personal believes
Judging (J)	Stable and organized, focusing on completing, organizing and planning
Perception (P)	Maintaining flexibility, dealing with problems as they arise

Table 10.2

Dimensions	*MBTI Characteristics*	*Guidelines*
Perceiving and information processing	Sensing	Dealing with facts and clear tangible data; using known things; practical approach oriented on procedures; connection with real, actual situations and scenarios
	Intuition	Dealing with abstract ideas and potential problems
Problem solving and decision making	Thinking	Providing clear, concrete information and rational premises; focusing on problematic cases and expecting logical solutions
	Feeling	Providing self-contribution, amplifying positive attitude; avoidance of criticism

Dashboard Is Built from Dependent Layers[*]

The main objective in dashboard development is to make it adaptable to the user's needs. It is very important that the designed dashboards not only deliver knowledge, but aid in the decision-making process. The different dashboard users have different requirements because every person has a different perception of reality.

The Five Planes

The user experience the development process is all about ensuring that no aspect of the user's experience with your site happens without your conscious, explicit intent. This means taking into account every possibility of every action the user is likely to take and understanding the user's expectations at every step of the way through that process. It sounds like a big job, and in some ways it is. But by breaking the job of crafting user experience down into its component elements, we can better understand the problem as a whole.

That neat, tidy experience actually results from a whole set of decisions—some small, some large—about how the site looks, how it behaves, and what it allows you to do. These decisions are built upon each other, informing and influencing all aspects of the user experience. If we peel away the layers of that experience, we can begin to understand how those decisions are made.

Building from Bottom to Top

These five planes—strategy, scope, structure, skeleton, and surface—provide a conceptual framework for talking about user experience problems and the tools we use to solve them (Figure 10.1).

On each plane, the issues we must deal with become a little less abstract and a little more concrete. On the lowest plane, we are not concerned with the final shape of the site at all—we only care about how the site will fit into our strategy (while meeting the needs of our users). On the highest plane, we are only concerned with the most concrete details of the appearance of the site. Plane by plane, the decisions we have to make become a little more specific and involve finer levels of detail.

Each plane is dependent on the planes below it. So, the surface depends on the skeleton, which depends on the structure, which depends on the scope, which depends on the strategy. When the choices we make don't align with those above and below, projects often derail, deadlines are missed, and costs begin to skyrocket as the development team tries to piece together components that don't naturally fit. Even worse, when the site finally does launch, the users will hate it. This dependence means that decisions on the strategy plane will have a sort of ripple effect all the way up the chain. Conversely, the choices available to us on each plane are constrained by the decisions we make about issues on the planes below it.

---

[*] Adapted from Garrett (2003).

The Surface Plane

On the surface you see a series of Web pages, made up of images and text. Some of these images are things you can click on, performing some sort of function, such as taking you to a shopping cart. The surface describes the finished dashboard (Figure 10.2).

The Skeleton Plane

Beneath that surface is the skeleton of the site: the placement of buttons, tabs, photos, and blocks of text. The skeleton is designed to optimize the arrangement of these elements for maximum effect and efficiency—so the skeleton describes screen layout (Figure 10.3).

The Structure Plane

The skeleton is a concrete expression of the more abstract structure of the site. The skeleton might define the placement of the interface elements on our checkout page; the structure would define how users got to that page and where they could go when they were finished there. The skeleton might define the arrangement of navigational items, allowing the users to browse categories of books; the structure would define what those categories actually were. Structure defines metrics correlation (Figure 10.4).

The Scope Plane

The structure defines the way in which the various features and functions of the site fit together. Just what those features and functions are constitute the scope of the site. Some sites that sell books offer a feature that enables users to save previously used addresses so they can be used again. The question of whether that feature—or any feature—is included on a site is a question of scope (Figure 10.5).

The Strategy Plane

The scope is fundamentally determined by the strategy of the site. This strategy incorporates not only what the people running the site want to get out of it, but what the users want to get out of the site as well (Figure 10.6).

Dashboard Solutions

There are a number of dashboard solutions on the market; drawing up requirements based on analysis mind share, dashboard type, and KPIs will help narrow the list. The tolerance for analysis will drive the graphical and numeric content of a

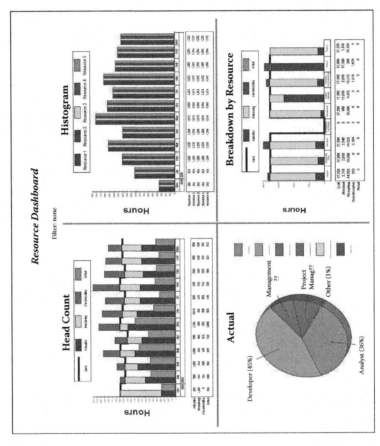

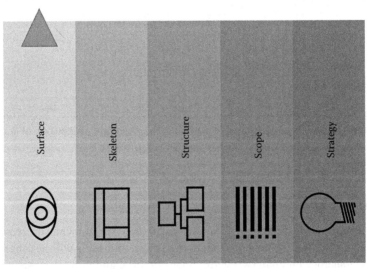

Figure 10.2 The surface describes finished dashboard.

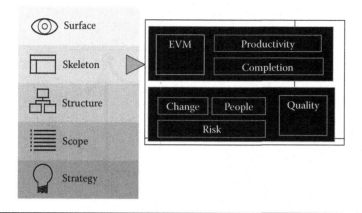

Figure 10.3   Skeleton describes the screen layout.

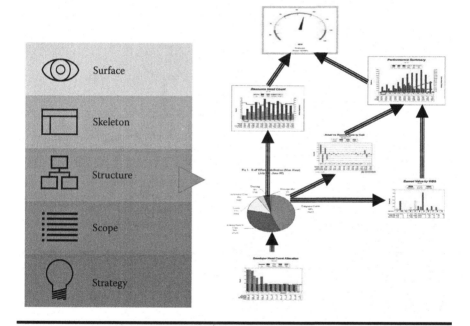

Figure 10.4   Structure defines metrics correlation.

dashboard. A clear picture of the types of dashboard your organization requires will help define where your solution lies between displaying cached results for a strategic dashboard and interactive updates for some operational dashboards. The nature of your key performance indicators will help you understand how much preaggregation is required before summary data can be displayed. This should launch you on the way with what, by definition, is a high-visibility project.

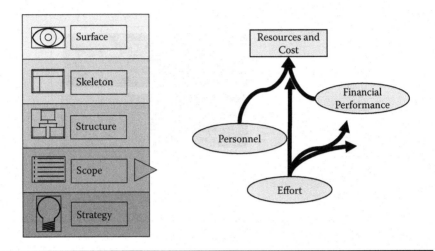

Figure 10.5   The scope plane.

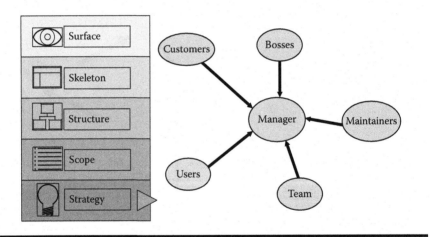

Figure 10.6   The strategy plane.

References

Annick Bourguignon, Véronique Malleret, and Hanne Nørreklit. 2001. *Balanced scorecard versus French tableau de bord: Beyond dispute, a cultural and ideological perspective.* Cedex, France: ESSEC Business School.

G. Chassang. 1989. Réinventer le contrôle de gestion, *Revue Française de Gestion Industrielle* 8,1/89, 53-63.

Dan Dubriwny and Kurt Rivards. Are you drowning in BI reports? Using analytical dashboards to cut through the clutter. http://intelligent-enterprise.informationweek.com/showArticle.jhtml;jsessionid=VZANM2TKQEEZ5QE1GHPSKH4ATMY32JVN?articleID=18300136

Stephen Few. 2004. Dashboard confusion. March 20. www.perceptualedge.com/articles/ie/ dashboard_confusion.pdf

Jesse James Garrett. 2003. *The elements of user experience: User-centered design for the web.* Indianapolis, IN: New Riders Publishing.

J.L. Malo. 1995. Les tableaux de bord comme signe d'une gestion et d'une comptabilite a la francaise. In *Mélanges en l'honneur du professeur Claude Pérochon.* Paris, France: Foucher, 357-376.

Conclusion

By implementing this framework, companies will be able to build their own defensive mechanism, which will evaluate and act (not react) on disturbing information from the outside environment. The source of the majority of organizational mistakes is decisions made based on individual response and reaction.

This is not about reacting and responding appropriately to the environmental factors. We should not react and respond to whatever outside conditions take place. We should set our own goals to determine our own course. And after that, within the context of our defined and quantified goals, we respond and react appropriately, which should further our organizational path to success.

> The situation gives rise to measurements
> Measurements give rise to estimates
> Estimates give rise to analysis
> Analysis gives rise to balancing
> Balancing gives rise to triumph
>
> **—Sun Tzu**

Conclusion

Appendix A: Business Activity Monitoring and Simulation

Joseph M. DeFee
Advanced Systems Division, CACI

Paul Harmon
Business Process Trends

Managing a Business in Real Time

Companies have always depended on processes. Historical processes may not have been as well analyzed as they are today, but there have always been business procedures designed to turn inputs into outputs in an efficient manner. Just as there have been processes that defined how materials flowed from their arrival to assembly and then to shipping, there have always been communication and control systems that attempted to monitor the process flows and deal with events that threatened to upset the expected flow.

Consider one example of how processes have historically been managed. Imagine a small hospital of thirty years ago. As today, this hospital had a customer life cycle process that managed customers from admission through treatment to discharge (Figure A.1). The first subprocess or activity was probably admissions. As patients came through the front door they were documented. The patient's medical history was determined, credit was established, and the patient was assigned to a specific ward for treatment. Over the course of time, the hospital had established expectations. In a normal week, roughly the same number of patients entered as were discharged, maintaining a predictable need for doctors, nurses, medicines, and beds.

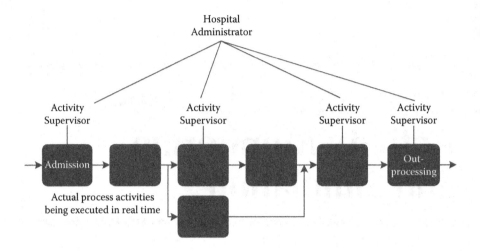

Figure A.1   A manual patient life cycle process with reports delivered by phone.

Consider what happened when a serious local infection began to manifest itself, or when a major fire or traffic accident resulted in a large number of patients all arriving at once. When a sudden, unexpectedly large number of patients arrived in the lobby, the supervisor in charge of admissions picked up the phone and called the administrator to alert her that there was a problem. The administrator would normally ask the nature of the emergency, and then consider possible actions. If the emergency was an accident, it was easier to deal with, in the sense that a few phone calls could probably determine the extent of the accident and number of patients that would be arriving at the hospital in the course of the next hour or two. Calls to other supervisors would result in still other calls to change shifts and make more doctors and nurses available. Still other phone calls would result in shifts of bed assignments to ensure that the emergency trauma ward had enough beds available. In the course of an hour or so, the hospital would adjust its activities and assign new resources to ensure that the patient life cycle process would continue to function effectively.

A harder problem would be an increase in flu patients. In this case, instead of getting a large, but known, increase in admissions over the course of a few hours, the hospital would need to deal with a number of unknowns. Admissions would begin to increase slowly, and then, as the flu spread, the increase would grow from day to day. Many variables would determine the overall course of the flu. Severity, the susceptibility of particular groups (like older people or youngsters), whether school was in session, the availability of flu shots, and many other things could limit the spread, or control the duration of hospital flu patients. Complicating matters, the flu might infect doctors and nurses, making it harder to smoothly adjust staffing schedules. Although most flu epidemics pass without serious consequences, there have been especially virulent epidemics, like the one following World War I, which killed millions of people. The alert hospital administrator has to try to plan for a variety of different scenarios, and then adjust her actions as she acquires more data on the development of the flu in the hospital's community, and in the nation as a whole.

Different industries have different kinds of problems. Most, however, have processes that are designed to run within set parameters, and those processes have communication and control systems in place to handle exceptional periods. Most exceptions are easy to understand and deal with, while some are much more challenging, involving, as they do, more complex interactions among variables over a longer period of time.

Historically, companies have relied on smart, experienced managers to gather appropriate data, interpret it correctly, and make decisions to minimize the effect of the changed circumstances on the daily functioning of company processes. As companies have become larger and processes have been disbursed over wider geographical areas, managing large business processes has become more difficult.

In the past thirty years, most companies have installed computers and used them to collect data and, in some cases, to automate processes. Thus, for example, our hospital admission office now enters new patient data via a computer terminal and can often access data from customer databases to determine a new patient's medical history and credit. Since most supervisors have access to computers, it is often possible for ward supervisors to check the admissions database to determine how many new patients will be arriving in the ward in the next hour. Similarly, it is possible for an administrator to check historical data and generate a report that describes how many patients were admitted during the flu season last year or during the last ten flu epidemics.

In essence, computers, which were originally installed to facilitate or automate the flow of patients, parts, or assemblies through a process, can also be used to facilitate monitoring and communication, and some can even support managers who have to make decisions to maintain the efficiency of a process in unusual circumstances.

During the last few decades, most companies have also become more sophisticated in their management of processes. To counteract a tendency toward departmental functions that don't communicate as efficiently as they might, most companies have designated managers who are responsible for large-scale business processes. In product-oriented companies, these managers are often called line managers. In other cases, managers are assigned to coordinate processes that cross functional lines, like our patient life cycle process. To support these managers, who are often responsible for managing processes that occur at several different locations and over long periods of time, software vendors are working to create tools that pull together all of the relevant information, highlight problems, anticipate problems, and assist in making decisions to ensure rapid successful adjustments of the process flow.

Business Activity Monitoring

In 2002, the Gartner Group coined the term *business activity monitoring* (BAM) to refer to software products that aimed at "providing real-time access to critical business performance indicators to improve the speed and effectiveness of business operations."[1] In the past year the term *BAM* has become quite popular.

Before using the term, however, it's important to emphasize that BPM is a misleading term. The emphasis should have been on business *process* monitoring. Unfortunately, Gartner already used the acronym *BPM* to refer to business process *management*, so Gartner apparently used *activity* to get a unique, new acronym. BAM has caught on, and we'll use it throughout this paper, but readers should remember that the emphasis in BAM is on pulling together information about large-scale processes, rather than on monitoring small-scale activities.

BAM and Other Decision Support Technologies

As we have already suggested, using computers to help smooth the flow of items through a process is nothing new. For many years, software designers have built triggers and alerts into software applications. Thus, for example, if admissions exceed some set number, an administrative terminal may sound an alert. One only has to think of an operator at a power plant to understand how a computer can provide the operator with a wide variety of alerts, and even provide diagnostic information to assist the operator in his or her job performance.

Similarly, marketing groups have analyzed data from sales for decades to determine shifts in customer preferences. In the past decade, many companies have invested in large data warehouses that consolidate data from many smaller databases, and business intelligence (BI) applications that use special algorithms to search massive amounts of data, looking for patterns that humans might overlook. The results of these efforts usually find their way to senior managers, who set strategy or design new products.

IT groups have also used ERP and EAI tools to analyze the flow of data between application components. The emphasis, in the case of IT, has been on fast, efficient data processing and smoothly functioning middleware, and not on drawing any broader meaning from the data. Still, it's easy to imagine how transaction data, relabeled and provided within the broader context of a business process model, could help business process managers understand how a process is working.

BAM proposes something that falls in between the immediate feedback that alert signals and triggers can provide operators and supervisors and the long-term trend reports that database reports and BI can provide senior managers (Figure A.2). BAM aims at providing a process manager with a broad overview of a major business process. As in the case of our example, it seems to provide a hospital administrator with an overview of the current status of the patient life cycle process. Or, it

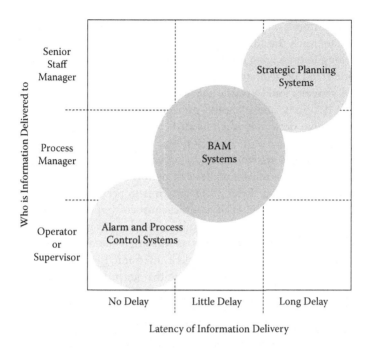

Figure A.2   One way of organizing the monitoring and decision support systems in use today.

seeks to provide a factory administrator with an overview of how an entire production line is functioning.

Figure A.2 provides one way of summarizing the range of monitoring and decision support systems in use today. Process control systems that provide information to operators and provide alerts to supervisors are mostly real-time systems that report to employees and supervisors who are very close to a specific activity. Similarly, systems that gather data, analyze them over hours, days, or weeks, and report to senior staff managers are mostly designed to aid in future planning. BAM systems are newer and less widely deployed. They aim to fill the middle ground between activity-specific and strategic planning systems by providing business process managers with near-real-time information about an entire process. Properly done, they allow the process manager to initiate changes in specific activities that keep the entire process running smoothly.

The Functions Required for an Effective BAM System

A BAM system cannot simply provide the administrator with the kinds of raw data or the signals that it provides plant operators or IT managers, or the administrator would be overwhelmed with inputs. Instead, someone must design a filtering system that draws data from a wide range of sources and then massages it so that only truly significant data reach the administrator. On the other hand, the BAM system can't spend too long in massaging the data, or it will be out of date, like the BI systems that provide trend data to strategists, and are only useful for future planning. A good BAM system should provide the administrator with enough information to enable good decisions, and it should provide the information in something close to real time so that decisions, when needed, can be taken in time to actually affect the ongoing performance of the process flow.

Any effective BAM system requires a collection of modules (Figure A.3). There are different ways the various modules can perform their functions, but all of the functions must be present if the BAM system is to perform as its strongest advocates suggest it will. The first set of modules must convert data about actual events into digital information. In most cases this can be done by simply monitoring databases and transaction events that occur as software is used to automate a process. Thus, the same data the administration clerk enters into the computer, as he signs in a new patient, can feed a monitoring system that keeps track of the rate of patients entering the hospital.

The second level or set of modules required for BAM must provide some context for the digital data being accumulated. The BAM system may depend on an explicit model of the actual business process, as illustrated in Figure A.3, or it may simply depend on a series of equations that establish relationships between data sources. One way or another, however, the system must be able to organize the data to reflect the process it is monitoring. The analysis of the relevance of the data, the generation of information about trends, and intelligent action suggestions all depend on an analysis of the process and the relationships between process elements.

Using its understanding of the process, the BAM system must apply some kind of logic to the data to identify problems, diagnose them, and recommend managerial actions. For example, the BAM system might apply a set of business rules. One rule might state that whenever patient admissions increase by more 10% of the expected rate for a given period, a signal should be set. Another rule might state that whenever a signal is set as a result of a 10% increase, the patients' ward assignments should be analyzed to determine whether the increase in patients was random, or whether there was a significant increase of patients for a particular ward. Still another rule might say that whenever patients are assigned to a given ward in excess of some historical number, the rule should post a suggestion on the administrator's BAM monitor that specific changes are to be made in the staffing of the ward. Rule-based systems can be used to accomplish a number of different tasks. For our purposes here, they simply provide an example of one way the process data can be analyzed so as to generate action recommendations.

Finally, any BAM system needs some way of presenting the information to an administrator. Most vendors speak of these monitor displays as dashboards.

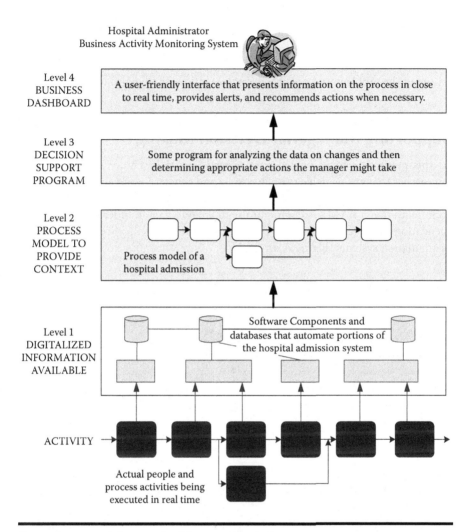

Figure A.3 Modules required for a serious BAM system.

The term is meant to reflect the fact that the displays often have dials, gauges, or other graphic devices that alert senior managers to changing conditions. Equally important, however, is a context for the information presented. If the manager is simply monitoring the admissions process, then several gauges might be adequate to let the manager know what is happening. If the manager is managing the entire customer life cycle process, however, the manager is probably going to need some general picture of the process as a whole to pinpoint the problem area. For example, admissions might be normal, but discharges might drop, creating a shortage of beds for the new patients. Or, abnormal delays in obtaining lab test results may delay procedures that result in longer patient stays. So, some kind of graphic should probably help the manager pinpoint the area of concern. Then, within each area, data ought to be summarized. Finally, if alerts are displayed, information about the nature of the problem and possible corrective actions should also be presented.

Supporting Managerial Decision Making

At this point, let's focus on what we termed level 3 in Figure A.3, the specific approaches that are available to analyze data and generate actionable recommendations to process managers. There are, in essence, three more or less independent techniques that a BAM system might use to analyze data in order to make recommendations to a manager: rule-based systems, business intelligence–based systems, or simulation systems (Figure A.4).

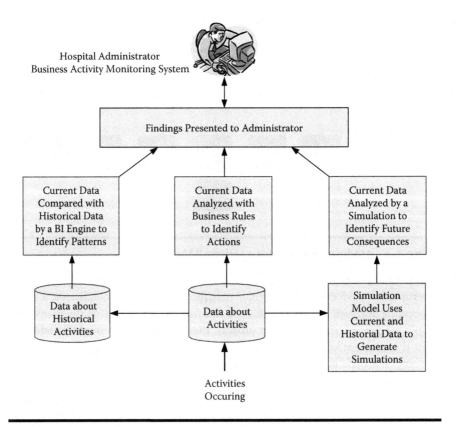

Figure A.4 Sources and nature of decision analysis.

Rule-Based Systems

The most straightforward approach, as we suggested earlier, is to use a set of rules to analyze existing data. Whenever the current data trigger a rule, it fires, either generating a recommendation or triggering still other rules that ultimately lead to a recommendation. There are different types of rule-based systems. The simplest are rule systems that are embedded in database management programs. The more complex systems rely on an inference engine that processes rules that are held in a rule repository.

BI-Based Systems

An alternative approach is to rely on historical data and business intelligence (BI) techniques. In this case, the BAM system might compare current data to historical data in an effort to identify a pattern. Such an approach might, for example, identify a slight increase in the use of certain medicines, correlate that with the season and a slight rise in admissions, and detect the onset of a flu epidemic before the doctors recognize that they are facing an epidemic. Using the same approach, the system might suggest to the administrator shifts in staffing and drug orders to bring today's activities in line with the staffing and drug order patterns that were relied upon during the last three years' epidemics.

BI is an umbrella term used to refer to a broad collection of software tools and analytic techniques that can be used to analyze large quantities of data. The data used by BI systems are usually stored in a data warehouse. A data warehouse consists of the data storage and accompanying data integration architecture designed specifically to support data analysis for BI. The data warehouse integrates operational data from various parts of the organization. Unlike operational databases, which typically only include current data, a data warehouse incorporates historical information, enabling analysis of business performance over time. Data warehousing is considered an essential, enabling component of most BI and analytic applications.

BI usually relies on pattern-matching algorithms derived from artificial intelligence (AI) research or, in some cases, on specially designed rule-based systems.

Simulation-Based Systems

Simulation systems rely on a process model and a set of assumptions about how work flows through the process. The assumptions are often based on knowledge of historical flows, but can be combined with current data. In essence, a simulation system projects future states of affairs. Thus, a trend that may be too small to attract attention today may, if unchecked, result in major problems in a few days or months. A simulation system can run repeatedly simulations with the latest data and alert managers of potential problems before they occur. It can also be used to determine how proposed changes will affect the process in the future.

Mixed Systems

In many cases, BAM products will combine various analytic techniques. Thus, simulation systems could also employ rules to facilitate certain kinds of analysis. Similarly, rule systems might also employ BI and other techniques.

Table A.1 provides a summary of some of the advantages and disadvantages associated with each analytic approach.

Obviously, there is no one best analytic technique for all situations. As a generalization, rule-based techniques are best for narrowly focused, specific analysis. BI techniques are best when there are a lot of historical data and you are reasonably sure that future situations will be like those that occurred in the past. Simulation techniques are best for more complex and changing situations.

Early Examples of BAM Offerings

Consider some early examples of vendors who are creating BAM solutions. The ERP vendors offer application modules. Their modules are designed to store information in a common database. Most integrate the flow of information between modules with a workflow system and rules. Depending on their existing technology, most have begun to create interfaces for business managers that are driven by information from the database. They have difficulty including data about applications other than their own. A good example of this approach is SAP's BAM offering.

Similarly, workflow vendors are well positioned to enter the BAM market. Workflow tools depend on an initial analysis of the flow of material and information between activities. They usually supplement their models of a process with rules to make it easy to control and alter the flow. Although most workflow systems are small in scope, some cover entire business processes, and some are capable of interacting with nonautomated processes by providing workers with tasks and recording when they indicate they have completed the tasks. For a good example of a BAM solution being offered by a workflow vendors, see SeeBeyond's BAM offering.

EAI vendors offer systems that integrate a variety of different applications. They also depend on workflow-like systems, supported by rules, to describe how various applications are related and how to manage the flow of data between applications. EAI vendors have also begun to create BAM interfaces that allow managers to see how applications are functioning. These systems usually have trouble including information about human activities that may play a role in a large-scale process. A good example of this approach is TIBCO's BAM offering.

IBM acquired Holosofx, a business process modeling vendor, and has begun to integrate this business modeling tool into its WebSphere middleware environment. Holosofx, at the moment, relies on its strength in monitoring IBM MQSeries workflow data, but it can also monitor other middleware data flows to provide a manager with a management dashboard. Expect to see a variety of BAM offerings from

Table A.1   Comparison of Analysis Methods

	Advantages	*Disadvantages*
Rule-based systems that analyze current data	• Can be provided for very specific tasks and can operate independent of other systems • Can be easily defined and tested • Are a well-understood approach	• Can become complex if the range of variables are extensive • Can become complex to test and maintain over time as the business changes • Difficult to graphically validate relationships to processes
BI systems that use historical data	• Have powerful algorithms for analyzing trends and patterns • Can pull together data from EAI and ERP systems and from best of bread applications	• Work best when used in conjunction with large amounts of data • Must create data warehouse as precondition to using BAM capabilities • Aren't designed to use a process context for reporting • Have not been designed to operate in real time
Simulation systems that project consequences	• Provide capability to model highly complex and dynamic processes • Provide better insight into the future predicted state of business, based on validated process flows • Can provide unique insight into longer-range situations • Notice gradual changes not so readily identified by other techniques • Can take advantage of both BI and rule-based approaches to provide even better simulation results at runtime	• Simulation technology is not so well understood at the user level • Development of complex simulation requires specialized knowledge • Requires an initial analysis and specification of a business process model

business process modeling tool vendors and middleware vendors. The problem with most of these approaches is that they have to be hand-tailored for each application.

In addition, a number of data warehouse/business intelligence vendors have begun to offer BAM modules. In this case, the vendors are already storing data and already have powerful BI tools to examine the data. What they usually don't have is a process model to provide context for the data, nor are they adept at providing analysis in near real time. However, most are working on BAM extensions to their suites. A good example of this approach is the Business Objects BAM offering.

Finally, a BAM solution is being developed by at least one simulation vendor, and that is the focus of this appendix. Like workflow, EAI, and business process modeling tools, simulation tools already rely on the creation of models of processes. Simulation tools are especially flexible in their modeling capabilities, since they are often used to model large-scale processes. Simulation tools normally rely on rules that incorporate statistical assumptions and on historical data to execute their models and generate data on possible future scenarios.

Most of the current products rely on rules to offer limited decision support. The two exceptions are the data warehouse/BI tools that rely on their BI algorithms to identify historic patterns and the simulation tools that can use current and historical data to run scenarios and project future states based on current trends.

Obviously, there are many combinations that are also possible. Many business modeling tools also support limited simulation, and increasingly, most of these tools can be integrated with offerings from more powerful rule-based tools, like those from Pegasystems and Fair-Issac.

There are no mature BAM tools. All of the offerings, to date, are early products that have been assembled from the features of the vendor's current product. As the market grows and matures, more comprehensive and specialized BAM offerings will appear.

Simulation

At this point, since our primary focus is on the use of simulation to support BAM, let's consider simulation in more detail. Simulation is the use of computing to mimic the behavior of a real-world system or process. Simulations are represented and executed from models that are abstractions of those real-world systems or processes. Simulation modeling is a broad topic that in its entirety is beyond the scope of this appendix. We will focus on discrete event simulation models since they are more likely to add value to business process analysis, business process management, business monitoring, and decision support. Discrete event simulation models are based on events that occur within and are acted upon in a business process. By using random occurrences of those events, the simulation can mimic the dynamic behavior of the business. There are commonly two types of implementations of discrete event simulation models:

- Probabilistic: The use of probability distribution functions to represent a stochastic process (this type of implementation is also commonly known as Monte Carlo).
- Deterministic: The events that are input into the simulation will produce the same set of results over time.

This section will focus primarily on probabilistic discrete event simulation models. These models are used to define the business work steps and, specifically, the entities that flow through the business, as well as the resources required to perform each work step. Once the process modeler has created the basic process diagram, a simulation expert must enter information about the flow of events. The timing and occurrence of the events are based on probability distribution functions, which reproduce the behavioral dynamics of a real-world business process. The developer of the simulation must choose probability functions that reflect the behavior of a given process. The process model and the information about the events are entered into a software program, which can then "execute" the simulation. By entering initial data, and executing the system, the modeler can determine future states of the process. As the simulation executes, the events are generated, the entities flow through the process, the delays are sampled, and the resources are used—all using probability distributions to produce the real-world randomness of the business process.

Consider a simulation of our hospital patient life cycle process. We have a probabilistic function that determines how many patients that enter admissions are routed to the maternity ward. This function is based on historical data. If we indicate that one hundred patients enter on Monday, our system will automatically assign a portion of them to the maternity ward. If we indicate that one thousand patients enter on Tuesday, the same formula will assign a proportionally large number to the maternity ward. As the number of patients entering the maternity ward increases, resources, ranging from beds and rooms to doctors and nurses, must be increased. By running different simulations, we can determine just what resource would run out first and develop a plan to deal with the constraint if we expect that we might one day have that number of maternity cases.

A Detailed Simulation Study

Now consider a more detailed simulation. In this case, consider what happens to patients entering the emergency room who need operations. This will illustrate how a discrete event simulation model can successfully support business process analysis. The purpose of this model is to consider the potential business impacts of opening a new emergency room facility that increases the number of treatment rooms by 50%. As with any good simulation model, the primary goals of the simulation are clearly stated:

- Examine the resource impacts (resource utilization, cost, etc.) from opening the new facility. Resources include physicians, nurses, support staff, supplies, and facilities.
- Examine the impacts to patient treatment cycle time. This particular hospital maintains an average treatment cycle time of 2.1 hours per patient. The new facility should seek to improve the cycle time at best and maintain the cycle time at worst.
- Examine the cost of specific activities in the operation (activity-based cost).

You will notice that the goals of the simulation are kept to a few key business metrics. This is one of the most important things to remember when applying simulation technology: don't try to model the whole world all at once. Models should be built incrementally or evolved to solve increasingly complex problems over time. The measurements need to have a business focus and not focus on technical problems that management is not immediately concerned with.

The model is made up of three basic ingredients: entities, activities or work steps, and resources. The primary entities in the model are the types of patients that may arrive randomly at the door of the emergency room. The model makes assumptions about the number of individuals who will show up within any given period, and what types of problems they will have. These probabilistic assumptions are based on historical data. Some types of patients arrive more often, on average, than others. Some will have higher priority than others, based on severity of the illness or injury. The work steps include the primary activities performed, ranging from triage to initial evaluation, to treatment, to outprocessing. The amount of time to perform each work step depends on the type of problem, and this, again, is based on historical data and is represented as a probabilistic function that introduces a realistic variation into each patient's treatment. For example, the amount of time to perform the triage may be a random sample from an exponential or Poisson distribution. The normal distribution would have a mean value and a standard deviation to represent, statistically, what occurs in the real world. The resources required to perform each work step are assigned and include such attributes as the number available, cost, and planned downtime. The number of each resource type may also be selected from a probability distribution in cases where a business has variations in the number of resources available. In other words, the model will consider things like employees taking leave or breakdowns in machinery.

Figure A.5 illustrates a screen shot of the emergency room process model. Notice that the model provides a concise, high-level view of the process. Each of the major subprocesses shown in Figure A.5 has been defined in more detailed process models. This is another important aspect of simulation models. Where possible, the overall model should be kept as general as possible to ensure it can be easily understood and that it will generate answers to the important business questions. Models with too much detail actually make it harder to identify and answer

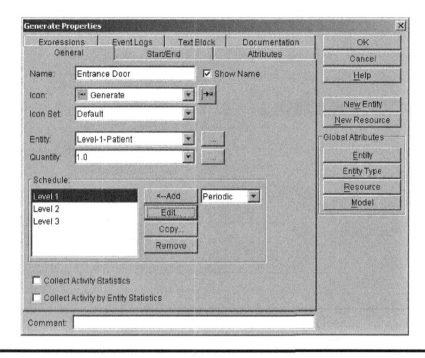

Figure A.5 SIMPROCESS screen showing top-level process flow model.

important questions. At any point in the analysis, if more granularity is needed, you can always drill down to the lower processes and model their subprocesses and activities to get the results needed. This technique allows you to have some processes modeled in detail while others are simply pass-through boxes. It lets you see the whole process at the higher levels and drill down in later spirals of analysis, if needed, without having to change the high-level model.

The patients (the key entities) in the model are categorized into three types:

■ Level 1: The most critical or severe, needing immediate attention.
■ Level 2: Critical patients needing attention but probably not in a life-threatening condition.
■ Level 3: Patients that do not need immediate attention.

The three types of patients arrive at the door at varying rates. Figures A.6 through A.8 show pop-up windows that SIMPROCESS™ presents to analysts who are entering the information needed to set up a simulation. The three windows require the entry of information about the activity that occurs at the emergency room entry door. In this case, the analyst has decided to enter three different rates to reflect the patient flow historically experienced by the hospital. Figures A.6 and A.7 focus on the arrival rates for level 1 patients.

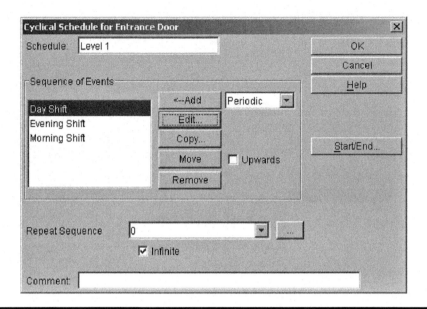

Figure A.6 SIMPROCESS screen showing entity definition.

In Figure A.6 we define the three types of patient entities that will flow through our business model. Since the patient types, levels 1, 2, and 3, arrive at the hospital at varying rates and at varying quantities over time, we must define separate interarrival schedules for them in SIMPROCESS. In Figure A.6 we have set up three schedules and named them level 1, 2, and 3, respectively, to correspond to the patient entity types. By choosing the level 1 schedule in the Figure A.6 dialog and the edit function, we can now describe the interarrival schedule for the level 1 patients, as depicted in Figure A.7.

The dialog presented in Figure A.7 allows us to create schedules within schedules. That is, the interarrival of level 1 patients varies, depending on the time of day it is. In this model, we have defined three interarrival schedules for the patients: day shift, evening shift, and morning shift. By selecting the shifts in Figure A.7 and selecting the edit function, we can define how the level 1 patients will arrive for each daily period, or shift. This concept can be extended, as necessary, to include varying the schedules for weekends, time of month, or season. This is an important and powerful capability when using simulation models since it mimics how the business really encounters patients statistically during different periods of time.

Once a shift is selected from the choices in Figure A.7, the dialog box shown in Figure A.8 is presented. This dialog box allows the user to define the types of patients (entities) that could appear during that shift. Patient quantity and rate of arrival are defined as well. Since the hospital manages by shifts and keeps its metrics by shift, it only makes sense to have the simulation model be consistent with the shift schedules.

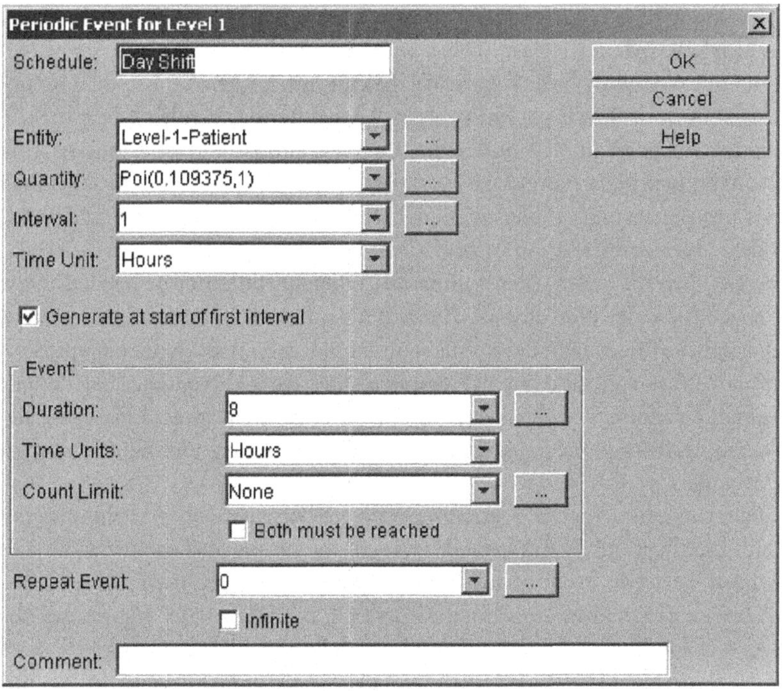

Figure A.7 SIMPROCESS screen showing entity schedules.

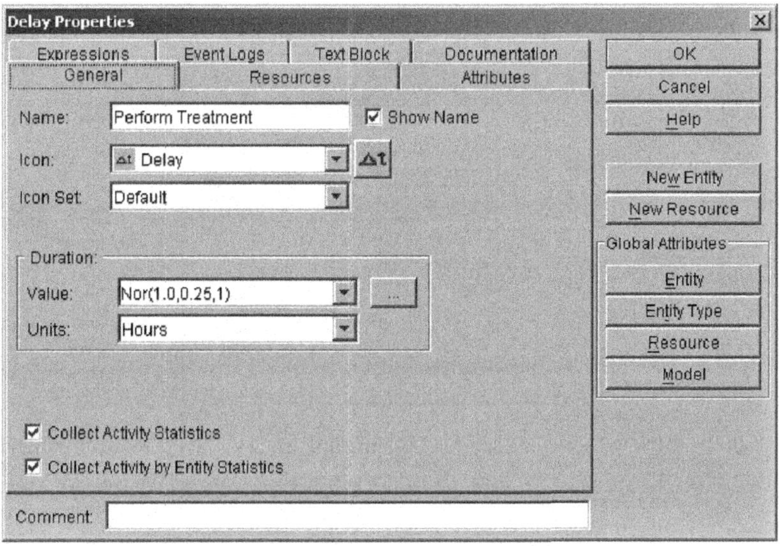

Figure A.8 SIMPROCESS screen showing patient arrival rates.

The interarrival rates for level 1 patients are 0.109375 patient on average every hour. This is based on the past history at the hospital, having an average of 111 total patients per day, with level 1 patients making up 2.775 of those on average. For the day shift, it is 0.875 patient over an 8-hour period, resulting in the 0.109375 per hour average. You will notice the use of a probability distribution function (Poisson) to provide a representative statistical curve of how the patients arrive. If we just use the average, then our model would not be probabilistic and would not provide a true representation of how things really occur. If events occurred in the real world at steady states, then simulation analysis would not be needed. However, that is not the case. Not only do the patients arrive at random, but resources fail (x-ray machine breaks), go down (person takes leave or is sick), are occupied or busy (physician takes varying times to diagnose and treat the patient), or deplete (for consumable resources, e.g., oxygen canisters) at random rates. Likewise, the time it takes to perform work steps varies and is not accurately represented by a steady-state average.

Once the entity (patient) arrival rates have been defined and the process flow diagram (see Figure A.5) has been developed, the timing and resources on the work steps must be set to account for the time delay that is required and exactly what resources are assigned or consumed to perform the work steps. Figure A.9 shows a pop-up window that an analyst could use to define the delay time and the resources required to perform one of the treatment steps (perform treatment) in this model.

In this model, we have defined the time to perform the treatment work step as a probability distribution function. We have used the normal distribution function

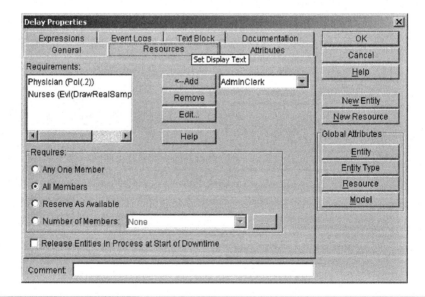

Figure A.9 SIMPROCESS screen showing activity delay time.

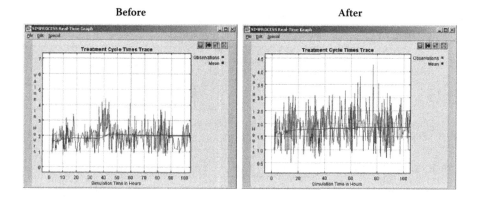

Figure A.10 SIMPROCESS screen showing required resources.

with an average of 1 hour and a standard deviation of 0.25 hour. When the simulation is run, the entities (patients) will flow through the system, and when they reach this work step, the time allotted to perform the task will be randomly sampled from the normal probability distribution function. This will create the randomness in the time it takes to do the task, just as the probability distribution function in Figure A.8 defined the interarrival rates of patients.

Figure A.10 shows the resources required to perform the actual treatment. Resources are globally defined in SIMPROCESS and can be used or assigned to any task in the process model where they may be needed. The number of resources available as well as the number required to perform a certain work step can also be randomly sampled, as described earlier using probability distribution functions.

You will notice that in this model, the number of nurses required is sampled using a probability distribution function to simulate how the real-world process works, since the same number of resources is not always the same, depending on the type of treatment. You will also notice that the physician resource is a shared resource, since physicians bounce between five or six patients on average. This model is sampling a Poisson distribution, with a mean of 20% of a physician's time, on average, being consumed by a single patient.

Additionally, resources can be required, based on different scenarios. In Figure A.10, we have specified that all the resource requirements (physicians and nurses in this case) are required at the same time to perform the work step. This means the entity (patient) will wait (this is where queuing and bottlenecks are discovered) at this work step until both resource types are available simultaneously before the task can start. In some cases, we may list substitutable resources and set the requirements to "any one member" to specify that the work step can start as soon as any one of the resource types are available to do the job. The use of the "reserve as available" option in Figure A.10 allows us to lock one of the resources needed as soon as it becomes available and wait until the others are available and lock them until all resources requirements are met.

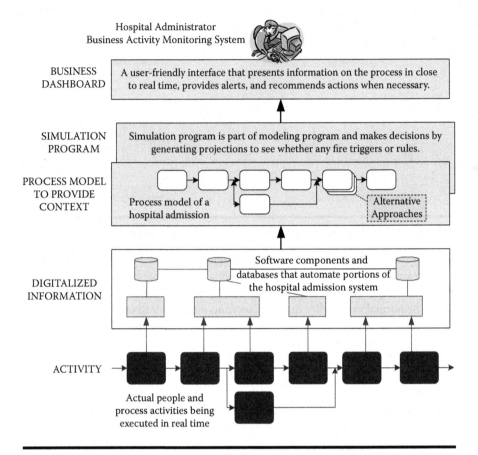

Figure A.11 Two SIMPROCESS screens showing patient treatment cycle time: before and after.

As can be seen in the use of probability distribution functions for all the key components of a SIMPROCESS model (entities, activities, and resources), we can simulate even the most complex dynamic behavior of any business process.

Recall the goals of the simulation model. We used the model to do *what if* scenarios that will be influenced by the new emergency room facility and 50% increase in treatment rooms. This model looks rather simple on the surface, but is a very powerful tool to do the *what if* analysis and determine whether the business metrics and goals can be met. Figure A.11 is a plot of the treatment cycle time (one of the most important business performance metrics), with the old facility plotted on the left and the new (50% additional rooms) plotted on the right. The plots in Figure A.11 are clipped for the first one hundred hours of simulation time.

Multiple simulations of *what if* scenarios were used to ensure the hospital could achieve its treatment cycle time business goals. For example, if the number of physicians, nurses, and lab technicians remain the same, the additional rooms will cause the treatment cycle time to go above three hours. This is due to patients getting in the rooms without enough resources to treat them, and hence waiting in the room for additional time (treatment time is counted from the time the patient gets to a room until the time he or she leaves the treatment room). The simulations quickly uncovered these types of problems and allowed the hospital to play additional *what if* games to find the right balance of resources and costs to make optimal use of the new treatment facilities and resources. The objective of all this is being able to avoid embarrassing impacts to treatment of patients (for this particular hospital, cycle time is one of its marketing nuggets), or worse, poor utilization of a new facility from an operating cost standpoint. As can be seen from the "after" plot in Figure A.11, the treatment cycle time is actually improved when adjustments are made to the physician and nurse resources. In the old facility, adding resources would not have improved treatment time since the bottleneck was the number of room resources.

Using Simulation for BAM

The "Simulation" section focused on how simulation models are used in traditional business process analysis (BPA). Models are developed and validated for an existing business process (an as-is model). Then, various changes (*what if* models) were imagined and tested, via simulation, to see if they would improve the efficiency of the process. In the simulation process, bottlenecks and specific inefficiencies were identified and eliminated.

Although this use of simulation is very common and valuable, most organizations use the simulation models developed in this manner during a limited improvement project and then set them aside as the new process is implemented.

It is possible, however, to use simulation to support BAM systems. In essence, the new process model is maintained in the simulation environment, and new simulations, using the latest data, are run periodically. Triggers or rules are used to identify problems. The current level of admissions at our hospital, for example, may be slightly higher than it was a week ago, but not high enough to trigger an alert. On the other hand, if a simulation is run using the past month's data, it may be determined that an underlying trend is present that will result in unacceptable rates of admissions in three weeks.

Data generated by the actual process would be used to run simulations. The simulation system would have alerts and rules to identify problems and suggest alternatives. In some cases, the simulation system might include alternative activities. If the system determined that the normal process would generate problems, it might try prepackaged alternative approaches to a specific activity to see whether a particular set of changes would result in an acceptable projection. This is one way in which a simulation might be able to combine alerting a manager about problems with suggested remedies.

The approach goes beyond what is available in today's simulation products. In effect, it changes the simulation from something done to test alternatives and makes it, instead, a way of dynamically determining what will happen in the future if the current state of the process is allowed to continue without change.

Obviously, this diagram greatly simplifies what is involved in using simulation for BAM. The developers need, for example, to identify the events or data items that will be monitored. Similarly, they need to insert triggers or create rules to determine when managers should be alerted. And they need to determine how frequently the simulation should be run, and how far ahead it should project. These are all decisions that will need to be made in the context of a specific company process. These decisions are not unique to the use of simulation. The same events, triggers, and information monitoring will need to be defined for any BAM solution. Simulation is merely providing an additional dimension to already useful BAM solutions.

Rule-based systems, by themselves, only look at the present for problems. BI systems use historical data to look for current patterns that might suggest problems, but can only identify problems that have already occurred before, in the past. Simulation systems can combine the best of both and add the ability to look for future states that suggest problems and then dynamically try alternative assumptions to identify changes that the manager could make today to avoid the undesired future state.

Companies that have already used simulation and have been happy with the results find the possibility of reusing their simulation investment to create powerful BAM systems exciting.

CACI, for example, has used simulation in the loop for real-time decision making for customers such as the Department of Defense (DOD). For example, DOD training systems are a good example of using simulations along with feeds from real-time operational systems to create scenarios for training purposes. The result is a hybrid tool that operates partially off validated probabilistic models along with real-world events at real time. This concept, when extended to more mainstream solutions such as BAM, opens up some interesting ways of significantly improving the benefits of BAM (especially if process modeling investments have already been made with BPA models).

A Case Study

If we consider the hospital example described above, we can get an idea of how this capability could be put to practical use. The process simulation models were already built as part of a business process improvement project and were extended to serve as a key ingredient in a simulation-based BAM solution.

Let's imagine a scenario of where this particular hospital—which has operational information systems that capture the key events in the business activities, such as patient sign-in, initial triage data, resource clock-in/out, and posttreatment data—can actually provide data to the simulation models in real time. The data feeds can be done at periodic intervals to get a "look ahead" on the impacts to patient treatment cycle time based on the current resources, patients received, expected future patient arrivals (see the "Using Simulation for BAM" section for simulation of patient arrivals based on empirical data), and the validated standard processes documented in the simulation modeling tool. Remember, the patient interarrival rates were based on probability distributions, as well as the activity delays and resource assignments. These probability distributions provided us a powerful tool to mimic real-world dynamics; however, if an unexpected peak occurs in any of the variables, the probability distribution function chosen may not have predicted a worst-case situation. These spikes may be statistically insignificant over a long period of time, but they could skew the performance of the business for several days or weeks, impacting the business goals as well as the profit and loss (P&L). When using the actual real-world data feed along with the probability distribution for future expected events, we get a hybrid model that is based on both real and simulated data. This is technically a preload of the model with current data, while the simulation will use expected events as it simulates to the future, for example, two weeks, one month, six months, etc. The result is the capability to alarm management with data to make decisions (such as call in temporary resources or change to a crisis process) based on the simulated future.

One might ask what the benefits of this would be over traditional BAM-type dashboards. The difference is that the current data and rules associated with alerting management from the traditional BAM solution may see only gradual changes in the variables of the business performance and may not have enough insight into the long-range impact to know to alert management. With the simulation-based BAM, we add another dimension to the BAM solution. We can look several weeks or months into the future and predict what impacts may be experienced in overall key business performance measurements while there is still time to affect those impacts. The hospital example we used in this section was based on the customer's very important business metric of average patient treatment cycle time. If certain run-time events drive the average up, due to unforeseen peaks, the hospital loses its ability to use its performance metric as a marketing tool. There are many other metrics that could be looked at, such as efficient resource utilization. In many cases, staffs are overworked and exhausted before management is aware of it, and exhausted staffs can create even more business performance problems, such as quality of service.

Another example situation that could arise in the hospital model is if a flu outbreak starts an upward spike of level 1 and level 2 patient types that are normally not expected. Since level 1 treatments can disrupt the primary process flow due to priority of patient care, and level 2 treatment takes longer on average to administer, the BPA model would not uncover those scenarios unless an explicit *what if* experiment were run. With the simulation-based BAM solution, the actual data affect the simulation and, in theory, "reprogram" the simulation and give a better future picture of the organizational performance.

The proposed simulation-based BAM does not have to have user intervention as in BPA simulation analysis. Once the model is built, it runs completely in the background and presents management dashboard data that are in a business metrics form. However, another consideration is to let the simulation run through multiple "fall back" or crisis process alternatives based on the real-time data, and present the user with choices that would then, in turn, be related back into BPM solutions for temporary process adjustments.

The dashboard information is described:

■ The actual real-time reporting (traditional BAM scenario) of business information includes the following graphical gadgets:
  – A meter to the left of the dashboard that depicts the running average of patients per day for the past month. The colors on the rim of the meter are used to help the manager quickly see the numbers that represent critical values (i.e., red indicates a critical situation).
  – A bar graph that depicts the total patients for the last month for each type of patient.
  – A thermometer gadget that depicts the utilization of treatment rooms. The fill in the thermometer changes colors to indicate critical values.
  – A trace plot on the far right that depicts the average treatment cycle time of all patients over the last month.
  – Two text values that depict the current levels of the most critical resources—nurses and physicians.
  – A text field to indicate the date of the dashboard information.
  – A text field that indicates the average treatment cycle time up to the last hour of reporting. This is important to see the difference from the thirty-day average and the last hour or so of activity. This field is used in conjunction with the next field.
  – A text field that is used with the previous field and indicates the average treatment cycle time for the previous twenty-four hours in this example. Obviously, this time span can be set to a wider range based on the business being monitored.

The data reported in were based on certain events occurring in real time, and as can be seen from comparing the data, the impact is minimal and probably not alarming to management based on the traditional BAM data. However, when the simulated data up through February 5 are provided, you can see the urgency of the problem as the key business metrics are affected. For example, the average treatment cycle time goes from 2.14 hours average over the last month to 2.83 hours for the last 24 hours of real-time data up through February 5. An interesting piece of information is that if you focus only on the last 24 hours in the actual data (2.09

hours average, which is less than the monthly average), you can see how not including simulated data can delay alarming management to a building problem.

The events that caused the situation to become critical are:

- Starting on January 15, the average arrival of patients increased by six per hour. This was due to a flu and cold outbreak.
- On January 30, one of the nurses became ill and had to take emergency leave for up to ten days.
- On January 31 at 4:00 p.m., one of the physicians and one additional nurse had to take emergency leave due to exhaustion and illness. Notice the number of nurse and physician resources on the dashboard have decreased from 7 and 3 to 5 and 2, respectively.
- An additional ten patients arrived on January 30 due to two separate accidents.
- An additional twenty patients arrived on January 31 at 11:00 a.m. due to multiple accidents.

Since the traditional BAM reporting does not simulate ahead to predict the queuing theory problems of the growing arrival rates and the drop in resources, as of 5:00 p.m. on January 31 the actual data are not showing any major impact to the business metrics. The simulated BAM data, however, predict significant problems growing rapidly over the next several days and risk driving the average patient treatment time significantly above the goals set by management. If the problem is allowed to spike the treatment time, it could take a couple of months of improved performance to pull the average back into line with management goals.

Simulation-based BAM solutions are achievable today. CACI's model-view-controller (MVC) architecture provides for separation of the simulation from the front-end analysis tool, therefore providing a server-based, GUI-less, and scalable capability. It provides connectors to outside applications through Java-based remote calls or XML, which are needed to feed the real-time data to the simulation tool. The example above is easily implemented with any vendor operational application with simple messaging capability.

Conclusion

Gartner suggests that BAM will become a major corporate concern in the next few years. Most large organizations will at least explore the possibility of improving business process management by creating systems that provide a broad overview of a process that can provide near-real-time information and advice to process managers. A variety of techniques will be used. Some BAM systems will, in fact, monitor subprocesses. Some will use rules to alert managers about specific real-time problems. Some will be based on simulation engines and use models that allow the system to project future events from the current state of the process and then dynamically generate alternative options to identify what changes, taken today, would maintain the process in the most efficient manner over the long term. We believe that simulation-based BAM will prove to be the most powerful and flexible approach to BAM and will increasingly be relied on by those with more complex processes.

Endnotes

1. Gartner Group, *Business activity monitoring: The Data Perspective*, February 20, 2002. For more information about SIMPROCESS, check www.simprocess.com.

The Authors

Joe DeFee is senior vice president and manager of the Advanced Systems Division Group at CACI. He has twenty-four years of information systems design, software development, enterprise architecture development, and business process reengineering experience. For the last twelve years, he has focused on business process reengineering, business process simulation technology, software reengineering, and aligning information technology to business objectives for customers. He is the coauthor of CACI's RENovate methodology, a formal methodology for modernizing customers' business processes and information technology.

Paul Harmon is the executive editor of *Business Process Trends* and the author of *Business Process Change* (Morgan Kaufmann, 2003).

Appendix B: Driving Auto Dealer to Performance against Strategic Objectives

By David Russo

> It's about management and change first, measurement and technology are second.
>
> **—Howard Rohm, Balanced Scorecard Institute**

Introduction

The dealership has experienced tremendous growth over the past nine years. This growth has been due largely to the driving personality of its owner, who installed processes, procedures, and systems, and hired and trained personnel while performing the duties of general sales manager.

Dealership growth stalled in 2003. While the revenue performance may be somewhat attributable to external economic factors, many of the problems related to process problems became more noticeable, causing the owner to rethink his strategy for getting back to growth in 2004.

In our initial conversation, Chuck was hoping for a way to articulate dealership strategy and align processes and personal goals throughout the organization toward achieving the strategy. We decided that a balanced scorecard (Robert S. Kaplan and David P. Norton, Harvard Business School, 1996) would best fit the situation to channel the energies, abilities, and specific knowledge held by people throughout the organization toward achieving long-term strategic goals.

The Proposal

This engagement will deliver the following pieces of information:

Strategy and goal setting:

1. Use industry standard methods for analyzing the business performance of each department in 2003 and forecast performance for 2004. Each department and job title will have associated performance measures (leading and lagging indicators) tied to a compensation plan to help create an atmosphere of ownership and control throughout the dealership.

2. Set strategy, targets, and goals for dealership and supporting departments. Use the strategy map technique to diagram the relationship between strategy, targets, and goals across the financial, customer, internal process, and learning perspectives.

3. Build a list of measurements and reporting methodology against the strategy map targets. The list of overall measurements won't exceed twenty-five items. The list of departmental measures will only be constrained by the necessary data to ensure compliance to targets and sufficient data to support process analysis and improvement if targets aren't being met.

4. Create marketing material to communicate strategy development to employees and customers.

Organization alignment:

5. Create organization chart, and job descriptions written against industry standards and dealership-specific roles and responsibilities.

6. Create employee handbook outlining the responsibilities of the dealership and the employees.

Process analysis and improvement:

7. Identify strategic processes and create multifunctional process flowcharts showing handoffs, inputs, outputs, and constraints across all the high-level processes.

8. Isolate the lever points in each process, and analyze the influencing factors on them as either people, process, or system.

9. Where the lever point can be controlled systematically, configure the system to minimize variations, and make sure variances would show up on actionable reports.

10. Where the lever point can be controlled by process, communicate the update to the entire dealership, and effect the change as quickly as possible. Train people to enforce the processes that drive efficiencies throughout their department and the dealership.

11. Where the lever point is controlled by people's actions, evaluate their operating environment and training, and then evaluate their compensation plans to ensure we reward the correct behavior. Communicate any changes in the compensation plans to the entire dealership to show how

compensation is applied to drive maximum efficiencies, customer satisfaction, and dealership profitability.

This engagement will also help each employee and group at Nissan of Keene meet the requirements to build the above list of documents, analysis, reports, and overall capabilities to manage the dealership.

The engagement is targeted for twelve weeks, but will be extended until the owner is satisfied his team is executing the full requirements of the balanced scorecard initiative.

Documentation to Be Developed

1. Policy manuals: Policy manuals are documents that state the goals of the system. These manuals clarify and simplify operational tasks. They indicate priorities and the hierarchy of decisions. Policy manuals state policies and guidelines that direct action, not step-by-step detailed procedures on how to carry out a given task. They enable managers, supervisors, and others to direct subordinates in a manner consistent with company policy.

2. Procedure manuals: Procedure manuals are documents that spell out in detail the steps involved in carrying out a given routine or action. They establish the daily procedures of the company by defining how each task is to be done, always in accordance with stated company policy. The procedure manual defines each specific step in handling such things as payroll, credits and collections, and returns of merchandise. Procedure manuals should be organized by department. The procedures related to the operations of a given department are gathered together in a single manual and placed in that department for easy reference by personnel.

3. Forms manual: Forms manuals are collections of all the business forms used in a system. They specify the layout, size, type of stock, and other relevant details for each form, and list the source of supply, order points, and storage information. They may include details on how to complete or fill out each form, and information for handling and routing. The manual should also specify the procedures to follow if modifications or revisions become necessary. Assembling all forms into a single manual facilitates the development of a comprehensive forms program. This ensures the consistent appearance, quality, and utility of the forms used within a system, reduces costs, and builds a better corporate image.

4. Data dictionary: A data dictionary is prepared for database management system software. It specifies the form, style, and content of the records in the database so that all entries will conform to a uniform standard. This greatly expands the utility of the database.

Dilership: The Way It's Meant to Be—Progress

Week 1: Create strategy map, organization chart, and high-level process chart showing "how work gets done." Start detailed flowcharts for key processes.

Week 2: Draft job descriptions against the organization chart, create/update employee handbook, and complete more detailed process flowcharts. Create Nissan of Keene profile presentation to communicate strategy to customer and employees.

Week 3: Compile measures of success template against strategy map for each department (sales, service, parts, and accounting), keeping the overall list of measures to twenty-five key items. We began an internal control audit to review cash transaction processes and valuable inventory access controls. Complete second draft of job descriptions and circulate to managers and key employees for input.

Week 4: Create draft measurement system plan, covering resources, systems, and people. Set 2004 business plan with targets on strategy map. Cascade targets to each department and create first-run reports against the plan.

Week 5: Create 2004 plan for service/parts using 2003 performance and Nissan standards for efficient operation and maximum customer satisfaction.

Week 6: Investigate parts process for handling internal part requests. The found process was being circumvented whereby the parts counterperson handling requests for items not requiring labor, instead of creating a nonlabor repair order, would create a parts invoice and put the transaction against policy accounts. This creates manual work for accounting and falsely improves the margin of a car sale when the parts aren't accounted against the deal before the accounting is finalized. Corrective action: Reinforced the process, updated system pricing on external parts sourcing (NAPA, local auto parts stores, other dealers) to be (fixed COST + xx), and updated the employee discount formula to comply with New Hampshire state law to be within the range of discount available to customers.

Week 7: More changes in ADP service department setup: technician schedules, shop schedules, technician deletions. We finalized the 2004 sales and parts and service business plan. Created measurement report of new and used vehicle sales and adjusted 2004 sales targets based on seasonality of 2003.

Week 8: We created the *Information Security Policy and Procedure Manual*, including updates to the employee handbook. Completed 2004 targets for each area, and defined reporting procedure.

Week 9: We conducted a competitive pricing study for reconditioning service offers and adjusted prices accordingly. Chief competitor is Buff-n-Shine in Keene, New Hampshire, the reconditioning department for the local Chrysler dealership. We also created a reconditioning service menu as a sales aid to the service advisors and to be left in the customer waiting area for additional selling opportunity.

Week 10: Generated the first report on the overall targets and reviewed with each department and job title. ADP consultant visited us and we worked with accounting, service, and parts. In accounting, we reviewed the process for using the forecasting feature so reports can show progress against targets and possibly help with trending analysis. In service, we created service menus that will drive recommended service detail to the service advisors when they are making appointments, and the detail would also be printed on service reminders mailed to customers. The service menu feature is meant to be a sales aid promoting the value of our service work. In the process of creating service menus, we edited the list of op codes in the systems, simplifying the SA job and improving price controls. In parts, we established a no-return policy for nonreturnable (J code) items less than $5.00 in cost and added a line stating the policy to print with the item description on invoices containing these items.

Week 11: The accounting office prepared the scorecard packages prior to the management meeting. The owner was happy for the one-page summary of operations, and department managers were quick to spot deficiencies in their areas. Two trouble areas were the age of warranty work not submitted and used car aging. The first creates larger accounts receivables with Nissan and, once aged a certain amount, can no longer be collected. The service manager made these submittals a priority, moved their work to the service advisors, and dedicated himself to making all submittals before the end of the week. Second, the aging of used car inventory creates inefficiencies on capital employed by the business. Sales managers need to make decisions more quickly on turning over trade-in vehicles, only keeping the ones likely to create deals meeting the targets and clearing out via auction or dealer-to-dealer transactions those vehicles that will not meet targets for the business.

Week 12: The managers ran the management meeting in the crisp fashion the owner was hoping for, and while there are still problem areas, they are more visible to everyone, and there is agreement that each area is working on the priority issues that benefit the entire organization.

Table B.1 2004 Targets (Overall)

Strategic Objectives	Strategic Measures			Strategic Measures		
	Core Outcomes (Lagging)	2004 Targets		Performance Drivers (Leading)	2004 Targets	
Financial				**Revenue mix**		
	Revenue	$20,761,262				
F1—Improve revenue	Revenue vs. plan	%		New	$12,448,044	
F2—Broaden revenue mix	Profit margin	15.00%		Used	$5,676,048	
F3—Reduce cost structure	Inventory (time on hand 30/60/90)	45–60 days new		F&I	$552,900	
	Total expenses as % of total gross profit	30–45 days used		Service labor	$996,968	
		78–84%		Service parts	$887,302	
				Parts	$200,000	
				Average profit/vehicle (new:Nissan CSI scores)	$1,715:$2,600	
Customer Perspective						
C1—Increase customer satisfaction with our people and products	Share of segments by vehicle (Polk)	Better than district and region			Better than district and region averages	

C2—Increase customer satisfaction after the sale	Market share—Nissan report	Better than district and region averages	Service department customer satisfaction via follow-up calls	
Internal Processes				
	New product acceptance rate	Best in district and region	No. customers interacted (Opps)	3,110/year
I1—Understand our customers	F&I (PVR)	$600/vehicle	No. customers to demo drive	80% (of customers who come in)
I2—Cross-sell products	Close ratio per salesman	30%	No. service walkthroughs	100% (of customers who demo drive)
I3—Minimize operational problems	Labor hours/repair order	2.0 customer pays	Vehicle delivery checklists:	100%
		~1.0 warranty	New and used	
		<3.0 internal		
I4—Deliver responsive service	Effective labor rate	$50.00	Comebacks—serviced right the first time	<5% of total customer pay and warranty repair order
	No. repair orders written	15/service	Turnover to F&I business	100%
	Parts revenue/repair order	$0.89:$1.00 of labor revenue		

(continued on next page)

Table B.1 (continued)   2004 Targets (Overall)

Strategic Objectives	Strategic Measures		Strategic Measures	
	Core Outcomes (Lagging)	2004 Targets	Performance Drivers (Leading)	2004 Targets
Learning				
L1—Develop strategic skills	Total gross per employee	$6,852	Strategic job coverage ratio	100%
L2—Provide strategic information	Average sales per salesman	186 units/year	Strategic information availability ratio	>90%
L3—Align personal goals	Employee satisfaction			

Table B.2 2004 Targets (Sales)

Strategic Objectives	Strategic Measures		Strategic Measures	
	Core Outcomes (Lagging)	2004 Targets	Performance Drivers (Leading)	2004 Targets
Financial			**Revenue mix**	
	Revenue	$18,676,992		
F1 — Improve revenue	Revenue vs. plan	%	New	$12,448,044
F2 — Broaden revenue mix	Inventory (time on hand 30/60/90)	30:54 days (new:used)	Used	$5,676,048
F3 — Reduce cost structure	Cost vs. plan	$	F&I	$552,900
			New — PVR	$500
			Used — PVR	$700
			Average profit/vehicle (new)	$1,517:$2,000

(continued on next page)

Table B.2 (continued) 2004 Targets (Sales)

Strategic Objectives	Strategic Measures		Strategic Measures	
	Core Outcomes (Lagging)	2004 Targets	Performance Drivers (Leading)	2004 Targets
Customer Perspective				
C1—Increase customer satisfaction with our people and products	Share of segments by vehicle (Polk)	Better than district and region averages	Nissan CSI scores—questions 1–3, 6–13	100%
C2—Increase customer satisfaction after the sale	Market share—Nissan report	Better than district and region averages	Nissan CSI scores—overall	Better than district and region averages
Internal Processes				
I1—Understand our customers	New product acceptance rate	Best in region	No. customers interacted (Opps)	3,110/year
I2—Cross-sell products	F&I (PVR)	$600/vehicle	No. customers to demo drive	80% (of customers who come in)

			No. service walkthrough	100% (of customers who demo drive)
I3 – Minimize operational problems	Close ratio per salesman	30%		
I4 – Deliver responsive service	% repeat customers	>75%	Vehicle delivery checklists: new and used	100%
			Accessories upsale $ (as part of vehicle gross $)	$200/vehicle
			Turnover to F&I business	100%
Learning				
L1 – Develop strategic skills	Revenue per employee		Strategic job coverage ratio	100%
L2 – Provide strategic information	Average sales per salesman	86 new		
100 used	Strategic information availability ratio	>90%		
L3 – Align personal goals	Employee satisfaction			

Table B.3 2004 Targets (Service)

| | Strategic Measures | | Strategic Measures | |
Strategic Objectives	Core Outcomes (Lagging)	2004 Targets	Performance Drivers (Leading)	2004 Targets
Financial			**Revenue mix**	
F1 – Improve revenue	Profit margin	15.00%	Service labor	$996,968
F2 – Broaden revenue mix			Service parts	
F3 – Reduce cost structure			Parts, wholesale	$887,302
			Revenue per repair order	$200,000
Customer Perspective				
C1 – Increase customer satisfaction with our people and products	Service referrals to sales	Count of referred vehicles to sales where vehicle is >5 years old and repair value >$1,000	Nissan Satisfaction Index (NSI) scores	>90%
C2 – Increase customer satisfaction after the sale				

Internal Processes

I1 – Understand our customer	ADP service advisor productivity report	No. repair orders/day ≥15 Op codes/repair order >2	Labor hours/repair order	2.0 customer pays ~1.0 Warranty <3.0 Internal
I2 – Cross-sell products	ADP service technician	Efficiency ≥115% Productivity ≥90%	Special order parts turnaround	<2 weeks from receipt to customer appt.
I3 – Minimize operational problems	Effective labor rate	$50.00	Comebacks—repairs/diagnosed right the first time	<1%
			Repair order mix	Customer pays: 60% Warranty: 20% Internal: 20%
I4 – Deliver responsive service			Vehicle delivery checklists (new:used:reconditioning)	100%

Learning

L1 – Develop strategic skills	Revenue per employee		Strategic job coverage ratio	100%
L2 – Provide strategic information	Employee satisfaction		Strategic information availability ratio	>90%
L3 – Align personal goals				

Table B.4 2004 Targets (Parts)

Strategic Objectives	Strategic Measures		Strategic Measures	
	Core Outcomes (Lagging)	2004 Targets	Performance Drivers (Leading)	2004 Targets
Financial			**Revenue mix**	
F1 — Improve revenue	Profit margin	>65%	Service parts	$12,488,044
F2 — Broaden revenue mix			Parts	$5,676,048
F3 — Reduce cost structure				
Customer Perspective				
C1 — Increase customer satisfaction with our people and products	Service referrals to sales		NSI scores	>90%
C2 — Increase customer satisfaction after the sale			Lost sales	<10%

Internal Processes

I1 – Understand our customer	Parts revenue/repair order	$0.89:$1.00 of labor revenue	Parts order efficiency (stock vs. order)	>90%
I2 – Cross-sell products	Inventory turns, gross	6–8/year	Parts credits > returns	Credits > returns
I3 – Minimize operational problems	Inventory turns, true	3–5/year	Special order parts shelf life	<2 weeks from receipt of item to wholesale customer delivery
I4 – Deliver responsive service	Parts inventory $	2.5 months worth based on average month cost of parts sales	Obsolete inventory	<10% ($ of total on-hand inventory)

Learning

L1 – Develop strategic skills	Revenue per employee		Strategic job coverage ratio	100%
L2 – Provide strategic information	Employee satisfaction		Strategic information availability ratio	>90%
L3 – Align personal goals				

Table B.5 2004 Targets (Service)

Strategic Objectives	Strategic Measures		Strategic Measures	
	Core Outcomes *(Lagging)*	*2004 Targets*	Performance Drivers *(Leading)*	*2004 Targets*
Financial				
F1—Improve revenue	Increase AP cycle time and discounts	100%	Internal controls audit plan	100% implemented
F2—Broaden revenue mix	Increase AR cycle time	100%	Actual cash flow vs. plan	100%
F3—Reduce cost structure	Cost vs. plan	100%	Contracts and vehicles receivables	≤3 days vehicles sales
	Cash and equivalent	= 1 month average expense	Accounts receivable – parts and service	<50% of monthly parts and service sales (excluding warranty, prep, internals)
			Finance receivables	<Current month F&I
			Warranty receivables	<110% of Nissan turnaround time

Customer Perspective

C1 – Increase customer satisfaction with our people and products	Nissan CSI scores		
		Decrease time for customer pays processes	
C2 – Increase customer satisfaction after the sale		Process financing institution supporting documents after vehicle delivery	<3 business days
		Process contracts to financing institution after receiving deal jackets	<2 business days

Internal Processes

I1 – Understand our customer	Close the books in a timely fashion	Month – by the 3rd Quarter – by the 5th Year – by the 10th	
		Prompt notification to dealership of Nissan delivery schedule	<8 business hours
I2 – Cross-sell products	Improve data integrity of form and in	Timely report generation for dealership	<8 business hours
I3 – Minimize operational problems			
I4 – Deliver responsive service			

(continued on next page)

Table B.5 (continued) 2004 Targets (Service)

Strategic Objectives	Strategic Measures		Strategic Measures	
	Core Outcomes *(Lagging)*	2004 Targets	Performance Drivers *(Leading)*	2004 Targets
Learning				
L1—Develop strategic skills	Revenue per employee		Strategic job coverage ratio	100%
L2—Provide strategic information	Employee satisfaction		Strategic information availability ratio	>90%
L3—Align personal goals			Personal goal alignment with job	>90%
			ADP updates: training and installation	Within 30 days of update notice

Appendix C: Development and Implementation of Human Capital Measures and Dashboards: Lessons Learned

The below reflect lessons learned by a program manager of business and technology solutions development at a large financial institution in the Northeast.

- Sponsorship
  - Creating a dashboard is a significant investment of time and money, and sponsorship should be clearly identified and committed to this endeavor.
  - If sponsorship is not clear and this project is in conflict with other priorities in the company, it should be postponed until full and consistent support can be ensured.
  - The opportunity to lose time and momentum with vendors and departmental involvement is high when sponsorship is not clearly voiced and the project prioritized.
- Project planning
  - Gather time commitments and support from the decision-making individuals well ahead of project initiation.

- Consider timing of the project in light of commitments from IT, budgeting, cyclical company commitments, etc. They all have a significant bearing on resources that you may need for your project.
◼ ROI—rationale
  - Focus the dashboard on measures that are directly related to company goals or solving a current and real (not perceived) business problem or process. This should be narrowed to two to four.
  - This should be decided upon from by C-level management and should not be ambiguous or left to the discretion of project participants and middle management to debate over.
  - Our development of thirteen corporate goals by a large committee was both painful and long. Gathering consensus was difficult, and in the end, we did not receive the full support of upper management as we had hoped and had to go back to the drawing board.
  - This should not be a guess and check game. The goals have to be absolutely clear to the working project team.
  - Identify your audience early and precisely. Who will use these measures and reports? Do they have authority to affect change? Do they have decision-making authority? Are these measures strategic or operational in nature? Who will be making the strategic and operational decisions based on these data?
  - Tie the goals to ROI. Tie the measures to the goals. If there is no direct tie, reconsider the measures.
◼ Validity
  - Validate the measures and reports with the end users.
  - Validate the measures for statistical significance. If there are not enough data to be statistically significant, don't use these data in the measure.
  - Validate the measure against the reality of data being used to make this decision versus professional training, management experience, intuition, relationships, or other influences. If the decision is important, but not one based on data, don't put it on the dashboard. For example, a decision on who should be promoted within a department will most likely not be data driven, but driven by personal observation of performance by the manager.
◼ Don't boil the ocean—managing volume
  - Too much information and too many measures do not make it either indicative or decision influencing. The risk of the project growing out of control and loss of focus is very high.
  - As drivers to the decisions are identified and measures relating to the drivers are developed, try to maintain focus. Try to narrow the measure to the most meaningful eight to ten.
  - Try to eliminate measures that indicate information that can't be acted upon. They may be relevant in retrospect and in understanding past performance, but if they do not define and help plan for the future, they

should be left for other types of reporting. If the measure does not guide in a decision, it should not be on the dashboard.

■ Creating input/brainstorming sessions
  - Be careful what you ask for and who you ask.
  - Understand the relationship and priorities of your input members.
  - Gather input from strategic leaders and decision makers that will be utilizing the dashboards. These activities are often delegated to departmental representatives, and in an effort to be inclusive and consensus driven, the input becomes overwhelming and difficult to manage.
  - Having to reject a solicited idea or 380 of them is difficult and can be avoided if input is asked in a pointed and direct way. No one feels good when his or her idea doesn't make the cut.
  - Attempt to keep this team very small. The more people in the mix, the more difficult it is to manage input and build consensus. A committee of sixteen people is ten people too big.
  - Choose people on this committee that are data oriented, decision makers, and have influencing skills. They should act as participants, validators, and liaisons to the rest of the company.
  - Focus these sessions to minimize negative, conflicting, or nonconstructive input.

■ Maturity of the organization
  - If there are organizational issues to resolve, pending restructurings or department consolidations that are planned, they should be resolved before project initiation. Otherwise, opposition will mount quickly to the dashboard, as it will be perceived as a vehicle to validate downsizing, etc.

■ Selecting measures
  - Take particular care to separate routine reporting functions and dashboard reporting.
  - The dashboard should not have every conceivable reporting vehicle within it.
  - Routine reporting should be a separate function or project.
  - Develop measures answer the question of why and how and not just what.
  - Consider correlation measures of previously unconnected factors. Correlation and modeling of two or three factors can often reveal hidden and valuable information.
  - Consider a projection feature for the dashboard report to be included.

■ Governance
  - Data
  - Process
  - Policy
  - Security

- – Change management
- – Consider the processes that will be affected by the new dashboard. Is the department that is responsible for its maintenance on board?
- ■ Managing opposition
  - – Identify risk areas, managers, and departments early in the process and develop a plan to mitigate these risks through the support of management and incentives to comply.
  - – Utilize the change management function to assist in buy-in and communication with these high-risk individuals.
- ■ Customization
  - – Customization is time-consuming and expensive. Buy a tool that allows customization instead of building a tool in-house.
  - – Minimize customization when possible by choosing the correct (best) measures that will be valid now and in the future.
- ■ Analyze by criteria
  - – The opportunity to view data in many different ways is enticing, but often not meaningful.
  - – Focus the criteria as narrowly as possible. In our case, the data could be seen in eighteen different ways, but when we focused the data to three different ways, the information became more clear and manageable. The first cut was by departmental level, the second was compared to competition (other departments, industry standards, external validation sources), and the third was over time.
- ■ Hierarchical information
  - – This is an important feature to consider when creating these reports. Will the decision be made on a department or organizational level? Will you need the data by department, location, profitability, etc?
- ■ Visualization
  - – If the data are not clear and attractive, the dashboard will not be used. Invest the time and money in getting a visualization expert to make all your efforts come alive on the screen.
  - – When it is all done, this will be the face of all your efforts.
- ■ Data dictionary
  - – Data dictionary and data mapping, especially in environments with many different data tracking systems, become increasingly complex. Plan for this to be a significant effort in time and resources.
- ■ Routine and self-service reporting
  - – This often comes up when dashboards are discussed and it is valid. The overall routine reporting should be made as flexible and available as possible, but should be treated as a separate project.
  - – Meaningful measures can be attached to these routine or customized reports that go to address efficiency, process, profitability, or operations of a particular function, but should not be the corporate dashboard measures.

- Roles
  - Identify the roles of the participants as clearly as possible at the onset of the project.
    - Project management, SME, validation group, statistical input, IT support, vendor participation, approval committee, governance, appeal/overriding protocols.
    - Allocation of resources: Analysis, communication, and consensus building will take the majority of time on your project. Select the correct resources for these functions. Failure to assign these critical tasks to the appropriate person will result in loss of time and credibility.
- Limiting population
  - Clean the data before you use them. Make sure the definitions from different sources are consistent. If one department is treated or tracked significantly different than the rest of the organization, consider making it the exception and not including it in the dashboards. Otherwise, the process of changing its reporting structure becomes a major subproject.
- Data security
  - This is a subject area that can become sensitive quickly. Role-based data access can be a solid way to differentiate rights and need-to-know debates.
  - Restricted populations need to be reviewed with the compliance and senior management early in the process to make sure that there is no breach of confidential information during and after the project.
  - Identify restricted data and populations that should not be used in the dashboard reports before embarking on measures development and protect the access to these data from the project team.
- Validation sessions
  - Conduct validation sessions both visualization perspective, measures perspective, and hierarchical perspectives.
  - Have the sessions model a potential decision that needs to be made and utilize the dashboard reports to assist in the decision. If the measures are not helpful to the decision that is linked to the company goal, rethink the measure.
- Don't build if you can buy
  - There are many vendors in the marketplace that have dashboard tools that can be utilized with a limited amount of customization. This is the optimal solution.
  - If you choose to build your own, the IT development and configuration time and costs are high and may not be the company's core strength. So, assume the development time to be tripled from that of a canned solution.
  - Consider this factor, because it will determine the course of the project in a fundamental way.

Appendix D: Clinical Trial Process Specification

I. **Document purpose:** The purpose of this document is to provide an overview of background and objectives of a small organization that sponsors clinical trial research. It specifies the details of the current process, starting from the phase of the study design through the data collection, and then closing out with a phase based on the analysis and conclusion. The organization goals and strategies follow. The document also proposes a solution for future processes that would be essentially applied to the software engineering framework to automate the system that would improve the process efficiency.

II. **Business overview:** A clinical trial is a process that has been conducted to allow collecting data on humans within a period of time. A clinical trial only happens when satisfactory information has been gathered for new drugs or experimental treatments, and also, it must be approved by health authority/ethics committee where the clinical trial is taking place.

Investigators (or the contract research organization [CRO]) invest their time in medical study cases in laboratories and perform tests on animals. If the test results are promising, then they proceed with a clinical trial. There are many types of clinical trials, for example, prevention trials, screening trials, diagnostic trials, etc. They all follow the same procedure:

1. Study design
2. Patient recruitment
3. Patient enrollment
4. Study conducted
5. Quality control
6. Reporting
7. Close out

III. **Current process model:** See Figure D.1.

IV. **Clinical trial logical mode:** See Figure D.2.

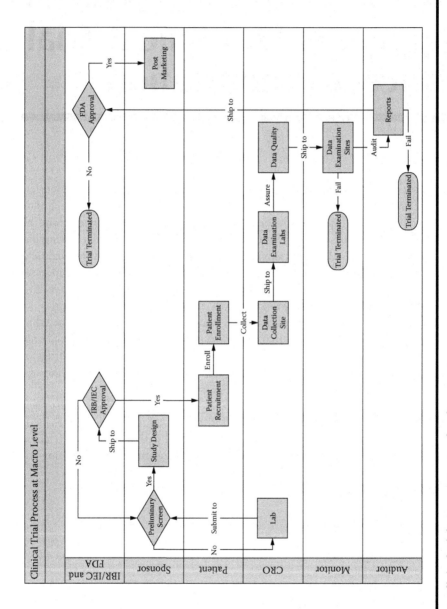

Figure D.1 Clinical trial process (macro level).

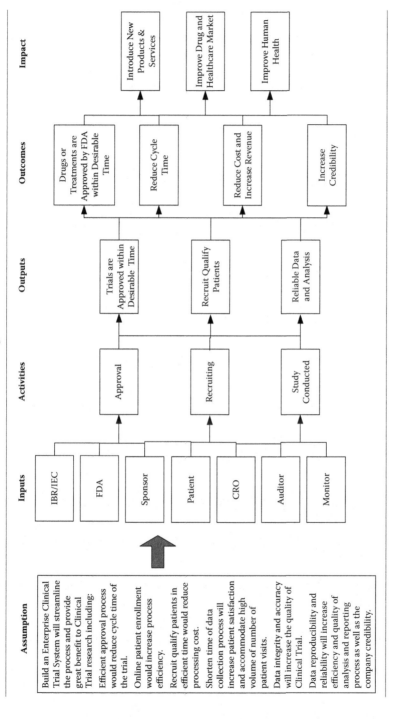

Figure D.2 Clinical trial logical model.

V. **Current process:** This document focuses on a small organization that sponsors clinical trials. It operates their business activities using a paper-based process. First, the paper forms are filled out and manually submitted to the institutional review board/independent ethics committee (IRB/IEC) for approval. Second, the sponsor works with multiple media for the patient recruiting process, where patients need to fill out a paper form and submit it at the research site. Third, data are collected from patients and stored in a data shadow system that operates in MS Office (Excel, Access, etc.). Data are manually collected and manipulated by business users.

VI. **Problem statement:** The current operation has a cumbersome process for approval and patient enrollment. It also creates a high risk of data that will lead to a wrong decision and conclusion for the clinical trial research. Here are the following issues regarding the inefficiency of processes:

1. Long time waiting for approval
2. Paper lost in patient enrollment process
3. Lack of data integrity
4. Lack of data security
5. Data are not compliant
6. Lack of data accuracy
7. Data inconsistent throughout the company
8. Difficulty of generating reports
9. Lack of data reproducibility

These problems have a major impact on the clinical trial process for this company as well as across the medical industry. First, they increase the cycle time of the clinical trial process because the company spends most of its time waiting for the documents to be approved. Second, the new drugs and new treatments are not fully tested and studied with accurate data, which may create side effects in humans. Consequently, many products have been recalled from the market after being used for several years, and lead into accountability issues for researchers, as well as affecting the company's reputation and credibility. Figure D.3 illustrates the process of problem analysis using the Fishbone model.

VII. **Root cause analysis:** Fishbone model.

VIII. **Objective statement:** Build an enterprise clinical trial system that will streamline the process, including reduce the cycle time, eliminate unnecessary cost, and ensure data quality and accurate analysis of the trial. It starts from the study design phase to patient's enrollment, data collection, reports and analysis, and then close out. The entire process should be automated, where all parties involved in the process could have access to the same system. The trial approval forms could be filled out, submitted, and approved electronically. Patients should be able to enroll online, and data should be easily

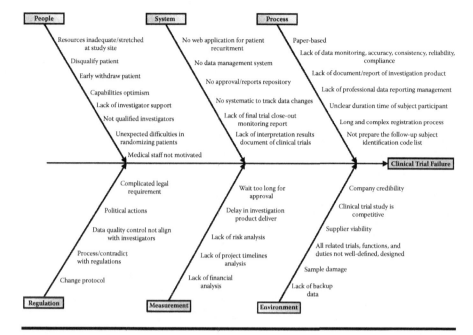

Figure D.3 Fishbone diagram.

collected and stored in a data management system. Data should be accurate, consistent, fully compliant, and reproducible.

IX. **Mission statement:** The mission of the clinical trial is to invent new drugs or new treatments to cure human or any other subjects. The clinical trial process must operate under government regulations to protect human subject safety and the integrity of the clinical trial.

X. **Critical success factors:** There are seven phases of the clinical trial. In order to be successful, each phase of the trial holds its own critical success factors in the following:

1. Study design: A planning stage where a number of tasks need to be completed, and information needs to be set up in the system for the automation process. Most important, the study needs to be approved by IRB/IEC before the trial can be started.

   a. Implement clinical trial approval functionalities in the system.

   b. Collaboratively work with IRB/IEC and investigators.

   c. Select qualified investigators/institution and obtain a list of names and addresses of investigators/institution in the system.

   d. Define, establish, and allocate all trial-related duties and functions.

   e. Define the financial aspect of the trial.

    f. Sign a financial agreement between the sponsor and investigator/institution.

    g. Define the insurance statement.

    h. Define the study statement.

    i. Define the type of trial: double-blind or placebo controlled.

    j. Define the duration time of the trial period.

    k. Define the measure method: randomization or binding.

    l. Identify data to be recorded.

    m. Get approval from the IRB/IEC.

2. Patient recruitment:

    a. Work with media.

    b. Specify payment method.

    c. Address cost of treatment of trial subjects related to injuries.

3. Patient enrollment:

    a. Implement patient-enrolled functionalities in the system.

    b. Define the duration time of subject participation.

    c. Provide a quick, easy, and online registration process.

4. Study conducted:

    a. Implement data management functionalities in the system to ensure data accuracy, reliability, consistency, and full compliance.

    b. Appoint an appropriate qualified individual to oversee conduct of trial, including handling, verifying, analyzing data, and preparing report.

    c. Establish independent data monitoring committee (IDMC) to access the process of a clinical trial.

    d. Document operating procedures and maintain written records of all IDMC meetings.

    e. Determine acceptable storage temperatures, conditions, times, etc., for collected samples.

    f. Determine package procedure to prevent contamination and unacceptable deterioration during transport and storage.

    g. Obtain documentation and dates of IRB/IEC reapprovals/reevaluations with favorable opinion, and any withdrawals or suspension of approval/favorable opinion.

    h. Ensure timely delivery of investigational products to the investigator.

    i. Maintain records of shipment, receipt, disposition, return, and destruction of investigation product.

    j. Maintain system for retrieving investigational products and documenting this retrieval.

    k. Maintain a system for the disposition of unused investigational products and for the documentation of this disposition.

5. Quality control:
   a. Require assurance and quality control data functionalities in the system.
   b. Provide direct access to source data/documents for trial-related motoring, audit, IRB/IEC review, and regulatory inspection.
   c. Ensure data quality control methodology aligns with agreement of institution/investigator.
   d. Maintain a list of individuals who are authorized to make data changes.
   e. Maintain adequate backup of data.
   f. Maintain blinding during data entry and processing.
6. Report:
   a. Implement report creation tool in the system.
   b. Ensure reports to be consistent with data source.
   c. Submit status reports to IRB/IEC frequently.
   d. Track that data correction follows compliance protocol.
   e. Retain essential document two years after last approval.
   f. Ensure data and reports are available upon request.
7. Close-out:
   a. Document investigational products are used or unused during trial.
   b. Complete subject identification code list for follow-up purposes.
   c. Establish final trial close-out monitoring report.
   d. Document completion of trial to IRB/IEC where required and, where applicable, to the regulatory authority.
   e. Document results and interpretation of trial.

XI. **Goals/key performance indicators/metric/measurement:** See Table D.1.

XII. **Risk analysis:**
   1. Adverse event
   2. Out of budget
   3. Out of project timelines
   4. Early terminated trial
   5. Data unorganized without structure or pattern
   6. Not enough data to understand the results
   7. A contingency plan for recovery is not in place should the results prove to be less than satisfactory
   8. Data fraud

XIII. **Six Sigma roles and responsibilities:**
   1. Institutional review board/independent ethics committee: An institutional review board (IRB), also known as an independent ethics committee (IEC) or ethical review board (ERB), is a committee that has been formally designated to approve, monitor, and review biomedical and behavioral research involving humans, with the aim to protect the rights

Table D.1   Goals/Key Performance Indicators/Metric/Measurements

	Goal	*KPI*	*Metric*	*Measures*
Financial	Increase revenue	Number of approved studies	Actual amount of approved studies	Design study
		Number of approved trials	Actual amount of approved trials	Trial
		Number of early terminated trials	Actual amount of early terminated trials	Terminated trial
		Number of approved drugs or experimental treatment	Actual amount of approved drugs or experimental treatments	Approved drugs or Treatment
		Hours spent on each test		Time
		Cost of internal and external staff		Salary
		Cost of materials and facilities		Material and facility
Customer	New drugs or treatments	Number of new drugs or treatment users	Amount of new drugs or treatment being used	Drug or treatment
	Patient satisfaction	Satisfaction index	Amount of complaints	Complaint
	Improve human health	Number of healed patients	Actual amount of healed patient	Healed patient
Internal processes	Reduce cycle time	Hours spent on waiting for approval	Actual hours spent on waiting for each approval	Approval process

Table D.1 (continued) Goals/Key Performance Indicators/Metric/ Measurements

	Goal	*KPI*	*Metric*	*Measures*
		Hours spent on waiting for patient recruitment	Actual hours spent on patient recruitment for each trial	Patient recruitment process
		Hours spent on waiting for patient enrollment	Actual hours spent on enrollment process for each patient	Patient enrollment process
		Hours spent on waiting for patient visit	Actual hours spent on each patient visit	Patient visit
		Hours spent on waiting for data examination	Actual hours spent on data examination for each test	Data examination
		Hours spent on waiting for data management	Actual hours spent on data management for each trial	Data management
	Improve process quality	Incidence rate of medical misadventure	Actual rate of medical misadventure	Adverse event
		Number of data discrepancies	Actual rate of data discrepancies	Data quality
		Number of reports does not meet compliance	Actual amount of reports does not meet compliance	Report quality
Organization	Increase creditability	Percent of recalled products	Amount of recalled products	Recalled product

and welfare of the research subjects. Their responsibilities are specified as follows:

    a. Review and approve protocol or amendments before starting study.

    b. Make sure informed consent form is signed accurately, complete, and easy to understand.

    c. Review any other written information to be provided to the subjects.

    d. Review advertisement for subject recruitment.

    e. Review any other documents given approval/favorable opinion.

    f. Approve final report for trial completion.

2. Sponsors: Clinical trials are sponsored or funded by a variety of organizations or individuals, such as physicians, medical institutions, foundations, voluntary groups, and pharmaceutical companies. Their responsibilities include:

    a. Provide the clinical trial system.

    b. Recruit and enroll patients.

    c. Provide up-to-date investigator's brochure following compliance trial protocol.

    d. Inform local investigator of the true history of drug, device, or treatment.

    e. Monitor the results of the study and form various sites (or call data monitoring committee [DMC] to review data the sponsor received).

    f. Collect adverse event reports from local investigator.

    g. Inform judgment to local investigator, whether the adverse event related into the treatment or not.

    h. Collaborate with local investigator, informed consent writing.

3. Investigators/institution: Most likely medical researchers (doctors, dentists) that are elected by sponsor. Investigators must have qualified education, training, and experience to assume responsibility for proper trial. They should be familiar with clinical trial protocols that are specified by IRB/IEC, and perform the clinical trial process following the investigator's brochure. Their responsibilities are:

    a. Guarantee the safety of subjects.

    b. Register for clinical trials.

    c. Conduct study according to protocol.

    d. Supervise study staff.

    e. Guarantee subjects give truly informed consent.

    f. Review adverse event report.

    g. Local investigator should communicate with IRB/IEC truthfully.

    h. Review relevant statistical tables, figures, and reports for the entire study at the sponsor's facilities, or other mutually agreeable location.

4. Monitoring: Acting as the main line of communication between the sponsor and the investigator.

a. The monitor is responsible for overseeing the progress of a clinical trial and ensuring that it is conducted, recorded, and reported in accordance with protocol.

b. Verifying that the investigator has adequate qualifications and resources and these remain adequate throughout the trial period, and that the staff and facilities, including laboratories and equipment, are adequate to safely and properly conduct the trial, and these remain adequate throughout the trial period.

c. Verifying for the investigational product that:
   i. Storage times and conditions are acceptable, and that supplies are sufficient throughout the trial
   ii. The investigational products are supplied only to subjects who are eligible to receive them and at the protocol specified dose(s)
   iii. That subjects are provided with necessary instruction on properly using, handling, storing, and returning the investigational product(s)
   iv. That the receipt, use, and return of the investigational product(s) at the trial sites are controlled and documented adequately
   v. The disposition of unused investigational product(s) at the trial sites complies with applicable regulatory requirement(s) and is in accordance with the sponsor's authorized procedures

d. Verifying that the investigator follows the approved protocol and all approved amendment(s), if any.

e. Verifying that written informed consent was obtained before each subject's participation in the trial.

f. Ensuring that the investigator receives the current investigator's brochure, all documents, and all trial supplies needed to conduct the trial properly and to comply with the applicable regulatory requirement(s).

g. Verifying that the investigator and the investigator's trial staff are performing the specified trial functions, in accordance with the protocol and any other written agreement between the sponsor and the investigator/institution, and have not delegated these functions to unauthorized individuals.

h. Verifying that the investigator is enrolling only eligible subjects.

i. Reporting the subject recruitment rate.

j. Verifying that source data/documents and other trial records are accurate, complete, kept up to date, and maintained.

k. Verifying that the investigator provides all the required reports, notifications, applications, and submissions, and that these documents are accurate, complete, timely, legible, dated, and identify the trial.

l. Checking the accuracy and completeness of the CRF entries, source data/documents, and other trial-related records against each other. The monitor should specifically verify that:

    i. The data required by the protocol are reported accurately on the CRFs and are consistent with the source data/documents.

    ii. Any dose or therapy modifications are well documented for each of the trial subjects.

    iii. Adverse events, concomitant medications, and intercurrent illnesses are reported in accordance with the protocol on the CRFs.

    iv. Visits that the subjects fail to make, tests that are not conducted, and examinations that are not performed are clearly reported as such on the CRFs.

    v. All withdrawals and dropouts of enrolled subjects from the trial are reported and explained on the CRFs.

m. Informing the investigator of any CRF entry error, omission, or illegibility. The monitor should ensure that appropriate corrections, additions, or deletions are made, dated, explained (if necessary), and initialed by the investigator or by a member of the investigator's trial staff who is authorized to initial CRF changes for the investigator. This authorization should be documented.

n. Determining whether all adverse events (AEs) are appropriately reported within the time periods required by GCP, the ICH *Guidance for Clinical Safety Data Management: Definitions and Standards for Expedited Reporting*, the protocol, the IRB/IEC, the sponsor, and the applicable regulatory requirement(s).

o. Determining whether the investigator is maintaining the essential documents.

p. Communicating deviations from the protocol, standard operating procedures (SOPs), GCP, and the applicable regulatory requirements to the investigator and taking appropriate action designed to prevent recurrence of the detected deviations.

5. Audit: The auditors are independent individuals appointed by sponsors to conduct a systematic and in-depth examination of trial conduct and compliance with the protocol, and the applicable regulatory requirements. An audit is separate from routine monitoring or quality control functions. The regulatory authority may also appoint an auditor to a trial.

a. Selection and qualification of auditors:

    i. The sponsor should appoint individuals, who are independent of the clinical trial/data collection system(s), to conduct audits.

    ii. The sponsor should ensure that the auditors are qualified by training and experience to conduct audits properly. An auditor's qualifications should be documented.

b. Auditing procedures:

    i. The sponsor should ensure that the auditing of clinical trials/systems is conducted in accordance with the sponsor's written procedures on what to audit, how to audit, the frequency of audits, and the form and content of audit reports.

    ii. The sponsor's audit plan and procedures for a trial audit should be guided by the importance of the trial for submission to regulatory authorities, the number of subjects in the trial, the type and complexity of the trial, the level of risks to the trial subjects, and any identified problem(s).

    iii. The observations and findings of the auditor(s) should be documented.

    iv. To preserve the independence and value of the audit function, the regulatory authority(ies) should not routinely request the audit reports. Regulatory authority(ies) may seek access to an audit report on a case-by-case basis, when evidence of serious GCP noncompliance exists, or in the course of legal proceedings.

6. Research assistant/study staff (at local sites):

    a. Including: nurses, laboratory technician, laboratory assistant, clinical assistant, laboratory supervisor, dental assistant, etc.

    b. Provide local IRB documents to obtain permission to conduct study.

    c. Assist study start-up.

    d. Identify eligible patients.

    e. Obtain informed consent.

    f. Administrate study treatments.

    g. Collect data.

    h. Maintain data files.

    i. Communicate with IRB/IEC and sponsor.

7. FDA (Food Drug Administration):

    a. Approve treatment after all phases are finished.

    b. Review protocols to approve clinical trial beginning.

    c. Get researcher's credentials.

IX. **SIPOC model:** See Figure D.4.

X. **Cost analysis:** See Figure D.5.

XI. **SWOT analysis:**

1. Strengths

    a. New drugs in high demand in market

    b. Strong and well-developed manufacturing base

    c. Proficiency in path-breaking research

2. Opportunities

    a. High-demand market

    b. Globalization

    c. Future growth

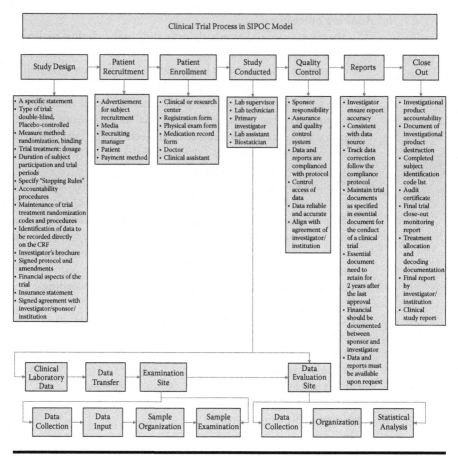

Figure D.4 Clinical trial process in SIPOC.

Actual Project Timelines
(Number in month)

Report, 5.0

Close out, 2.7

Study Design, 12.0

Quality Control, 13.4

Recruitment, 38.0

Study Conducted, 22.0

Figure D.5 Project timelines and cost.

    3. Weaknesses
        a. Small number of discoveries
        b. Fragmented capacities
        c. No data management system
        d. Manual process
    4. Threats
        a. Competitive market
        b. Loss market share
        c. Compliance issue
        d. Change protocol
        e. Unsustainable partners
XII. **Process measurement:** See Table D.2.
XIII. **Future process proposal by team:**

Table D.2   Clinical Trial Process Measurement

Time	Number of days waiting for study to be approved	Number of patients being recruited for each day	Enrollment rate per site per month	Average time spent on site per visit	Average time spent per test	Average time spent on audited report	Time of waiting for trial to be approved
Quality	Number of not approved studies or number of change protocols	Number of disqualified recruited patients	Percent of patients failed to register	Number of patient withdraws and number of data collected outside of cycle time	Number of failure tests	Number of failure reports	Number of disapproved trials
Productivity	Number of approved studies	Number of qualified recruited patients	Number of patients enrolled	Number of patient visits and number of data collected within cycle time	Number of completed tests	Number of compliance reports	Number of approved trials
Cost	Setup cost per study	Recruiting cost per trial	Patient payments	Study conducted cost	Assurance and quality control cost	Report auditing cost	Closed out cost

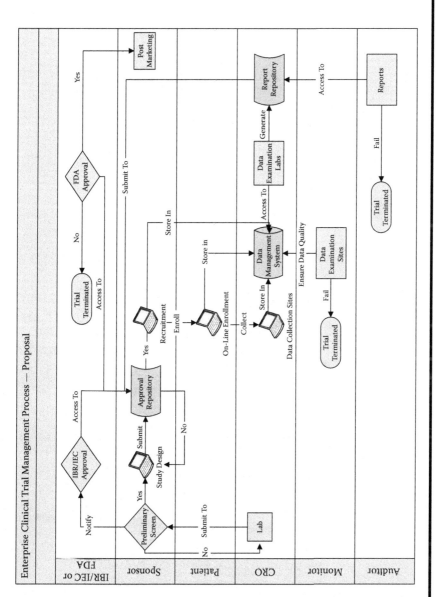

Figure D.6 Enterprise Clinical Trial Management Process—Proposal.

Index

Printed in the United States
by Baker & Taylor Publisher Services